THE TEETH ARE SMILING . . .
BUT WHAT OF THE HEART?

Studies in Society

Titles include:

THE TEETH ARE SMILING

The persistence of racism in multicultural Australia

Edited by Ellie Vasta and Stephen Castles

ALLEN & UNWIN

First published 1996
Allen & Unwin Pty Ltd
9 Atchison Street, St Leonards, NSW 2065 Australia
Phone: (61 2) 9901 4088
Fax: (61 2) 9906 2218
E-mail: 100252.103@compuserve.com

National Library of Australia
Cataloguing-in-Publication entry:

The teeth are smiling: the persistence of racism in
multicultural Australia.

  Bibliography.
  ISBN 1 86448 055 6.

  1. Pluralism (Social sciences). 2. Racism—Australia.
  3. Australia—Race relations. 4. Australia—Ethnic relations.
  I. Vasta, Ellie. II. Castles, Stephen.

305.800994

Set in 10/12 pt Times by DOCUPRO, Sydney
Printed by SRM Production Services Sdn Bhd, Malaysia

10 9 8 7 6 5 4 3 2 1

Contents

Acknowledgments

The editors thank Colleen Mitchell of the Centre for Multicultural Studies, University of Wollongong, for her meticulous work in preparing the final manuscript of this book. We also thank Elizabeth Weiss of Allen and Unwin for her support and assistance throughout the project.

Ellie Vasta and Stephen Castles

Contributors

Ellie Vasta is a Senior Lecturer in Sociology at the University of Wollongong. Ellie's research has concentrated on Italians in Australia with emphasis on Italo-Australian women and the second generation; and on the relationship between multiculturalism, culture, identity and difference. She is co-editor (with Caroline Alsorso, Stephen Castles and Gaetano Rando) of *Australia's Italians: Culture and Community in a Changing Society* (Allen & Unwin, 1992). Her current research is concerned with the theme of political mobilisation in western Sydney as it relates to multiculturalism and issues of identity, culture and difference.

Stephen Castles is Professor of Sociology and Director of the Centre for Multicultural Studies at the University of Wollongong. He has been studying migration, ethnicity and racism for many years and has worked in Germany, Britain and Southern Africa. His books include *Immigrant Workers and Class Structure in Western Europe* (with Godula Kosack, Oxford University Press, 1973), *Mistaken Identity: Multiculturalism and the Demise of Nationalism in Australia* (with Bill Cope, Mary Kalantzis and Michael Morrissey, Pluto Press, 1988), and *The Age of Migration: International Population Movements in the Modern World* (with Mark J. Miller, Macmillan, 1993).

Jock Collins' current research is on racial discrimination in the Australian labour market, ethnic small business and ethnicity and sport in Australia, and comparative immigration studies. He is the author of *Migrant Hands in a Distant Land: Australia's Post-War Immigration* (Pluto Press, 1991), co-author of *A Shop Full of Dreams: Ethnic Small*

Business in Australia (Pluto Press, 1995) and editor of *Confronting Racism in Australia, Canada and New Zealand* (Business, UTS, 1995). Jock Collins is an Associate Professor of Economics at the University of Technology, Sydney. He is a political economist who specialises in interdisciplinary studies of ethnicity, class and gender in contemporary Australian and Canadian societies.

Wendy Holland is Head of the Centre for Indigenous Australian Cultural Studies at the University of Western Sydney Macarthur. Her current research is concerned with the cultural politics of 'race'/identity and representation as it relates to 'Aboriginality'. She is currently involved in a research project entitled 'Dimensions of health and well-being among Aboriginal adolescents in South-Western Sydney' and funded through the Australian Rotary Health Research Fund.

Carol Reid's current research is on comparative indigenous education and the health and well-being of Aboriginal adolescents. She is author of 'Sick to Death: The Health of Aboriginal People in Australia and Canada' in *Racial Minorities, Medicine and Health* (eds B. Singhboloria and R. Singh, Firmwood, 1994). She has written a number of articles on indigenous education in Australia and Canada. Carol Reid is a lecturer in the Faculty of Education at the University of Western Sydney Macarthur. She is a sociologist and ex-teacher who specialises in studies of education for cultural diversity and interdisciplinary studies of indigenous issues in Australia and Canada.

Kalpana Ram is a Research Fellow at the Gender Relations Project, Research School of Pacific and Asian Studies, Australian National University. Her major publication is *Mukkuvar Women: Gender, Hegemony and Capitalist Transformation in a South Indian Fishing Community* (Allen & Unwin, 1992). She is currently researching themes concerning the reproductive embodiment of women across different caste and class settings in south India.

Jeannie Martin is a Senior Lecturer in the Faculty of Humanities and Social Sciences at University of Technology, Sydney. She has written on migrant women, multiculturalism and racism and the media. She co-edited *Intersexions* with Gillian Bottomley and Marie de Lepervanche (Allen & Unwin, 1991), and was co-author (with A. Jakubowicz, H. Goodall, T. Mitchell, L. Randall and K. Seneviratne) of *Racism, Ethnicity and the Media* (Allen & Unwin, 1994).

Janet Chan is a Senior Lecturer at the School of Social Science and Policy, University of New South Wales. Her research interests have been in criminal justice reforms in areas such as sentencing, corrections, and policing. Dr Chan's publications include *Doing Less Time: Penal Reform in Crisis* (Institute of Criminology, University of Sydney, 1992); *Preventing Juvenile Property Crime* (NSW Juvenile Justice Advisory Council, 1994); *The Price of Justice? Lengthy Criminal Trials in Australia* (Federation Press, 1995 forthcoming); and *Changing Police Culture* (Cambridge University Press, 1996 forthcoming). She is currently involved in a research project 'Police Culture and Professionalism: A Study of Recruits' jointly funded by the Australian Research Council and the New South Wales Police Service and has been appointed Associate Professor and Director of the Institute of Criminology, University of Sydney for 1996.

Fazal Rizvi is Professor of Education at Monash University. He has written extensively on the expression of racism in Australian society and schools; multiculturalism as a public policy; problems of democratic reforms in education; and ethics and educational administration. He is currently working on two major projects: one concerned with the cultural practices of marketing higher education to Asia, and the other related to the role of OECD in shaping recent educational policies in Australia. He is a member of the Australia Foundation for Culture and the Humanities.

1

Introduction: Multicultural or multi-racist Australia?

Stephen Castles and Ellie Vasta

Australia advanced proudly into nationhood and the twentieth century as an openly racist society. Will we enter the twenty-first century with a genuine commitment to anti-racism? That is the central theme of this book.

The racist world view dominant among Australians in the early part of the century had two central components: racism against Aboriginal and Torres Strait Island peoples, and racism against immigrants. For the first group, a set of popular, religious and scientific beliefs in the inferiority of indigenous peoples was matched by a set of practices of exclusion, control and discrimination tantamount to physical and cultural genocide. With regard to immigrants, exclusion of non-Europeans was the purpose of one of the earliest laws passed by the new Federal Parliament: the Immigration Restriction Act of 1901. This was the legal expression of the White Australia policy which was supported by most Australians irrespective of class or political persuasion (Willard 1923). Non-British Europeans (such as Italians and Germans) were not excluded, since their pioneering skills and labour were needed, but they were kept in positions of inferiority through discriminatory practices, including restrictions on land ownership, exclusion from certain occupations, and prohibition of foreign-language schools and newspapers.

We have come a long way since then. Most Australians now see themselves as tolerant and unprejudiced, willing to give everyone a fair go, whatever their colour, culture or origins. Overtly racist laws and policies towards both indigenous people and immigrants were abolished in the 1960s and 1970s. Multiculturalism—introduced in the 1970s and continually reaffirmed and refined in the 1980s and 1990s—seeks to

1

provide a new inclusionary definition of Australian national identity. Cultural diversity is seen as crucial to our future, both in terms of interethnic relations and in terms of the need to find a new place in the Asia-Pacific region. Racism should have no place in this new Australian world-view.

Moreover, government policies explicitly recognise the existence of barriers to equal participation in economic, social and political life, based on race, ethnicity, gender, religion and culture. The *National Agenda for a Multicultural Australia* (OMA 1989) declared that it was the duty of the state to overcome such barriers. A wide range of laws, policies and agencies exist for this purpose. The Native Title Act of 1993 (which was a response to the *Mabo* decision of the High Court) appears particularly symbolic as a measure of atonement for past wrongs against indigenous people, and as part of a strategy of national reconciliation (see Goot & Rowse 1994). The *Mabo* decision raises such issues as the importance of an economic base for indigenous Australians, the protection of Aboriginal heritage, the relationship between indigenous and non-indigenous law, and the position of in-digenous rights in the Australian Constitution (Pearson 1994). *Mabo* has an anti-racist potential. In the light of such developments it might appear that multicultural Australia is not only a non-racist country, but even an anti-racist one.

But is this really the case? The actual experience of members of minorities, especially those who are visibly different, does not fit in with this comfortable image. They report frequent instances of verbal abuse, discrimination and even violence, as was documented a few years ago by the Human Rights and Equal Opportunities Commission in its *Report of the National Inquiry into Racist Violence* (HREOC 1991). Aboriginal people have the most frequent experience of racism, often at the hands of the police and other government officials, but people of Asian appearance also report many instances of abuse or violence, while discrimination and prejudice of various kinds still affects immigrants of non-English-speaking background (NESB) in general. The heated debate surrounding the Racial Vilification Bill of 1994 was indicative of widespread unwillingness to confront racism.

While it is widely believed that Australian racism has declined since the 1960s, we have no accurate way of knowing whether matters have got better or worse in recent years. There is no systematic monitoring of incidents of racist violence or discrimination—unlike the USA, where special legislation in the late 1980s introduced monitoring of 'hate crimes', or Britain, where the police and Home Office collect systematic data on racially motivated crimes. The various bodies set up under federal and state laws to combat racial discrimination and vilification do not provide any comprehensive information on the incidence of such practices—they merely respond to complaints. For instance, HREOC received 458 complaints under the Federal Racial Discrimination Act in 1993–94, while the New South Wales Anti-Discrimination Bureau received 329 complaints on grounds of racial discrimination and 86 on grounds of racial vilification (ACTU 1995, p. 5). But there is strong evidence that only a small percentage of such cases is actually reported (ACTU 1995, pp. 10, 15). This is partly because of lack of information on the part of victims of racism, partly because of the complex and lengthy procedures faced by those who do complain, and partly because existing laws are weak and rarely provide effective remedies. For example, the NSW Anti-Discrimination Board received 448 complaints on grounds of vilification over a five-year period; of these, three cases were eventually recommended for prosecution, but not in fact proceeded with (ACTU 1995, p. 10). In the light of this, people may feel that complaints are a waste of time.

But even if we have no way of quantifying racism, there is ample evidence that it is a widespread and serious problem. Here are just a few examples taken from the Australian Council of Trade Union's overview of racism for the year 1994 (ACTU 1995):

- Jewish organisations reported increasing numbers of anti-Semitic incidents.
- A survey of engineers showed that employment prospects were significantly affected by race, with a clear bias in favour of Europeans.
- 1994 was the last year that Federal government departments were required to report publicly on their equal opportunity programs. This requirement has been abolished, although only 9 per cent of recent appointments to the Public Service were NESB people.
- Attorney General's Department had 519 members in its statutory and non-statutory bodies, of whom only two were NESB people.
- The NSW Ombudsman released a discussion paper which suggested that 'the behaviour of some police officers was often racist and negative stereotyping was part of a learnt police culture'.
- Mr Downer, then leader of the Federal Opposition, admitted appearing on the platform of a meeting organised by the racist League of Rights.
- The National Committee for Discrimination and Employment has 'fallen in a heap' according to the ACTU, and there is no coordinated

strategy by federal and state authorities to combat discrimination in employment.

- Federal and state bodies concerned with implementing multicultural policies and combating discrimination were demoralised and marginalised, and had their resources cut.

Thus, despite multiculturalism, the official response to racism and marginalisation of minorities is ineffective and evasive. All available social indicators show that Aborigines and Torres Strait Islanders are still highly disadvantaged with regard to health, housing, education, employment, life expectancy and social conditions. They suffer exclusion, discrimination and racist violence. Immigrants too experience discrimination of various kinds. However, the experience of various groups differs, and they cannot be dealt with as a single category.

White immigrants from highly developed countries often have incomes and conditions at or above the national average, and suffer little or no discrimination. The experience of the pre-1970s Eastern and Southern European settlers was frequently marked by discrimination and socio-economic disadvantage. This group—now often nearing or past retiring age—still faces serious problems of exclusion and poverty. Their children—'the second generation'—may have achieved upward mobility, but still find themselves treated as 'wogs' in certain contexts. Their bicultural identity is often conditioned by experiences of racism.

More recent immigrants from Asia, Latin America and the Pacific Islands vary greatly in characteristics like education, qualifications and language skills. Immigrants and refugees without recognised skills may experience a double exclusion: they have high rates of unemployment or are forced into low-paid informal sector jobs, while at the same time suffering racial discrimination, harassment or even violence. Highly skilled non-European immigrants often do very well in the labour market (though not always, for barriers to skill recognition and employment still exist), but they may still suffer various forms of personal racism on account of being visibly different.

So racism *is* still a problem in multicultural Australia. We should not forget that the name Australia was until recently synonymous with racial exclusion and white dominance, to the point that many people in Asia and Europe are still surprised when told that Asian immigration is now common. The two centuries in which racism was an almost universal tenet have left their mark on institutions, social practices, intellectual discourse, popular ideas and national culture. The anti-racism of official policies and public rhetoric is often only skin-deep: it masks the continuing reality of differentiation and discrimination based on biological and cultural markers which are linked to discourses of race and ethnicity. There is no single racism in Australia, no simple black–white divide. Rather, there is a whole range of intersecting sets of ideas and practices among different groups, which in turn interact with ideas and practices concerning class and gender. Thus, in the title of this introductory chapter we echo the notion of a 'multi-racist' society coined for Britain by Cohen and Bains (1988): Australia is in the contradictory position of being both a multicultural and a multi-racist society. This is another way of saying that multiculturalism is incomplete and unstable, as long as it coexists with various forms of racism.

Discourses of tolerance and diversity are not unimportant—indeed they are a great step forward compared with our racist past—but they can only be seen as genuine anti-racism if they are matched by a commitment to fundamental change in institutions, attitudes and practices. In principle and (in the long run) in practice, multiculturalism and racism in any form are incompatible. Yet, as the contributions to this book show, a commitment to fundamental change is still missing in many areas of Australian life. Contemporary Australia has shown a capability for change and innovation, but much remains to be done if we are to enter the twenty-first century as a non-racist society.

Social science and racism

Australian anti-racists still have a major task ahead of them. Achieving change is above all an issue of political practice, but social scientific analysis is a vital precondition for such practice. A central problem of anti-racist movements throughout the world has been their frequent failure to keep up with changes in racist ideologies and practices (see Taguieff 1988). We hope that this book will help contribute to an awareness and understanding of contemporary Australian racisms, especially those which seem able to coexist with the ostensibly anti-racist tenets of multiculturalism.

We have already indicated that there is no single *racism* in Australia, but rather a range of *racisms*, which affect different groups in different contexts. However, at the same time it is important to be aware of the *unity of racism* as a process of social differentiation which has played a central role in Western society since the beginnings of modernity and colonialism. In the Australian context this means understanding that both indigenous people and immigrants have been subjected to processes of racialisation, as a means of controlling them and subordinating them to the interests of the dominant group.[1] The forms and effects of racialisation have been very different. Above all, racism against indigenous people has been much more brutal and destructive than against immigrants. Yet the ideologies, practices and interests on which they have been based are essentially the same.

In Australia, there has always been a dichotomy between studies of the situation of Aboriginal people, and studies of immigrants and their descendants. This dichotomy has reflected the administrative division between Aboriginal affairs on the one hand and immigration and ethnic affairs policy on the other. Frequently a division has been made between the study of race relations (concerning indigenous people) and the study of ethnic relations (concerning immigrants). There is no theoretical or analytical basis for this division, and it tends to undermine understanding of the process of racialisation as well as making it harder to develop anti-racist perspectives.

It is in this context that we can see one of the central dilemmas of Australian social scientific work on racism or race relations. Social scientists have played a major role in shaping attitudes and policies on racial and ethnic difference. But on the whole there has been little effort to understand the common roots of practices of discrimination and exclusion towards both indigenous people and immigrants. To do so would mean admitting that racism arises out of the structure and culture of our own society, rather than out of the specific characteristics of the racialised groups. Thus social scientists have not only ignored the unity of racism, but have often denied the existence of racism altogether.

In the nineteenth century, Australia with its great wealth of cultural groups became an El Dorado for anthropologists. These helped create myths of separate and 'authentic' indigenous cultures, and somehow missed the reality of how colonialism was destroying Aboriginal society. Anthropology became both an instrument of control and a way of asserting the superiority of the dominant group. Immigration studies were carried out by sociologists, demographers, economists and others, who addressed issues like: How many more people does Australia need? What types of people (based on ethnic origins) can Australia assimilate? How can immigrants be absorbed without changing the existing society and culture? What policies are most conducive to assimilation? In other words, the perspective of social science on difference until recently has been that of the dominant group in society: first the British colonial power, then the emerging Anglo-Australian ruling class. Indigenous people and immigrants were represented and objectified in academic and policy debates, and had little or no opportunity to represent themselves.

However, since the 1960s another, more critical, approach has developed. Australian social scientists began to support calls for Aboriginal rights and the abandonment of the White Australia policy. The work of people like Rivett (1962) and Yarwood (1964) was influential in debates on immigration policy. Writers like Rowley (1970), Lippmann (1973) and Stevens (1970) showed some of the brutal realities behind Australia's frontier myths. Social scientists began to take on a critical function as agents for change in official racist policies. This was possible for three reasons. The first was the world-wide movement against racism connected with decolonisation and the revulsion against Nazism. The second was the fact that oppressed groups in Australia were finding a voice and putting difficult questions to the people who had hitherto claimed to represent them. When Aboriginal people began to question the European scientific notions of truth against their own 'dreaming' versions of truth, and began voicing their own experiences of repression, then intellectuals were forced to re-examine their own role. At the same time, people of immigrant background began to take a part in immigration policy debates and immigration research and began to question the racist effects of assimilationism and the White Australia policy.

The third reason for the growth of critical analysis was, of course, that official policies were failing. The White Australia policy and the denial of rights to Aboriginal people had become international embarrassments, while the doctrine of assimilation was rapidly collapsing in the face of community formation and ethnic mobilisation. Critical knowledge was needed, because large sections of Australia's political class were beginning to understand the need for change. Social scientists were to play a major role in the development of the new discourses for dealing with diversity: Aboriginal self-management and multi-culturalism.

To say this is to point to one of the fundamental problems of critical social science in a modern democratic country: people who are trying to work for change, emancipation and equality are at the same time contributing to new strategies of control and conflict management within a system based on economic and political inequality. This dilemma of social scientists mirrors that of both Aboriginal and immigrant political activists in Australia, who have to walk a narrow line between pressing for real change and becoming coopted into the consultative structures of a multicultural welfare state.

There is no space for a detailed review of the great volume of recent work relevant to the study of racism in Australia, but a few observations can be made. To start with, most research still follows the administrative division between Aboriginal affairs and policies towards immigrants. There are some exceptions, however, such as Yarwood and Knowling (1982), Pettman (1992) and Markus (1994), who try to examine racism as a whole, and to link it to other central issues in Australian society. Many social scientists see themselves as agents of change. Some anthropologists have been involved with Aborigines in their struggle against the vestiges of racism and colonialism, for instance by giving expert evidence to support land rights claims. Scholars like Reynolds (1981, 1987a), Cowlishaw (1988), Bennett (1989) and Eades (1993, 1994) have changed our understanding of the various dimensions of unequal power relations between indigenous and non-indigenous Australians.

In immigration studies, sociologists such as Jeannie Martin (1978) and Jerzy Zubrzycki (1977) played a major role in the 1970s in exposing the failure of assimilationist policies, and showing the extent of immigrant social disadvantage. Zubrzycki was highly influential in the development of the Fraser Government's model of multiculturalism. Zubrzycki's approach rested on a conservative culturalist perspective in which ethnic group difference was to be promoted and respected. In turn, this concentration on a static and traditionalist concept of culture was criticised by social scientists who focused on the political economy of racism (Collins 1991; de Lepervanche 1980, 1989; Jakubowicz 1981, 1989a).

Recent work sets out to link issues of ethnicity, class and gender with the role of the state and with the politics of identity and community (see for example Alcorso 1991, 1993; Bottomley & de Lepervanche 1984; Bottomley et al. 1991; Castles et al. 1992a, 1992b; Collins 1991; Jupp 1984; Jupp & Kabala 1993; Lever-Tracy & Quinlan 1988; Martin 1984, 1991a; Vasta 1993a, 1993b). Such analyses have played a role in the redefinition of multiculturalism by the Australian Labor Party (ALP) Government of the 1980s and 1990s, with its dual focus on principles of cultural diversity and of social justice.

It should be noted that most work in this area is not explicitly on racism, but on various aspects of the situation of Aboriginal people or of immigrants. An implicit critique of racism is frequently present, but coherent and systematic analyses are rare. Even where racism is dealt with as a central theme, there is generally a failure to adequately analyse its causes and its changing forms. As Cowlishaw (1988, p. 267) points out, such important works as Stevens (1970) and Yarwood and Knowling (1982) reduce racism to biological difference, especially that based on skin colour. Social and cultural dimensions of racism are ignored. In a recent work, Markus (1994) provides a comprehensive history of race relations in Australia up to the early 1990s, yet his chapter on 'the idea of race in western culture' barely goes beyond the nineteenth century. This lack of up-to-date theorisation of racism is a serious problem, especially at a time when racist ideologies are everywhere shifting from biological to cultural principles.

In any case, the tradition of social science based on the gaze of the dominant group is still strong. It exists above all in the administratively orientated research commissioned by government departments and special agencies like the Bureau of Immigration, Multicultural and Population Research. Such work reproduces willy-nilly the bureaucratic division of labour and the policy concerns of those who hold political power. This is not to question the soundness of such work, nor the integrity of those who carry it out. Indeed, highly critical approaches are sometimes to be found in official reports (a few examples out of many are: Morrissey et al. 1992; Moss 1993). But it is important to realise that the funding structures which determine most research in the field almost inevitably lead to short-term approaches, compartmentalised choice of themes, lack of theoretical reflection, and a top-down perspective.

The issue of representation of difference in the social sciences is a significant one, particularly for indigenous Australians. As they have become more publicly politicised, social scientists have come under attack not only for their representation of blacks as Other, but also for positioning themselves as the purveyors of knowledge about Aborigines in a way that created 'truth-effects' which ultimately reproduced the power of whites over blacks (Attwood & Arnold 1992; Cowlishaw 1988). Over the past few years two significant debates have emerged within Aboriginal studies and anthropology. The first concerns a discussion about representation which took place in *Oceania* in 1992 (see Hollinsworth 1992; Mudrooroo et al. 1992). Its starting point was the concern expressed by white scholars that Aboriginal stress on blood lines and biological continuity was damaging to the Aboriginal cause for social justice. The argument was that biological essentialism could lead only to racial hierarchies and new forms of racism. According to this view, racial hierarchies should not be accepted from any person or group.

The other closely related debate refers to recent work which not only describes the power relations between Aborigines and whites but also examines Aboriginal resistance. In her research in a rural area of New South Wales, Cowlishaw (1988) illustrates how drinking, swearing and general 'unruly' behaviour operates as an oppositional culture to white authority. The critics of this position argue that such resistance is self-destructive and ultimately does not change racist structures and practices. Lattas (1993, pp. 245–6) has argued that such critiques are indicative of a 'new paternalism' in Aboriginal studies. White scholars now have to share the task of representation with the voices of indigenous peoples, yet still try to preserve their role as 'experts' who can help decide on how to constitute the identity of the Other. Thus:

> when Aborigines seek to give a mythological content to, or to reclaim, a primordial past for themselves then they are accused of essentialism and of participating in their own domination . . . This is identity without content and without a primordial past; it is identity stripped to the bare logic of being simply a relation. The demand that Aborigines produce their popular consciousness along the lines of a social theory of identity is a request that they become conscious of themselves as purely relational identities; they are to be resisters without producing an essence for themselves (Lattas 1993, pp. 245–6).

Or, to put it in more directly political terms: 'myths of the "Other" permeate relations between indigenous and non-indigenous people . . . As objects of this history, indigenous Australians have created their own myths in order to survive an oppressive system' (see Chapter 6). Ultimately, as Lattas (1993, p. 254) asks, should we treat Aboriginal essentialism as something which is dangerous and false, or do we accept it as a process which provides a sense of continuity and groundedness? Cowlishaw gets to the core of the matter when she suggests that some academics believe that if they get their theoretical frameworks correct, then they can rest free of political anxieties. However, she continues: 'No theory can guarantee political correctness, as it is in the *uses* of theory that its effects are manifested' (1993, p. 183).

Social scientists do have to share responsibility for the attitudes, practices and policies which arise from their work. The economic and social constraints of scholarly work in a period of erosion of academic independence are issues which have to be negotiated, but they are not a justification for reproducing ideas of domination and hierarchy. No researcher today can work outside official structures of funding and control. Yet the very complexity of issues of cultural difference and the growing ambiguity of the interests of state and capital in this area provide a space in which critical knowledge is needed and even encouraged. This makes it possible to develop alternative ideas on issues of difference, equality and participation. The dilemma of the social scientist is to avoid cooption into mechanisms of domination over minorities. There is no easy way to achieve this, but the key must lie in cooperation and negotiation with members of minority groups, and participation in the development of anti-racist strategies.

Plan of the book

The authors of this book share a commitment to social scientific study of racism, as a basis for the improvement of anti-racist strategies and policies. Beyond this, there has been no attempt to achieve unanimity of approach or conclusions. The book does not claim to be comprehensive: some important areas of racism in Australian society are not covered. Rather, we have presented some general theoretical and analytical aspects, together with a series of case studies of particular aspects of racism.

In Chapter 2, 'The racisms of globalisation', Stephen Castles discusses the changing character of racism at the international level. He argues that beyond the wide range of national and local racisms it is possible to discern general trends. These include the growing intensity of racism in many areas, its increasing role in global politics, the shift in emphasis from biology to culture, and the increasing complexity of links between racism and other forms of differentiation, such as nationalism and sexism. Castles argues that current developments can be explained through an analysis of globalisation, and the way it has precipitated crises of economic, social, cultural and political relations in various countries.

Chapter 3, 'Dialectics of domination: racism and multiculturalism' by Ellie Vasta, examines the question: has multiculturalism overcome previous racist constructions of Australian social relations and national identity? She argues that multiculturalism contains contradictory elements: it is a strategy for 'managing ethnic diversity' and hence for maintaining the domination of the majority over minorities, yet it also points to the possibility of new forms of social and cultural relations. Critics are right to say that multiculturalism has not been able to fully resolve the dilemma of reconciling universalism of rights in a democratic state with differences in needs and values of various groups. Yet multiculturalism does provide a framework in which unequal power relationships can be questioned, and issues of identity and participation can be worked through.

Later chapters develop and apply analyses of racism to particular sites of intergroup relations. In Chapter 4, 'The changing political economy of Australian racism', Jock Collins examines the labour market as a key sector for the reproduction of racist attitudes and practices. He describes exclusionary forms of racism which lead to high rates of unemployment for indigenous people and some immigrants, as well as inclusionary racism through which members of minorities are employed in jobs below their ability. Collins analyses the way in which conservative economic and sociological theories explain (or explain away) racial discrimination. He points to the economic contradictions of racism: it may strengthen the position of employers through divide-and-rule strategies, but it also reduces productivity, wastes human potential, and undermines efforts to internationalise the economy.

Chapter 5, 'Mis/taken identity' by Wendy Holland, explores some of the complex forces that have shaped the identity of Aboriginal and white Australians. She discusses differences in the experience of racism by indigenous people and immigrants, and examines how racism, sexism and class relations interact. Holland's personal account of how the education system deals with race and difference shows the extent to which anti-Aboriginal racism is still deeply entrenched in Australian society. Holland's analysis of her black and white identities reflects the multiple strategies she has lived in multi-racist Australia.

A case study of an initiative at the University of Western Sydney which has attempted to challenge the marginalisation and exclusion of indigenous students in tertiary education follows in Chapter 6, 'The Aboriginal Rural Education Program: a case study in anti-racist strategies'. Carol Reid and Wendy Holland show that anti-racist coalitions of indigenous and non-indigenous educators are vital for bringing about change, and discuss the difficulties of achieving such coalitions.

In Chapter 7, 'Liberal multiculturalism's "NESB women": a South Asian post-colonial feminist perspective on the liberal impoverishment of "difference" ', Kalpana Ram shows how Western liberal scholarship splits up immigrant women's experience into two fragments: the 'here' of Australia and the exotic 'there' of the place of origin. Her account focuses on resistance against arranged marriages as a site to examine the intersection of multicultural and feminist issues. She argues that liberal multiculturalism actually produces a certain version of difference based on older Western understandings of 'other cultures'. To respond to this, minority feminisms need the tools of post-colonial theory which can demonstrate the hybridity within both 'tradition' and 'modernity'. However, immigrant feminism can in turn reveal certain critical blind spots on the part of a masculinist post-colonial theory.

In Chapter 8, 'Signs of the times: race, sex and media representations', Jeannie Martin examines how languages of sexism and racism intersect in media representations of identity and difference. The study focuses on television advertising, and its image of 'Australian-ness' centred on the 'blonde Aussie mum' as a bearer of timeless Anglo traditions. In contrast, non-Anglo women are represented as exotic and natural, potentially offering sex and other services to Anglo men. For non-Anglo men, the gender distinction is blurred: they are often seen in feminised, domestic roles. Martin calls for a 'politics of rep-resentation' by minorities and women, concerned with both control and content of media products.

In Chapter 9, 'Police racism: experiences and reforms', Janet Chan draws on both Australian and overseas research to describe the ways in which racism is manifested in police work, and how the problem is being addressed by government. She analyses the reasons for the apparent ineffectiveness of reform policies, showing that police racism is not a matter of personal prejudices, but rather a result of the social practices through which the role and culture of the police are con-structed in our society.

In Chapter 10, 'Racism, reorientation and the cultural politics of Asia–Australia relations', Fazal Rizvi argues that it is impossible to separate attempts to forge new relationships within the Asian region from the racisms within Australia. 'Asia-literacy' initiatives are unlikely to succeed unless they consist of much more than just learning about other cultures. A program of anti-racism that is serious about estab-lishing a more equal and productive relation with Asia must take into account the ambivalence and contradictions that seem inherent in our representations of Asia. Australians have to recognise that their attempts to negotiate a new relationship with Asia are tied inextricably to the way they see themselves as a multicultural society.

Towards an anti-racist republic?

We started this introduction by asking will Australia enter the twenty-first century with a genuine commitment to anti-racism? The contri-butions of the various authors provide ideas and information which may help in answering this question. These final paragraphs present some personal reflections by the editors.

It is argued in several places in this book that the whole issue of racism in multicultural Australia is marked by contradictions—indeed, the very title of the book is consciously contradictory, for there simply shouldn't be racism in a multicultural country. Yet racism does exist in many sites, such as in the labour market, education, the media and policing. Indeed, if this book has one general conclusion, it is that racism is alive and strong in Australia.

It is important to work through such contradictions, if we are to help provide the knowledge needed to bring about change. Australia cannot long remain both multicultural and multi-racist. We are still in the middle of a process, which started in the 1960s, of moving away from a racist world-view. It is not a linear process: in some cases racist attitudes and practices have been replaced not by non-racist ones, but by new forms of racism. The shift from biological to cultural racism, the repressive nature of some discourses of tolerance, the racist content of some environmental theories and the difficulties in overcoming our ethnocentric ideas about Asia are all indicative of the complexity of change.

So what are the central contradictions that we need to understand? A first one is the gulf between the rhetoric and the practice of anti-racism in Australia. Not only government, but most community leaders (including politicians, media commentators, industrialists, trade unionists and spokespersons for interest groups) claim to oppose racism and to support measures to combat it. Anti-racism is the dominant discourse and nobody admits to believing doctrines of white or Anglo superiority. Yet racist attitudes and practices are still to be found in almost every social sphere, and in every significant social grouping. Indigenous people and people of non-English-speaking background continue to experience structural and personal racism as part of their daily lives.

The second contradiction concerns the specific dualism of both racism and anti-racism in Australia: the division between issues concerning indigenous people and issues concerning immigrants (a division which many chapters of this book attempt to transcend). Racism against both grew from the same historical and cultural roots, but it took different forms and constructed indigenous people and immigrants in different ways. In turn, the politics of resistance of indigenous people and immigrants took different and separate forms. This has facilitated divide-and-rule strategies by the dominant group and the state. It is only recently that attempts have been made to assert the need for joint anti-racist action by indigenous people and immigrants. An anti-racist struggle can succeed only as a unified struggle against all forms of discrimination and hierarchisation based on physical or cultural difference. Furthermore, to be effective, anti-racist struggles need to operate both within and outside the state apparatus.

The third central contradiction concerns the weakness of the social democratic welfare-state model in a period of globalisation and economic rationalism. Multicultural policies put forward by the ALP Government claim to reconcile social justice and economic efficiency, within a capitalist economy. Yet capitalism (especially in its neo-liberal form) is based on setting differential values for different types of human capital. Race, ethnicity and gender remain key mechanisms for legitimating labour market segmentation. The social-democratic model cannot deliver on its promise of social justice. All it can do is counter some of the more blatant forms of discrimination. This is worth doing, but it is a far cry from equality or social justice, and it is no coincidence that extremes of wealth and poverty have increased everywhere in recent years. That is why funding for welfare and community relations activities so often seems paltry and tokenistic. Multicultural policies are marginal compared with the big-ticket areas of government action, such as education, social security, transport, etc. Anti-racism must therefore mean not only striving for improved social justice and community relations policies, but also seeking to gain a much higher priority for such sectors within the total constellation of government action.

This leads on to the fourth contradiction: that between the public and the private sectors in a capitalist society. The state can try to achieve greater equality in the provision of the services and resources which it controls (for instance through policies of access and equity). But the state has much more limited possibilities of influencing what happens in the private sector, which is crucial for economic, social and cultural relations. For instance, if employers dislike limits put on their power to hire and fire through equal opportunities policies, they can move production offshore. Similarly, the government can introduce guidelines on how the media should treat issues of difference, but has little power to intervene in actual portrayal of minorities by commercial media. Anti-discrimination and anti-vilification laws have a symbolic value, but have proved blunt instruments in practice. Adoption of international human rights covenants might provide some improvement, although so far these have proved difficult to enforce.

The fifth contradiction concerns the principle of participation which is at the core of multicultural policies: previously excluded groups should be empowered to take part in the making and implementation of policies which concern them. The principle is excellent, but it does not fit easily with a form of representative democracy which has historically shown little willingness to give a fair place to women, indigenous people or immigrants of non-English-speaking background. So far there is little sign of greater real empowerment for minorities through the initiatives of recent years. Two things are needed: first a struggle to secure equal representation in parties and political institutions for people who do not belong to the traditional male Anglo ruling group; secondly, the introduction of effective systems of participation in decision-making for minority groups particularly affected by certain policies or decisions. In the case of indigenous people, this should take the form of self-determination and veto rights where vital community interests are at stake.

In view of all these contradictions, it is clear that the development of anti-racism has to be based on both analysis and practice, both social scientific research and political action. Neither of these can be carried out adequately from the top down by government, however enlightened its policies. The first step in achieving change is to analyse racist attitudes and practices and explain their causes. Although academics and intellectuals can contribute to a systematic understanding of racism, a key role in analysis has to be played by members of excluded and discriminated groups, who often have the clearest view of the meaning and consequences of racism.

The second step is to bring about changes in attitudes, practices and institutional structures. Government has a central role in devising and implementing anti-racist strategies, but it cannot and will not act without substantial pressure from civil society. The political mobilisation of groups disadvantaged and marginalised by racism is crucial. However, it is also important to mobilise other groups who oppose racism not as its victims, but because of their concerns for equality, solidarity and social justice. In Western Europe, for instance, anti-racist movements have grown in response to the realisation that extreme-right anti-immigrant movements threaten democracy and human rights for everyone. Anti-racist coalitions at the grassroots level and at a more general political level are vital levers for change. Anti-racism and anti-sexism need to be made a central element of discourse in every context where political opinions and political will are formed.

Thus we can conclude by saying that anti-racism cannot succeed in isolation from other social struggles: it must be part of a much broader campaign for greater equality and more democracy in Australian society. In the current political constellation, a major site for this campaign is likely to be the debate on Australia's move to a republic. Anti-racists should not accept the idea of simply replacing the present foreign monarch with an Australian president, while leaving the existing Constitution and many discriminatory structures in place. Rather, we should call for a fundamental democratisation of Australian economic and political institutions. An anti-racist republic can be based only on the full realisation of principles of equality, social justice and political participation for all.

2

The racisms of globalisation

Stephen Castles

What are the images of racism in the mid-1990s? Among the most dramatic are the massacres of Rwanda, 'ethnic cleansing' in Bosnia, urban riots in the USA, skinhead attacks on asylum seekers in Germany, and—closer to home—the heated debates on the Native Title Act of 1993, and the (subsequently withdrawn) Racial Vilification Bill of 1994. Less visible, but no less important, are the countless expressions of everyday racism, which reduce the life chances of ethnic minorities in many countries. On the level of international relations too, racism has not lost its importance: the North–South divide is often a euphemism for the domination of the peoples of formerly colonised countries by Europe and North America—joined now by Japan and a small circle of newly industrialising countries.

Yet the images have changed: in the 1960s, racism usually meant overt segregation (e.g., in the US Deep South or in South Africa) or explicit racial exclusion (like the White Australia policy). Racism was often linked to colonialism or neo-colonialism (the political and economic control of former colonies without direct rule). The Vietnam War was a site of racist confrontation: the use of weapons of mass destruction by the USA against a rural people struggling for independence appeared as a continuation of the 'civilising mission' of the West, which had justified centuries of barbarity. The labour migrations of the 1960s gave rise to a 'colour bar' in Britain, which kept black immigrants out of dance halls, rented rooms and jobs. Western European countries like Germany and France also used discriminatory practices to exploit migrant workers, although here people were reluctant to speak of racism, using instead the euphemisms 'xenophobia' or 'hostility to foreigners'.

The late 1960s and the 1970s appeared to be a 'liberal hour', as overt racism declined under the pressure of anti-colonial struggles and civil rights movements. The concept of the Third World emerged as a global symbol of the movement against white domination. The international campaign against apartheid—which was to take so long to bear fruit—was emblematic of the new climate. Desegregation and affirmative action set a new political agenda in the USA. Racial selectivity in immigration systems was abolished in Australia and other countries (though not everywhere). Indigenous peoples fought for and obtained political rights—only to find that this did not mean the end of discrimination and marginalisation.

Today, no mainstream politician speaks openly of the racial superiority of whites over other races. The few academics who still put forward the tenets of 'scientific racism'—the conventional wisdom of the biological and social sciences up to the 1940s—are considered eccentric. Many countries now have anti-discrimination laws and equal opportunity measures. Yet racism persists. Some of its targets are the same as before (indigenous peoples, migrant workers, ethnic minorities in developed countries) but there are new ones, including minority ethnic[1] groups in former colonies, and national minorities in the emerging states of Eastern Europe. These do not easily fit into the traditional white/black schema of racism. The dividing line between racism and nationalism has become less clear. There are new types of discrimination and exclusion, as well as new ideologies to justify them. As many authors have argued (for instance, Balibar 1991a; Cohen & Bains 1988; Gilroy 1992; Miles 1993), it is no longer useful (if indeed it ever was) to speak of racism as if it were an homogeneous phenomenon. We need to examine specific *racisms*, as they affect particular groups in various locations and times.

In this chapter, my aim is to discuss current international patterns of racism, and some of the theoretical and political debates that arise from them. In the first section, I will examine some of the problems that arise in defining racism in a rapidly changing context. The second section briefly examines the various types of racism to be found in the contemporary world. The third section attempts a theoretical explanation which links racism with the crises caused by global restructuring.

My main argument is that trends towards globalisation of politics, economic relations and culture are central to understanding the changing nature of racism. *Globalisation* designates the latest stage of a process—often referred to as *modernisation*—which began with

European colonial expansion in the fifteenth century. Modernity implies increasingly integrated capitalist production and distribution systems, linked to secular cultures based on the principle of rationality. Modernity has meant colonisation of the rest of the world, not only in the direct sense of political control, but also through diffusion of Western cultural values. Racism—as an ideology which justified European domination—has always been part of modernity.

The concept of globalisation has been used since the 1970s to refer to an acceleration of international integration based on rapid changes in political and economic relations, technology and communications (see Featherstone 1990; King 1991; Robertson 1992). Racism is an integral part of the politics and culture of this new stage: we may refer to this tendency as the *globalisation of racism*. But current developments also involve new types of racism, taking on differing and shifting forms with regard to various target groups and locations. These I refer to as the *racisms of globalisation*—the central theme of the chapter.

Why do these international debates matter in a book on Australian racism? Australia is not cut off from the discourses and practices which construct global patterns of racism. Indeed, it never has been: racism towards indigenous people and non-British immigrants was shaped by the ideologies and policies towards 'inferior peoples' prevailing in Britain's global empire. It was not until Australia was likened to South Africa and had difficulties in establishing good relations with emerging Asian nations in the 1960s that policies began to change. Most recently, the Federal Government has told us that we should celebrate 'productive diversity' as a major asset in our search for a place in the dynamic Asia-Pacific region. New international issues—such as the moral panic on South–North migration or the revival of ethnic nationalism—have direct effects on Australia, just as our own debates on multiculturalism are receiving increasing attention elsewhere. We cannot discuss racism in multicultural Australia without being aware that this country is part of a shrinking world.

Defining racism

There is a confusing plethora of literature on race and racism. For instance the useful collection by Rex and Mason (1986) of *Theories of Race and Ethnic Relations* includes Weberian, Marxist, anthropological, pluralist, rational choice, sociobiological, symbolic interactionist and identity theory approaches. These are mainly sociological theories, but one can find other works by philosophers, historians, economists, jurists, psychologists, discourse analysts and cultural theorists. Any study of racism is necessarily interdisciplinary, for a full understanding can be achieved only through examination of all the factors—historical, economic, political, social, cultural, etc.—which make up a given situation of racism.

If racism is a global phenomenon with a multiplicity of shifting forms, any theory of racism needs to be broad enough to take account of their diversity, without losing sight of their essential unity. This is a tall order, which has led some observers to argue that 'rather than talking about racism in the singular, analysts should . . . be talking about racisms in the plural' (Gilroy 1987, p. 38). But this point of view ignores the obvious existence of common patterns and trends in racist ideologies and practices, which imply some commonality of character and causality. We need both the singular and the plural. Goldberg (1993, p. 41) argues for:

> a general but open-ended theory concerning race and racism. The theory would have to account for historical alterations and discontinuities in the modes of racial formation, in the disparate phenomena commonly addressed in racialised terms, as well as in those expressions properly considered racist. It must also enable and encourage opposition to racist expression, for ultimately the efficacy of a theory about race and racism is to be assessed in terms of the ways in which it renders possible resistance to racisms.

The last point seems specially important: a theory of racism must not only explain why racism comes about, but also help combat it. To be a useful guide to understanding and action, a theory of racism should:

- explain why racism exists in many different societies, both in the past and the present;
- explain the varying forms of racism within any one society, as well as in different societies;
- explain why racism becomes more or less severe at certain times; and
- provide ideas for strategies to combat racism.

Traditions of racism

The concept of racism is comparatively new. According to Miles (1993, p. 81) it was first used in connection with Nazi ideas on race in the 1930s. However, discourses and practices of hierarchisation based on the notion of race are much older (see Miles 1989, Chapter 1). Since ancient times, groups of people have come into contact with each other through trade, migration or warfare. This has given rise to notions of group boundaries, marked by area of origin, language, culture, physical appearance or other characteristics. Non-belonging to a specific group was frequently used as a criterion for discrimination or hostility. Practices akin to modern racism played a part in processes of territorial expansion, in which one ethnic group subjugated others, occupying their land and exploiting their labour.

Systematic ideas of racial hierarchy appear to be connected to European colonialism: from the fifteenth century onwards, religiously inspired views on the barbarity and inferiority of the indigenous peoples of Africa, Asia and America were used to legitimate invasion, genocide, slavery and exploitation (Cohen 1987; Potts 1990). In the eighteenth and nineteenth centuries, attempts were made to justify racism on the basis of scientific theory. Races were seen as biologically distinct entities, made up of people with different phenotypical characteristics. They were thought to form an unchanging hierarchy, in which the capacities and achievements of the members of each race were fixed by natural determinants. Domination by the 'superior race' was inevitable and desirable, because it was thought to lead to human progress (Husband 1982; Miles 1989). Goldberg (1993, pp. 41–3) argues that racism is itself a discourse which 'emerges with modernity and comes to colonise modernity's continually reinvented common sense'.

Within Europe, racial categorisation was crucial in the rise of nationalism from the eighteenth century. The attempt to base membership of a nation-state on belonging to a specific race or ethnic group required the creation of national myths, since all peoples were in fact the result of historical processes of migration and intermingling. Taken to a logical conclusion, this ideology requires policies to exclude members of other races or to deprive them of rights. The Nazis went to this extreme, defining Jews and Gipsies, who had been part of German society for centuries, as aliens, and physically destroying them. It is important to remember that this most extreme form of racism was carried out by one white group against others, showing that skin colour is not always a crucial marker.

Economic exploitation also played a part in the emergence of racism. Mercantile capitalists accumulated wealth through slavery and indentured labour—systems of labour mobilisation based on ideas of racial hierarchy. During the Industrial Revolution, racism against white immigrant workers (such as Irish in Britain or Poles in Germany) was widespread, foreshadowing racism against migrant workers after 1945.

After the defeat of fascism in 1945, UNESCO convened a series of

symposia to debate the legitimacy of the concept of race. Their statements demonstrated the invalidity of racial classifications in the terms
of both the natural and social sciences (Montagu 1974). A *race*,
therefore, is not a biologically defined group, but a social construction
arising out of *racism*. Action against racism became a declared aim of
the United Nations and other international bodies, laid down in a
multitude of resolutions and conventions. However, at the same time,
racist policies and practices continued unabated in many areas.

Social scientists are faced by a dilemma. The term *race* has no
scientific basis, yet racial categorisation is a crucial factor in social
structure and action. Many people believe that they belong to a specific
race, and that this is important for their social identity: in other words
racism helps to define both the *Self* and the *Other*. This can include
discourses of hierarchy, in which members of dominant groups assert
their superiority, but also discourses of solidarity, in which oppressed
groups (such as black Americans or indigenous peoples) assert their
unity and equality. Race may not be a biological fact, but it certainly
is a social reality. So should social scientists speak of race? Some
scholars have decided that the term is unacceptable yet indispensable,
so that it should be used, but only in quotation marks. Others continue
to use the concept of race without reflection, especially in the context
of research on *race relations*. I will use the term *race* here, because
of its significance in social discourses, but in a critical sense based on
two postulates:

- that race is not a biological reality;
- that race is constructed through racism—a set of ideologies and
  practices imposed by dominant groups on less powerful groups.

Racism, sexism and class

Racism, like sexism, is a social phenomenon embracing both discourse
and practice, which involves making predictions of social behaviour on
the basis of allegedly fixed biological or cultural characteristics. The
imposition of such categories leads to the 'inferiorisation' of certain
groups. This takes specific forms: 'racialisation' of phenotypically or
culturally defined groups and gender oppression against women.
Indeed, racism and sexism are closely linked: dominant ethnic groups
attribute to subordinate groups the characteristics seen in patriarchal
terms as feminine—weakness, dependence, emotionality, unreliability.
Similarly, patriarchy classifies women in the same terms as inferior
races—as exotic, passionate, savage and unpredictable. However,

racism is even more arbitrary than sexism in the sense that sex *is* a biological reality, even though ideas on gender, based on this substratum, are social constructions. For race, there is no such reality; it is whatever racists have the social power to define it as. Here lies perhaps the most crucial point: racism always implies the power (which can be political, economic, social or cultural) to impose a definition of the Other on the subordinate group.

Racism is also linked to sexism in the more direct sense that black, immigrant and ethnic minority women experience racial and gender oppression simultaneously. Here the question arises as to which of these forms of oppression has primacy—an issue of considerable importance for strategic discussions in the women's movement. Minority women's groups have often argued that race has been the primary source of oppression. Mainstream feminist groups, on the other hand, have often argued for the primacy of gender, and tended to ignore the experience of black and immigrant women (Martin 1986, p. 246). The emergence of organisations such as the Immigrant Women's Speakout Association of New South Wales and the Association of Non-English Speaking Background Women of Australia (ANESBWA), is one reaction to the neglect of issues of racism by mainstream feminism (Vasta 1993b, p. 10).

According to Essed, racism and sexism 'narrowly intertwine and combine under certain conditions into one, hybrid phenomenon. Therefore it is useful to speak of *gendered racism* to refer to the racist oppression of Black women as structured by racist and ethnicist perceptions of gender roles' (1991, p. 31). Balibar (1991b, p. 49) argues that 'racism always presupposes sexism'. They are not simply analogous forms of oppression of weaker groups by dominant groups, but rather 'a historical system of complementary exclusions and dominations which are mutually interconnected'. To put it more simply, the type of social order which subordinates women is also likely to racialise ethnic minorities.

It is tempting, then, to portray both forms of domination as mechanisms designed to sustain male ruling-class power in capitalist society. Wallerstein (1991, p. 33), for instance, sees racism as 'a magic formula' which makes it possible simultaneously to minimise the costs of labour-power and to minimise the protests of the labour force. By 'ethnicising' the workforce—dividing it up on racial and ethnic criteria—capitalists can pay workers differently and at the same time gain mass support for this hierarchy. According to Wallerstein (1991, pp. 34–5), just as 'ethnicisation' permits very low wages for some segments of the workforce, sexism reinforces exploitation by forcing women to do unpaid work in the household, or to take low wages outside it.

There is certainly a sound historical basis for the argument that racism, sexism and class domination are linked, but Wallerstein's interpretation here seems problematic. It comes close to the classical Marxist argument that class domination had primacy over other forms of domination, and that class struggle was therefore more important than gender or racial emancipation. This led to the concept of 'false consciousness': the idea that all workers 'really' had the same interests, but were duped by the capitalists into accepting divisions based on race, gender, skill-level and nationality (see, for instance, Cox 1959). This approach has been criticised by feminist and ethnic minority scholars (see Anthias & Yuval-Davis 1983; Barrett 1980; Brah 1991; Hartmann 1979). They see the idea of the primacy of class as a form of functionalism, which reduces both racial and gender oppression to mere mechanisms of ruling-class manipulation. However, the total unity of the working class has never existed: racism and sexism have always played a part within labour movements, as well as in the wider society. There is thus no justification for according primacy to class domination over racism and sexism. All three are forms of 'social normalisation and exclusion' (Balibar 1991b, p. 49) which are intrinsic to capitalism and modernity, and which have developed in close relationship to each other.

Nationalism and democracy

Racism and sexism provide legitimations for hierarchy and differential treatment in liberal democratic societies ostensibly based on ideologies of universalism and equality (Wallerstein 1991). Here we see the link to another important constituting factor of modernity: the nation-state and the accompanying ideology of nationalism. Recent debates have raised the issue of whether nationalism automatically leads to racism, i.e., that racism is a sort of supernationalism (see Anderson 1983; Goldberg 1993, p. 79; Nairn 1980). Against this may be put the idea of 'good and bad nationalism' (Balibar 1991b, p. 47). 'Good national-ism' is the one that helps construct a nation-state or which provides the focus for a struggle for emancipation of an oppressed group (like African-Americans). 'Bad nationalism' is the one that subjugates other nations and oppresses internal minorities. But does a good nationalism turn bad once it has gained power? Is there an automatic link between the encouragement of national feeling as a way of building identity and community, and the development of hatred and contempt for members of other national groups?

These are questions that cannot be discussed fully here, but it is vital to grasp that the nexus between racism and nationalism is central to modern nation-states. This is obvious in the case of authoritarian regimes: there is no better way to legitimate an undemocratic regime than to claim that it represents national feelings and interests against other nations or against internal minorities which are conspiring against it. A national community is based on the fundamental equality of being a member of the nation (portrayed as superior and sacred) against all the rest of the world, who are excluded from membership. This equality masks and legitimates political domination and economic exploitation. The nation is worth dying for, even if one is at the bottom of the social order. Thus, replacing the politics of class with the politics of race stabilises ruling-class domination.

But what of democracies? Why do they too generate racism? A democratic nation-state also has a strong need to define its boundaries. If being a citizen confers rights, then it is essential to define who is not a citizen and therefore should not enjoy the rights. Being a citizen implies equality and political community—enshrined in ideals such as the French Declaration of the Rights of Man and the US Bill of Rights—but it also implies exclusion and domination of non-citizens. And this is not simply a conceptual issue. The whole history of democratic nation-states is full of this ambiguity: colonialism, treatment of internal ethnic minorities (such as Jews or Gipsies), exploitation of immigrant workers. Ivo Andric (1994, p. 265) draws out the fatal essence of the nexus between democracy and nationalism in his famous novel about Bosnia, pointing out that in 1914 'the rulers of human destinies drew European humanity from the playing fields of universal suffrage to the already prepared arena of universal military service'. The right to vote, in the nationalist model, is linked to the duty to die for your country, and this in turn requires racism towards members of other nations.

Nationalism required the construction of myths of common origins, traditions and culture—i.e., of ethnicity—in order to achieve the integration of the 'imagined community' of the nation (Anderson 1983). Within this basic scheme, there are many variations. At one extreme, the 'German model' defines membership of the nation almost exclusively on myths of descent. To this day the principle of *ius sanguinis* (law of the blood) restricts naturalisation of foreign immigrants, leading to the marginalisation of 7 million permanent inhabitants of the country. At the other extreme is the French 'Republican model', which claims to base national belonging simply on membership of the political community. This model was used to assimilate the peoples of colonies into French culture, just as it is used today to assimilate immigrants. However, there is a catch: political assimilation requires possession of the necessary civic virtues, which in effect means assimilation into French culture (see Schnapper 1991; Weil 1991). Assimilation is racist in the sense that it hierarchises cultures, and legitimates their destruction as a precondition for equality.

It is hard to imagine a nationalism without an ideology to legitimate the exclusionary boundaries of the nation-state. Some nationalists deny the link to racism by claiming to see all nations as equally sacred. But that only applies as long as the other people stay 'at home', and as long as there are no existing internal minorities. These conditions are never realised in practice, particularly in an increasingly mobile world. Thus the link between nationalism and racism is very strong. The important question for Australia is the extent to which a pluralist concept of the nation and a multicultural model of national identity can overcome racism.

Exclusion and exploitation

Racism does not always seek to exclude or exterminate the Other. It is equally common for racists to seek to inferiorise and exploit minorities. (See Balibar 1991b, pp. 39–40.) Indeed, the racism of inferiorisation comes first historically: colonialism subjugated the peoples of occupied areas in order to exploit their labour. However, the racism of exclusion and extermination was applied if the colonised group stood in the way of the colonisers' economic aims, as with Australia's indigenous peoples. The racism of inferiorisation applies equally to modern situations of migrant labour: denial of rights forced Western Europe's 'guestworkers' of the 1960s to take the jobs no-one else wanted. Similar practices apply in Middle East labour recruiting countries today. The racism of exclusion and extermination is used against ethnic minorities which are seen either by the state or by certain sections of the majority population as a threat. Nazi anti-Semitism is the classic example, and 'ethnic cleansing' in former Yugoslavia is similar in character.

Sometimes the two types of racism exist side by side and are linked to class interests. The ruling class is more likely to be interested in the racism of exploitation, while workers may favour exclusion. For instance German employers today see a need for labour from Eastern

Europe, partly because it is easily exploitable; German workers call for its exclusion just because they fear the competition. The racism of exclusion may lead to inferiorisation: in Japan, official policies exclude unskilled workers, leading to large-scale entry of illegal migrants, who can be easily exploited by employers (Esman 1992; Sekine 1990). US agricultural employers have done the same with undocumented Mexican workers for many years.

In conflicts like this, we can see the links between racism and class. Again, they are ambiguous: employers may use the racism of inferiorisation to exploit migrant workers, while local workers, fearing competition, may use the racism of exclusion to keep them away. Debates on the White Australia policy in the late nineteenth century were full of such ambiguities (de Lepervanche 1975). It is here that we can see the core of rationality in certain racisms, which have their origins in the desire to protect class interests. Clearly, the distinction between exclusion/extermination and inferiorisation/exploitation is important for analysing specific racisms. It is important to realise that racism does not depend on the characteristics of the dominated groups, but rather on the interests and culture of the dominant group.

Biology and culture

Until recently the criteria for defining racism's Other were mainly biological: they focused on phenotypical features, especially skin colour (compare Taguieff 1988). Anti-racists accordingly saw racism as being mainly about white practices towards non-white people. Recently, cultural factors (such as religion, language and national origins) have been more strongly emphasised. Sometimes these are linked to biology through assumptions on the genetic origins of cultural practices. Nazi propaganda claimed that the Jewish religion and lifestyles were an expression of some biological essence. The more invisible the Jewish characteristics, the more dangerous they were—a case of racism without phenotypical race. In fact, the reduction of racism to white racism against non-whites is recent and linked to post-1945 anti-colonial and civil rights movements. Many older forms of racism focused on culture and national origins (compare Miles 1993, Chapter 3). Phenotypical and cultural racism have always existed side by side and have been closely linked.

The shift back to culture since the 1970s, which caused some observers to speak of a 'new racism' (Balibar 1991a; Barker 1981), has several causes. One was the increasing public unacceptability of biological racism after the defeat of Nazism. Another was the growth of ethnic minorities in Western Europe who could not sensibly be called black, but who were culturally distinct on the basis of religion (especially Islam), dress, lifestyle and values. Ironically, this led to problems for some British anti-racists, for whom it was axiomatic that the targets of racism were black: they went on tours of the Continent to identify 'the blacks' and were surprised to find that Turks and North Africans rejected the label. A third issue was the increasing evidence of racism against minority groups within African or Asian countries, which clearly could not be put in white/black terms.

Racism today is not just a 'colour' issue. Yet colour is not irrelevant, since global power relations are still structured by the aftermath of colonialism: in a world split into rich North and poor South, being white is still an indicator of power and privilege. As Balibar (1991a, p. 44) points out, media discourses on the racisms of the Third World reinforce white racism, by encouraging the idea that 'three-quarters of humanity are incapable of governing themselves'. When donor agencies like the World Bank today make 'good governance' a condition for loans, they are acting in the tradition of the 'civilising mission' of the West.

What has been said so far implies that there is no difference in the essential character of racism, whether it is directed against a group defined on the basis of phenotypical characteristics (a 'race') or against a group defined on the basis of culture (an 'ethnic group'). Race and ethnicity are similar social constructions, serving to define Self and Other. The main difference, as Goldberg (1993, p. 76) points out, is that ethnicity uses a rhetoric of cultural content, whereas race uses a rhetoric of descent, but these are 'rhetorical tendencies, not fixed conceptualisations'. Indeed, race and ethnic group are sometimes used as alternatives, as with Jews, Blacks or Hispanics in the USA. This does not imply that racists in a given location treat all minority groups in the same way: for instance, there is clear evidence that Australian racism is most virulent against Aboriginal peoples, then against Asians, and then other immigrant groups (HREOC 1991). Similarly German racists targeted Turks more than European immigrants until recently. Significantly, after reunification in 1990, European immigrants of Gipsy ethnicity came in for as much hostility as Turks. The point is that racism chooses its targets according to its own perverse inner logic, rather than on the basis of some fixed hierarchy.

The 'culturalisation of racism' (Essed 1991, p. 14) is also linked to the new discourses of tolerance, which are so important for multi-culturalism. Today, the term *racism* is almost invariably perjorative:

nobody admits to being a racist. Ideas of racial hierarchy are rejected, and the principle of equal opportunity is espoused by politicians of all persuasions. If some groups—especially people of non-European origin—are socio-economically and politically disadvantaged, this is attributed to cultural values which are seen as backward or inappropriate for a technologically advanced society. The acceptance of cultural pluralism is compatible with a belief in the superiority of the dominant culture. The very idea of tolerance for minority cultures implies a belief in the superiority of the dominant one: immigrants and ethnic minorities can keep their own values and cultures, but they cannot complain if this leads to their marginalisation. Moreover, if black people do not do well despite all the welfare measures and equal opportunity policies, then it must be their own fault. Emphasis on cultural difference is therefore a new ideology of legitimation for a covert racism without claims of biological superiority (Essed 1991).

Fixation on older definitions of racism as notions of biologically based hierarchies allows more subtle racisms based on cultural markers to claim to be benign and progressive (Barker 1981). The 'new racism' is a 'racism without race' (Balibar 1991a, p. 23). It no longer speaks of superiority, but rather of immutable differences that make coexistence between varying cultural groups in one society impossible. Socio-biological theories of 'natural aggression' and 'inevitable conflict' within 'nations of tribes' provide a pseudo-scientific argument against immigration and multiculturalism. And even multiculturalism may be seen as a new and more sophisticated form of racism, in the way it legitimates the power of the dominant group to proclaim and manage hierarchies of acceptable and unacceptable difference.

One way of dealing with this problem of constant change in the rhetoric of racism is to examine it as a form of culture. Goldberg (1993, p. 9) sees 'racist culture' as 'one of the central ways modern social subjects make sense of and express themselves about the world they inhabit and invent'. Racist culture has its expressions and objects, its meanings and values, which constitute a 'way of life'. Goldberg provides a powerful argument that racism is a central and enduring element of the modern world—however much its particular forms of expression may change. Racism has been intrinsic to the way of thinking of modernity. Moreover, although it has been important for centuries, the peak period of racism as a dominant ideology justifying European world conquest was only recent: the late nineteenth and early twentieth centuries. And let us not forget—above all in Australia—that racism was an accepted world view, openly held by the majority of the population only thirty years ago.

Commonsense and everyday racism

Overt racism may be less frequent than in the past, but it remains deeply embedded in our traditions and culture. As van Dijk (1993, p. 7) argues:

> this undeniable progress has only softened the style of dominance of white Western nations. Far from abolished are the deeply entrenched economic, social and cultural remnants of past oppression and inequality; the modern prejudices about minorities; the economic and military power or the cultural hegemony of white over black, North over South, majorities over minorities.

Racism is still part of *commonsense*: the accumulated, taken-for-granted and often contradictory set of assumptions used by people to understand and cope with the complex social world around them. In ostensibly non-racist societies like Australia, the influence of past ideologies and practices makes itself felt indirectly through discourses in the media, politics and popular culture. The received ideas of racist culture are not expressed openly, but rather in the form of ahistorical commonsense notions about the character and achievements of specific groups, and about the inevitability of competitions and conflict between different races. This hidden and often unconscious power of racist discourse allows elite groups to claim enlightened and meritocratic views, while in fact applying racist definitions of social reality (van Dijk 1993).

People do not need to have conscious racist beliefs to act in a way which reinforces racist structures and ideologies. As Essed (1991) argues, racism has become part of the systematic, recurrent, familiar practices which make up everyday life. She defines 'everyday racism' as:

> a process in which (a) socialised racist notions are integrated into meanings that make practices immediately definable and manageable, (b) practices with racist implications become in themselves familiar and repetitive, and (c) underlying racial and ethnic relations are actualised and reinforced through these routine or familiar practices in everyday situations (p. 52).

Beliefs about racial hierarchies and ethnic differences are so much part of our culture and traditions that we continually learn them in all the different parts of the socialisation process (in the family, school, peer groups and through the media). In our daily life, we tend to act on unconscious racist beliefs, and thus reproduce racist ideologies and practices as part of social structure and action.

A *working definition*

In the light of the above discussions, is it possible and useful to define racism? The danger of a formal definition is that it tends to simplify and fix something that is complex and constantly changing. On the other hand, a general definition of racism brings out the essential unity of certain types of normalisation and differentiation of people. It is therefore a valuable yardstick for analysis and political action, because it can help in assessing whether certain ideas, practices or situations can properly be seen as racist. I will provide a working definition here, on the understanding that it is useful only in the context of detailed analyses of specific racisms. The definition has three elements.

1 Racism is not an aberration or a result of individual pathology. It is a set of practices and discourses which are deeply rooted in the history, traditions and culture of modernity. Racism exists in a variety of forms in all modern societies, and plays a crucial role in consolidating nation-states, by providing an instrument for defining belonging or exclusion. That is why increasing racism in decolonised nations is part of the process of modernisation. Racism is linked to democracy in the sense that it reconciles ideologies of universalism and equality with the practices of hierarchisation and segmentation which are central to the economic and social order. Racism is closely interrelated with other forms of social normalisation and control, particularly sexism and class domination.
2 Racism is the process whereby social groups categorise other groups as different or inferior, on the basis of phenotypical characteristics, cultural markers or national origin. This process involves the use of economic, social or political power, and generally has the purpose of legitimating exploitation or exclusion of the group so defined. The dominant group constructs ideologies of the inherent difference and the inferiority of the dominated groups. The power of the dominant group is sustained by developing structures (such as laws, policies and administrative practices) that exclude or discriminate against the dominated group. This type of racism is generally known as *institutional racism*. More spontaneous types of prejudice or discrimination arising out of a racist culture are generally known as *informal racism*. These two types are closely related in that they are both expressions of group power or dominance. For this reason,

as Essed (1991, p. 37) points out, the concept of individual racism is misleading: racism always implies a group process.

3 Racism takes many forms of varying intensity, which may be seen as a continuum. Acceptance of even the apparently milder forms—in the form of commonsense or everyday racism—can pave the way for the more violent ones. The forms include: prejudiced attitudes; discrimination (in legal status, employment, housing, eligibility for services and access to public places); verbal or written abuse; incitement to hatred, discrimination or violence; harassment designed to intimidate or insult; physical violence; and genocide. All these practices may be seen as forms of violence, in the broad sense proposed by Galtung (1988, pp. 281–2): violence should be taken to include any practices, whether carried out by individuals, social groups or institutions, which restrict the freedom or self-realisation of human beings, and which are based on the ultimate threat of physical harm. In other words, all forms of racism are essentially violent, for they reduce people's life chances, and are ultimately based on the threat of physical harm.

The globalisation of racism

Racism has increased in significance in many parts of the world in recent times. It is my hypothesis that the forms it takes are closely linked to processes of decolonisation, modernisation, and international economic and cultural integration. In other words, most contemporary racisms are closely related to globalisation and to the way this brings labour transformations—often of a disturbing or even traumatic nature—at the national and local levels. In this section I will give a brief summary of some of the types of racism to be found in various settings.[2]

Oppression of indigenous peoples

The USA, Canada and Australia originated as white settler colonies, based on dispossession of indigenous peoples. In the USA, the destruction of Native American societies is part of the myth of nation-building and also an element in the widespread glorification of violence. In both the USA and Canada, indigenous people's movements since the 1960s have led to changes in public awareness and policies. However, most Native Americans (0.8 per cent of US population) and Native Canadians (2 per cent of total Canadian population) remain socio-economically marginalised and lacking in political power. The same applies to Australia's indigenous peoples, as will be discussed in Chapter 6.

Discrimination against indigenous peoples is also to be found in Latin America. In the Andean area and Central America, the origins of the rural peasant population are Indian or *mestizo* (mixed European and Indian), while the urban population is of European immigrant background. Class and other power relations therefore have strong ethnic aspects. There have been many cases of serious human rights abuses, including massacres of indigenous people (for instance in Guatemala) (US DoS 1992, p. 620).

Most Asian countries have long-standing national minorities—often marginalised through territorial expansion of dominant groups. For instance, the People's Republic of China has 55 designated ethnic minorities, making up 8 per cent of the total population. Most members of these groups are said to have living standards below the national average. In other Asian countries, minorities are categorised as 'tribal peoples' or 'hill tribes'. Such groups are to be found for instance in Bangladesh, India, Thailand and Vietnam. Minorities consisting of indigenous peoples overrun in the past by more powerful settler groups exist in Japan and Taiwan. All these groups experience some degree of socio-economic disadvantage and political exclusion (US DoS 1992, pp. 1402–3).

Racism connected with decolonisation and nation-building

Many forms of racism are part of the legacy of colonialism. European powers carved out new administrative entities with no regard for existing ethnic boundaries. Many post-colonial states include several ethnic groups, while members of a specific ethnic group may be citizens of two or more adjoining states. A further legacy of colonialism was the introduction of indentured workers from other areas (such as Indians in East Africa), who sometimes became economically successful but vulnerable minorities. Decolonisation and the formation of new nation-states has frequently involved domination, discrimination or exclusion of minorities (Castles & Miller 1993, pp. 140–3; Ricca 1990).

One consequence has been the rapid growth in refugee movements. An estimated 20 million people have had to seek refuge outside their countries, while at least the same number are internally displaced (UNFPA 1993, pp. 31–4). The overwhelming majority of refugees have their origins in less-developed countries, and seek refuge in other such countries. Political upheavals are often linked to ethnic conflicts as well. In Africa, political and economic struggles frequently express themselves as battles for dominance between tribes; many of the Indo-Chinese refugees are ethnic Chinese, who suffered racism as well as political persecution. Other refugee movements with this dual character included those of Tibetans to India and Nepal, East Timorese to Australia and Portugal, and Burmese ethnic minority groups to Thailand and Bangladesh. Such refugees often also find themselves victims of racism while on the flight, or in their new country of refuge (NPC 1991, pp. 68–91).

Zolberg et al. (1989, pp. 227–57) argue that the main cause of refugee movements is not poverty and underdevelopment, but the generalised and persistent violence that has resulted from rapid processes of globalisation. New states have been formed under conditions determined by colonial experience, as well as by neo-colonial power relations (domination of world trade by the industrialised countries). The result is weak states, underdeveloped economies and poor social conditions. This has been the context for ethnic conflicts and political struggles, leading to impoverishment and denial of human rights. Moreover, during the Cold War, local conflicts became internationalised, with the major powers supporting opposing sides, and sending weapons and even troops to intervene in struggles in Africa, Asia and Latin America.

In the former Soviet Union more than 60 million people live outside their nationality's administrative region, creating an enormous potential for conflict as new nation-states are created. Such states are generally based on membership of specific ethnic groups, which often means discrimination against minorities. Some of these are in turn fighting to establish their own states, or seeking to link up with other states in which their own ethnic group has power. In Russia itself many ethnic minorities exist, and the political and economic unrest following the collapse of Soviet power has led to the emergence of nationalistic and anti-Semitic movements. Conflicts have arisen as groups deported under Stalin have sought to regain their old territories (US DoS 1992, pp. 1284–7; see also Brubaker 1992). The conflict in Chechnya in 1994–95 is one of the most extreme examples.

In Eastern and South-Eastern Europe, the collapse of communist states has led to explosive ethnic conflicts based partly on long-suppressed historical issues and partly on current problems of rapid economic and political change (see Schierup 1993). Conflicts and refugee exoduses have affected Bulgaria, Romania and Albania. 'Ethnic cleansing' in the ruins of Yugoslavia has evoked widespread horror. The failure of supranational bodies like the European Community and the

United Nations to stop the fighting shows vividly that racism can present a major threat to democratic states and to the international community.

Migrant labour

Recruitment of migrant labour frequently involves racist practices: the division between national and non-national, or between dominant ethnic group and minority is a way of segmenting the labour market and forcing down wages. Migrant labour was a major factor in post-1945 economic growth in most industrial countries. Britain, France and the Netherlands encouraged labour migration from former colonies. Most immigrants were citizens of the immigration country, and differentiation was generally based on classical phenotypical racism. At the same time, nearly all Western European countries recruited foreign workers in Southern Europe, Turkey and North Africa. Here the legal division between national and non-national was the basis of a whole set of discriminatory laws and practices against migrant workers.

In the 1960s, the USA abolished discriminatory immigration rules, leading to large-scale entries from Asia, Latin America and the Caribbean. Non-European immigrants have encountered considerable racism. The fear of mass Hispanic immigration has become a major factor in US politics, leading for instance to the 1994 invasion of Haiti. In contrast, most Asian immigrants come legally and have secure legal status as refugees or highly skilled workers. Their economic situation is therefore often better than that of Hispanics. Nonetheless, Asians frequently report racial harassment and attacks.

Since the 1970s, foreign labour has been important for the Arab Gulf oil states, and since the 1980s for the newly industrialising countries of Asia. Labour movements are a result of growing capital mobility, uneven economic development, improving transport facilities, and increasing awareness of opportunities in distant areas—all typical aspects of globalisation (Castles & Miller 1993). The millions of foreign contract workers in the Gulf states lack civil, political and social rights, and are subject to economic exploitation, discrimination, and arbitrary deportation. Such practices are even more severe in the case of undocumented (or illegal) workers, who are totally lacking in legal protection, even though their employment is often widespread and tacitly tolerated by the state (as in the USA, Italy, Japan, and many other countries). In turn, the competition of rightless migrants often provokes a racist reaction from local workers.

Women play a growing part in labour migration: patriarchal stereotypes in both sending and receiving countries facilitate their exploitation, not only in traditional female occupations such as domestic service
and the sex industry, but also in advanced industrial sectors such as
electronics. Women in domestic service are frequently subjected to
sexual abuse, as has been well documented in the case of the Gulf
states. Here again, we see the links between gender discrimination and
racialisation.

Racism against old and new minorities

Many forms of racism are continuations of long-standing patterns.
However, they often take new forms, due to new migrations which add
additional elements to existing ethnic mixtures. In the USA, despite
government action following the civil rights movement of the 1960s,
racism against African-Americans (12 per cent of the US population)
continues. Distinctions between whites and blacks in income, occupational status, unemployment rates, social conditions and education are
still extreme (Hacker 1992; Marable & Mullings 1994). Racial violence
and harassment remain serious problems (ADL 1988). Such phenomena
have led some observers to regard racism as a permanent and unchange-
able feature of US society, which blacks have to learn to live with (Bell
1992a). The increasing complexity of interethnic relations is leading to
new types of conflict and to a politicisation of issues of culture and
ethnicity. The Los Angeles riots of 1992 were indicative of such trends.

Western European countries have a long history of ethnic conflict
and a deeply entrenched culture of racism. Racism expresses itself in
conflicts on the status of territorial minorities (such as Basques in Spain
or Corsicans in France), discrimination against historical minorities
(like Jews and Gipsies), as well as in attitudes and practices towards
the new ethnic minorities, which developed through post-1945 labour
migrations. Racism has intensified since the late 1980s when the end
of the Cold War coincided with a serious recession, and with an
increase in entries of asylum-seekers. The most dramatic signs of
tension are increasing racist violence, the rise of the extreme right, and
confrontations between ethnic minority youth and the police (Wrench
& Solomos 1993). Growing cultural diversity feeds into a moral panic
which portrays 'Fortress Europe' as under threat by unpredictable
influxes from the East and the South, evoking the 'Mongol hordes' of
a distant past. Neo-Nazis and skinheads now portray themselves as the
'defenders of the European idea' against invasion, while mainstream

political leaders outdo each other in putting up barriers to stop immigration.

Explaining the racisms of globalisation

There are many racisms throughout the world today, but they have an essential unity as a mode of exclusion based on socially constructed markers of biological or cultural variation, and of national identity. In this section I will argue that contemporary racisms are closely linked to the process of globalisation. The central question is: why does globalisation give rise to new forms of racism, and in many cases to an increased prevalence and intensity of racism? My hypothesis is that globalisation leads to fundamental societal changes, which are experienced as crises of the national economy and social relations, as crises of culture and identity, and as political crises. In turn, these shifts in the character and forms of expression of racism have led to a crisis of anti-racism. This section will concentrate on highly developed countries. The links between racism and the crisis of the South—characterised by decolonisation, economic dependence, weak states, and generalised violence—have already been hinted at in the last section.

Just as racism has always been an integral part of modernity, the current shifts in racism are linked to a general crisis of modernity. The French sociologists Wieviorka and Lapeyronnie and their collaborators argue that the recent rise in racism in Western Europe is the result of 'the decomposition of national industrial societies' (Wieviorka 1994, p. 25). The 'national industrial society' is the model which evolved in the nineteenth and twentieth centuries and became the norm for modern nation-states. It articulates three elements—society, state and nation—in a particular form. The society refers to an economic and social system usually based on rational (as opposed to traditional or religious) principles, within a bounded national territory. The state refers to a political system based on secular (and usually democratic) principles, capable of regulating economic and political relations and change. The nation refers to a 'people' defined both on the basis of belonging to the territory of the state and having a common cultural and ethnic background (Lapeyronnie et al. 1990, pp. 258–62).

Until recently, the social and political identity of citizens of highly developed countries was based upon the articulation of their own particular society, state and nation, within a world of nation-states. The whole of classical sociology takes this 'national society' for granted (Lapeyronnie et al. 1990, p. 259). Even the critics of capitalism based their politics on national units: social-democratic demands for economic reform and welfare policies addressed the state; communists called for world revolution, but were organised nationally. That helps to explain why the left was shattered by globalisation: capital became international much sooner than its opponents did.

Globalisation has destabilised the 'national industrial society'. The central dynamics of economic life now transcend national borders, and have become uncontrollable for national governments. Deindustrialisation of the older industrial nations has led to profound social changes, and has eroded the political basis of the labour movement. This in turn has severely weakened one side in the political conflict between capital and labour, which was a central organising element of society (Wieviorka 1991; 1992; 1993). Capital may appear to have won, but at the price of a social and political disorganisation which is highly threatening. The same is true at the global level: the end of the Cold War seemed at first to offer the chance of a stable global order, but unpredictable and uncontrollable conflicts soon emerged. Such uncertainties apply to culture too: rapid communication, travel and mass media offer an enormous and often confusing range of choices. Cultural openness is enriching, but it also questions one of the basic elements which integrated national societies: the myth of distinct and homogeneous national cultures (Anderson 1983; Gellner 1983). All these changes are ambivalent: they offer new horizons and possibilities of emancipation, but they can also lead to social and psychological insecurity, and threaten feelings of identity and community.

If we accept this idea of the 'decomposition of the national industrial society', the question is: how does this lead to new racisms? To answer this we need to look at the effects of restructuring on the societies of highly developed countries.

Economic and social crises

Globalisation has been experienced initially as a process of economic and industrial restructuring. Until the 1960s, capitalist expansion was based mainly on investment in existing industrial countries, leading to a long economic boom, rising wages and upward social mobility for many. The stereotype of the 'affluent worker' was born. But from the 1970s, investment patterns changed: capital moved offshore to establish factories in low-wage countries. Oil-rich countries and newly industrialising countries took an increasing share in world trade. Investment in the older industrial countries focused on labour-saving technologies. Full employment gave way to rising levels of joblessness. Qualified workers belonging to the old 'labour aristocracy' found their skills devalued by new technologies. The crisis of restructuring has occurred everywhere, but its effects have been felt most strongly in the older industrial areas, with their outmoded heavy and mechanical industries.

The economic crisis is always also a social one. Housing and urban infrastructure have declined as fast as the industries which used to help finance them. The decaying cities of the North and Midlands of Britain—the oldest industrial country—symbolise the end of an epoch. The industrial city was a central site of modernity, serving as a focus for national capital, political power and national culture. This does not imply homogeneity and consensus: it was not only ruling-class political power and culture that was centred in the city, but also that of the labour movement and its counter-culture. The post-industrial city is very different: manufacturing is declining, the ownership of productive and reproductive capital is integrated into complex international networks, political power is fragmented and opaque. At the same time, recent immigrations have made the big cities highly diverse in their ethnic composition. The spatial organisation of the city is now based as much on ethnicity as class, the two combining in complex and conflictual forms (Cross & Keith 1993; Davis 1990; Sassen 1988).

The globalisation of finance has led to a fiscal crisis of the state, which cannot be resolved at the national level. The welfare states which developed after 1945 were based on the need for maintaining political legitimacy and ensuring collective reproduction of labour power at a time of full employment. Their material basis and their ideologies of solidarity and compassion have been eroded through deindustrialisation and limitations on national economic autonomy. The Thatcher and Reagan Governments of the 1980s used the new ideology of economic rationality as a legitimation for changes designed both to privatise the crisis and to bolster the profits of international investors. The gradual roll-back of social security policies has led to a high degree of insecurity for large sections of the population. The 'two-thirds society', in which a large part of the population are decoupled from real participation in society, creates the potential for marginalisation and exclusion of minorities.

These economic and social changes have coincided with the settlement of large numbers of immigrants in the cities. Many local people have seen the newcomers as the cause of the threatening changes—an interpretation encouraged by the extreme right, but also by many mainstream politicians. Paradoxically, disadvantaged local people often share a common fate with ethnic minorities. Both are subject to the same processes of polarisation: a new middle class of highly trained managers, professionals and technicians is growing, but so is a new lower class of low-skilled workers employed in casual and insecure jobs. Minorities are affected disproportionately, as are new immigrants, who can no longer find entry-level jobs in factory and construction work. These groups are often pushed into the ghettoes of large public housing projects. Here, marginalised members of the majority population are face-to-face with the immigrants and minorities, whom they have come to blame for their own fate. The potential for racism is obvious, and it is indeed in such 'ghettoes of the disadvantaged' (Dubet & Lapeyronnie 1992) that racist violence and extreme-right mobilisation are most extreme.

Crises of culture and identity

The crisis of modernity also expresses itself in cultural terms. This happens at three levels. At the level of national culture, there is a feeling of uncertainty and loss, arising from the swamping of distinctive cultural practices and forms by a commodified international culture, produced in global cultural factories like Hollywood. Nations which used to define their uniqueness through traditions of language, folklore and high culture now find all this slipping away. Intellectuals and governments combine to maintain the purity of the national language, and to restrict the import of foreign cultural artefacts: the resistance of the French Government in 1993 to the opening of cultural markets to world trade in the GATT round was symbolic both of this struggle and of its futility.

A second level relates to the supposed threat to national culture through imported ethnic cultures. By maintaining their languages, folklore, cultural practices and religions, immigrants are seen as undermining national culture. Racists who attack women in Islamic dress claim to be defending the nation, or even European culture—a stereotype which links up with older racist notions on the threat of the Other to Christianity and civilisation. But this level is closely linked to the first: it is only because global influences make national culture so precarious that immigrant minorities appear as a serious danger.

The third level of culture is connected with the central role of the idea of superiority over non-European peoples in colonialism. If migrants from former colonies to France, Britain and the Netherlands have the same rights as local people, that questions century-old traditions of hierarchy. The problem is all the more acute in a situation of decline: in Britain immigration from the Caribbean and the Indian sub-continent coincided with deindustrialisation and social crisis, and with a rapid loss in significance on the international stage. Immigration could be portrayed as a revenge of the colonised peoples, which was undermining the nation (compare Cohen & Bains 1988; Layton-Henry 1992; Solomos 1993). Similarly, the decline of French culture has been linked by the extreme-right Front National to the loss of the colonies and the immigration of North Africans.

In such situations, racism against minorities takes on a central role: it helps to recreate a threatened community. Racism is a form of white ethnic solidarity in the face of the apparent cultural strength of immigrant groups (compare Wieviorka 1991). If British workers lose their jobs, and find their social security and environment declining, they can blame the alien influences which are undermining the nation. Hating immigrants helps to maintain an illusion of national unity and pride. Racism can help strengthen group and personal identity in a situation of crisis.

It has become fashionable to claim that racism today is a working-class phenomenon. Extreme-right groups recruit mainly from working-class sub-cultures such as skinheads and football fans. Conflicts between local people and immigrants occur mainly in working-class neighbourhoods. Ruling-class racism, like the support of German industrialists for the Nazis, or the support of Australian elites for the White Australia policy, seems to be a thing of the past. Capital is international, and will chase profit regardless of colour, culture or creed.

But caution is needed in accepting this judgement. Firstly, racism should not be seen as a working-class phenomenon, but rather as one product of the current decline of working-class culture and organisation. In the face of multinational cultural industries, popular cultures have lost much of their power to deal with change. Secondly, the absence of overt racism should not lead us to think that racism has declined in the middle or upper classes. As van Dijk (1993) shows so convincingly, racist discourses and beliefs have not lost ground among elites. Rather, they do not take open and violent forms, because elites are not as directly threatened as workers, and because they have the power to contain threats in more subtle ways. When elites do feel threatened, the ugly face of racism can quickly reappear, as the Australian mine-owners have shown through their campaigns against Aboriginal land rights.

Political crises

Economic, social, cultural and identity crises are, of course, not separate phenomena but different facets of the crisis of modernity, as expressed in the dissolution of the national society. All these dimensions are political: the erosion of the nation-state through globalisation leads to crises of both ruling-class and working-class politics. Racism should be seen not as a result of the crisis, but rather as one form of expression of the crisis (Balibar 1991c, pp. 204–27). One aspect of the crisis is the *racialisation of politics*, through which political discourses of many kinds are structured by attaching deterministic meanings to socially constructed physical and cultural characteristics. For example, the increasing role of ethnic difference in urban restructuring has led to a racialisation of social relations and politics at the local level: every conflict of interest now has an ethnic dimension, and racism becomes a way of expressing group interests (Ball & Solomos 1990).

At the national level too, social dislocation has been accompanied by a political crisis. The decline of working-class parties and trade unions, and the erosion of local communicative networks have created the social space for the growth of racism (Wieviorka 1991; 1993). Disadvantaged groups have found themselves without political representation in mainstream parties, which has led to a decline in confidence in democratic institutions. Many people have turned to extreme-right groups which provide a monocausal explanation for the crisis: that the nation is being undermined by immigration and minorities. Thus organised racism—often leading directly to violence—is both a psychological and a political response to processes of rapid change, which are often incomprehensible and always uncontrollable for those most affected.

This points to the need to analyse the links between economic change, political ideologies and popular attitudes. In many cases, the political response to restructuring has been a neo-conservative model which emphasises natural inequality, deregulation of markets, reduced state intervention, and a return to traditional values of family and nation. The attack on the welfare state helps to create the social conditions for racism, while the ideology of neo-conservatism provides a fertile climate for blaming 'deviant' minorities for social problems. These themes are taken up in the media and in popular discourse, helping to create a new 'commonsense' racism.

Extreme-right organisations take this ideology a step further by reinterpreting it as a call to violence. They recruit poor white urban youth, who seek to overcome their own powerlessness through violence against minorities with even less social power. At the same time, ideologies of equality and tolerance help legitimate elite racism. In this 'racism without race', powerful groups maintain that there is equal opportunity for all irrespective of ethnic background. Those groups which are disadvantaged or excluded must therefore be the victims of their own 'inferior cultures', and of their refusal to adapt to the superior majority culture.

The crisis of anti-racism

Racism is an integral part of the crisis of modernity, in all its economic, social, cultural and political facets. The failure to realise this is an important factor in the crisis of anti-racist thinking, which is still often fixated on older forms of racism—above all on the biological racism which was a central part of Western culture until at least 1945 (see Taguieff 1988). Even more serious, most anti-racists still see racism as something peripheral to social and political life—what Paul Gilroy has called the 'coat-of-paint theory of racism' (1992, p. 52). The idea is that racism is an unpleasant anomaly which is alien to the basic notions of humanism and liberal democracy. Racism can therefore be combated by legal, educational and psychological strategies which will deal with the ugly aberration without changing the overall social and political system. This approach has two main aspects, which may be called official anti-racism and critical anti-racism.

Official anti-racism refers to the role of the state. Throughout the history of modernity, the state has had a crucial role in constructing racism. In more recent times—since the international struggle against Nazism—the state has also had a role in combating racism. Most modern states have signed UN human rights declarations and have a whole gamut of anti-racist laws and policies. Australia is a case in point with its Federal Racial Discrimination Act, Human Rights and Equal Opportunity Commission, State Anti-Discrimination Boards, and so on. Sometime there is a tongue-in-cheek cynicism about such institutions: for instance, the strong German anti-racist laws do not apply to non-citizens, while strict naturalisation rules stop most of the seven million foreign residents from becoming citizens. But on the whole, anti-racism based on the UNESCO declarations of the post-war period has become part of the ruling consensus.

And yet, as discussed above, exclusion and exploitation based on racist criteria are as widespread and serious as ever—though they may have changed in form. Clearly, official anti-racism is ineffective. There are several reasons for this. One is the weakness and unwieldiness of laws on vilification and discrimination. Prosecutions are rare, and the effects on social behaviour are peripheral; the rules are often merely symbolic gestures. More important is the fact that official anti-racism is generally based on outmoded concepts of overt, biological racism. It is blind to the more subtle and pervasive expressions of cultural racism, as embodied in dominant political and economic institutions, everyday life and commonsense discourses. This is not surprising, for to recognise that racism is a central part of our social and political life would imply the need for radical changes, and thus undermine existing power relations. Official anti-racism thus has an ambivalent character. It does represent a break with the overtly racist ideologies of the past, but it sometimes serves as an excuse for new forms of exclusion and exploitation of minorities.

Critical anti-racism refers to movements which have developed since the 1960s, generally linked to ethnic communities as well as to left-wing political organisations, trade unions and church groups. Critical anti-racists have pointed to the hollowness of official policies, and have shown how laws and institutions have been inadequate in combating the widespread discrimination and marginalisation of minorities. But most anti-racist groups have concentrated on old-style biological racism, especially in its neo-Nazi guise. Racism has been analysed as something peripheral to capitalist society, and therefore excisable without other basic changes. Anti-racists have courageously fought against racist groups and exposed official hypocrisy. But their demands have generally been for better legislation, stronger anti-racist institutions, and more comprehensive community strategies. All these things are needed, but they will not in themselves alter the basic causes of racism, which are deeply embedded in our social order and culture.

Moreover, the fixation of anti-racism on legislation and rules for securing equality have opened the door to a new conservative critique, based on the slogan of 'political correctness'. By exposing and carica-turing alleged excesses of affirmative action and quota systems, espe-cially in the USA, the new right has endeavoured (with some success) to label anti-racists as opponents of equality and democracy. The powerful critique of political correctness is designed to legitimate inequality and racism, by appealing to the principles of individual rights and equality.

Anti-racism therefore needs to reinvent itself, in response to the transformation of racism. It is essential to understand that racism is a basic element of our society, and has played a crucial role in its evolution, from the very beginnings of modernity. It is equally important to realise that globalisation has not interrupted the continuity of racism, but yet has led to a whole gamut of new racisms. These are closely linked to the crises connected with restructuring, which are occurring everywhere, albeit in a variety of specific forms. The culturalisation of race, and the idea of 'racism without race' are widespread expressions of these developments. At the same time some of the older forms of racism—such as discrimination against indigenous peoples and ethnic nationalism in new nations—continue unabated. Anti-racism therefore needs a multi-faceted strategy, which takes account of the strength, diversity and mutability of racism, as well of its fundamental importance in modern society.

3

Dialectics of domination: Racism and multiculturalism

Ellie Vasta

In Western democracies with large immigrant populations, multi-culturalism has become a central theme of debate. The dilemma is how to incorporate increasing numbers of immigrants, while retaining national institutions and cultures. Public policies have to be developed in order to deal with a growing cultural diversity. At the same time, multiculturalism hits at the core of ideas about national identity. At a time when migratory flows have increased to unprecedented levels, there is a tendency to cling to myths of a historical national identity that has always been there, consistent and unchanged. As a country which dramatically increased its immigrant population in the post-war years, Australia has developed a relatively successful model of integration. Nevertheless, the Australian version of multiculturalism contains a number of contradictions and problems which are not easily resolvable and which require continuous debate, analysis and development.[1]

One major contradiction concerns the relationship between universalism and pluralism. Liberal democratic societies have long prided themselves on the idea that all members of society have equal rights. In recent decades, movements of women and of minorities of all kinds have shown the hollowness of this claim: some groups of people are more equal than others, both before the law and in socio-economic and political terms. This has led to the demand to recognise people as collective bearers of a culture, which implies the need for differential treatment of groups with differing cultures and social positions (Taylor 1992; see Young 1990a). Thus a tension exists between universalism and difference, and various societies attempt to deal with that tension through special public policies which address the needs and values of the various groups.

In Australia (and a few other countries) multiculturalism has emerged as a policy designed to deal with specific needs of ethnic minorities, which a universalist model of assimilation could not address adequately. The key question is: does multiculturalism overcome the previous racist construction of social relations and national identity? In this chapter, I will argue that while many explicit forms of racism (such as admission policies based on 'race' or ethnicity) have been abolished, other forms of racism persist, usually in covert forms. Indeed, some critics argue that multiculturalism itself is a form of racism, and thus a new form of domination. Many people therefore believe that much stronger anti-racist strategies need to be included in multiculturalism. In discussing this issue, the problem emerges that it is often quite hard to disentangle *anti-racist critiques* of multiculturalism from *racist critiques*. The discourse of equality is used both by those who want to combat the structural ethnic biases built into our institutions, and by those who wish to abolish anti-discrimination measures on the grounds that they 'discriminate against the majority'.

Multiculturalism developed in Australia from the early 1970s as a result of the failure of the previous strategy of assimilation, and in response to growing ethnic political mobilisation. In the early stages of multicultural policy, the main stress was on the significance of ethnic communities and on the legitimacy of cultural maintenance. More recently, especially since the Federal Government's 1989 policy statement *National Agenda for a Multicultural Australia* (OMA 1989), the emphasis has been on the social and cultural rights of citizens, and the need for the state to pursue active policies to combat discrimination and to achieve social justice. Multiculturalism has given rise to a plethora of special government agencies, and to a set of policies and measures designed to achieve 'access and equity' for members of minorities in all areas of government involvement. Multiculturalism has had less structural impact in the private sphere, but it has had considerable influence on debates on culture, identity and Australia's place in the world.

I do not intend to present a systematic account of multiculturalism here—that is unnecessary in view of the wealth of literature on the theme (see, for instance, Castles et al. 1992a; Castles 1994; Collins 1991; Foster & Stockley 1988; Freeman & Jupp 1992; Martin 1991a). Rather my aim is to examine debates on the relationship between multiculturalism and racism. In order to do so, it is necessary to separate analytically between two major aspects of multiculturalism (which, however, are often intertwined in policy and practice): firstly, multiculturalism provides principles for a social policy for migrant settlement; secondly, it is also concerned with the relationships between cultural diversity, ethnic identities and national identity.

In its first aspect, multiculturalism is meant to combat socio-economic inequality, insofar as this is caused by barriers based on 'race', ethnicity, culture, religion and gender. If such inequality persists, then multiculturalism can be seen as failing in its task of combating racism. The state itself has a contradictory position: on the one hand it claims to work for social justice, on the other it calls for economic rationality and deregulation of markets. Yet economic rationalism is based on the notion of inequality as a key factor in efficient distribution of resources (see Chapter 4). The question here is: can multiculturalism as a public policy overcome this contradiction?

However, it is in multiculturalism's second aspect—that of ethnic and national identity—that racism remains most significant. Since white invasion, Australian national identity has been structured in racist dominance: over indigenous people, through genocide, dispossession and destruction of their cultures; and over migrants, through the White Australia policy as well as through institutional and interpersonal discrimination against each new group of entrants (de Lepervanche 1975). Racism has been a central element in the construction and expression of power relationships between majority and minority groups. These, in turn, have directly influenced the construction of ethnic and national identities. The dominant national identity (usually referred to as Anglo-Australian identity) has been based on myths of Britishness and of the taming of a 'savage land'. The identities of Aboriginal people and migrants have been developed in a context where they have been positioned as Other. This raises the following question: has multiculturalism brought about major shifts in Australian national identity, such as to displace Anglo-Australian ethnic identity from its position of dominance? I shall argue that this is not the case, although multiculturalism does have the intrinsic potential to achieve such shifts.

As a public policy, multiculturalism is concerned with the management of cultural differences. It is in this apparently innocuous objective that all the ambivalence of multiculturalism arises: it is simultaneously a discourse of pacification and emancipation; of control and participation; of legitimation of the existing order and of innovation. Multiculturalism is part of a strategy of domination over minorities by the majority, but also points beyond this, to the possibility of new forms of social and cultural relations. As such, multiculturalism is a power relationship, and has something of the intrinsic ambivalence of power that Hegel demonstrated in his analysis of the master–slave relationship in *The Phenomenology of Mind* (1967). Charles Taylor (1975, p. 149) characterises this as the 'predicament of the master in the master–slave relation who has his world made over to reflect him by the labour of the slave, but who remains limited in his self-certainty'. It is not only the identities of minorities which have been structured in racist relations. The majority identity too has its roots in a history of domination over minorities. Multiculturalism has been adopted because the old racist identity can no longer work, yet in its present form it does not in itself provide an adequate framework for a new identity.

In order to understand the power relationships which operate around 'race' and ethnicity, we need a workable definition of racism as a mode of exclusion based on socially-constructed markers of biological or cultural difference (see Chapter 2). Two main aspects are significant in our context: institutional and interpersonal racism. The former refers to cultural biases and forms of majority dominance which have become part of institutional structures, so that the apparently impartial application of general rules can in fact lead to discrimination of minorities. Interpersonal racism refers to the way in which the taken-for-granted practices of social interaction are based on embedded historical patterns of domination and subordination. Philomena Essed (1991, p. 50) calls this phenomenon 'everyday racism':

> Everyday racism is the integration of racism into everyday situations through practices (both cognitive and behavioural) that activate underlying power relations. This process must be seen as a continuum through which the integration of racism into everyday practices becomes a part of the expected, of the unquestionable, and of what is seen as normal by the dominant group. When racist notions and actions infiltrate everyday life and become a part of the reproduction of the system, the system reproduces everyday racism.

Since the inception of the policy, there has been continuous debate about the successes and problems of multiculturalism. Over the past few years some critics have spoken of the 'demise of multiculturalism'. Others have called for some sort of 'post-multiculturalism' without positing any real alternatives. Yet others support the continuation of multiculturalism simply on the basis that it is better than assimilationism. Defenders of multiculturalism often argue that anti-multicultural positions are intrinsically racist, and therefore unworthy of further discussion. Some attacks on multiculturalism are indeed based on racist world views, but others are motivated by the experience of deficiencies and contradictions of current policies. We clearly need to go further than simple labels.

In this chapter I will analyse a number of current positions on multiculturalism, and attempt to understand what their implications are for social relations and for the construction of group identities and national identity. Four major debates will be discussed: the first is the relationship of Aboriginal Australians to multiculturalism; the second concerns the argument that multiculturalism separates and differentiates, thus undermining national unity; the third is the position that multiculturalism actually discriminates against migrants; and the fourth concerns the debate as to whether multiculturalism preserves, creates or masks inequalities, especially those based on class and gender.

Multiculturalism and Aboriginal Australians

Since its inception, multiculturalism has specifically referred to migrants and their place within Australian society. Until recently, little attempt has been made to examine the implications of multiculturalism for indigenous people, who had been generally omitted in discourses on cultural diversity. Since 1788, those in power had lumped Aboriginal people together as a homogeneous group, first to be exterminated and, when that failed, to be assimilated, which also failed. When new, ostensibly non-racist, discourses on majority–minority relations emerged in the 1970s, they were completely separate for migrants and indigenous peoples. For migrants there were the principles of multiculturalism and access and equity, administered through bodies like the Office of Multicultural Affairs and state ethnic affairs bodies. For indigenous people there were discourses around improvement of socioeconomic and cultural conditions and self-management, administered first through the Department of Aboriginal Affairs, and then through the Aboriginal and Torres Strait Islander Commission (ATSIC).

This bureaucratic separation to some extent reflects the wishes of many Aboriginal people: they see the cultural divide as being between themselves as Australia's original people and all those who have come since 1788. In other words, many Aboriginal people see society in terms of biculturalism (not multiculturalism) as has been successfully put forward by Maori people in New Zealand.

Aboriginal people's scepticism about multiculturalism is linked to their experience of a much more extreme form of racism than was the case of immigrants. In the colonial period, their communities, cultures and way of life were systematically destroyed. Even today, nearly three decades after the 1967 referendum which formally granted them full citizenship, large numbers of Aboriginal people are dispossessed of their land, unemployed and socially excluded. In terms of living conditions, health, life expectancy and education, Aboriginal people appear as a Third World population on the margins of a rich, white society. They are still subject to extreme forms of racism, from the police and other officials (see HREOC 1991). The promise of integration and social mobility that Australia held out to post-war immigrants never applied to the oldest Australians. This has been a source of tension: Aboriginal people have resented the fact that new groups were better treated than themselves, while immigrants often took on the racist stereotypes of Anglo-Australian society. Thus racism divides and differentiates between minorities.

Although Aboriginal people have always resisted white racism (Reynolds 1987a), it was not until the 1960s that a more public struggle against racism was mounted, influenced by the US civil rights movement and colonial liberation struggles. Aboriginal people had no reason to trust the state. Their initial experiences had been of colonisation, with its attendant violence and destruction. This had been followed by paternalistic forms of social control, known first as 'Aboriginal protection', then as 'assimilation' and finally as 'Aboriginal affairs' (Pollard 1989; Bennett 1989). Under the assimilation policy for instance, many Aboriginal children were forcibly removed from their families and placed with white families or in institutions.

Many Aboriginal people have a deep and justified mistrust of the state and the dominant group it represents. Hence their unwillingness to support and cooperate with new bodies designed as bridges between the state and the indigenous population, such as ATSIC. Such bodies and their ideology of self-management are all too often seen as new forms of paternalism or social control. Multiculturalism is rejected for similar reasons, and above all because its central concept of ethnicity is seen as unacceptable: Aboriginal people refuse to be seen as one ethnic group among others. On the other hand, Aboriginal people do support measures which involve real rights or control of resources, as embodied for instance in the Native Title Act of 1993 and the subsequent social justice package (see Goot & Rowse 1994).

The position of Australia's indigenous people is one of the great dilemmas for multiculturalism: it can never function as a model for national identity unless it includes and is accepted by Aboriginal people. And it cannot do this until it faces up to the racism which has always been at the root of white–black relations. On the bureaucratic level, there is a gradual realisation of this: an Aboriginal Reconciliation

Council has been established within the Department of Prime Minister and Cabinet, and this is beginning to work with the National Multicultural Advisory Council. There is a tendency to speak of 'cultural diversity' rather than multiculturalism as the policy model, in the hope that this will be more acceptable to Aboriginal people. Official statements on policies for Aboriginal people (such as the Native Title Act) have linked them to the notion of our multicultural society. But what is still lacking is a serious anti-racist policy, designed to deal effectively with discrimination and racist practices at all levels of society, including within the bureaucracy itself. The community relations strategies of the 1990s have been strong on rhetoric, but have been so poorly funded and so sporadically implemented that they can only be seen as tokenistic.

The same applies to minority politics. There have been calls for a more active coalition politics between Aboriginal and immigrant groups. But at the moment, these 'unifying narratives' have yet to be substantiated. If Aboriginal and migrant groups cannot forge a coalition politics against racism, then the struggle against racism is seriously weakened. This has to be taken seriously because multiculturalism and Aboriginal politics have so far touched only the tip of the iceberg and have not much changed the structures of racism in Australian society. Multiculturalism and the Aboriginal struggle for equality and recognition are only a first step. Anti-racism must be multi-dimensional. Until Aborigines and immigrants form their own alliance outside any state apparatus in order to combat racist structures and cultures, then the struggle against racism will continue to be fragmented.

Multiculturalism separates and differentiates

The argument that multiculturalism separates and differentiates is becoming increasingly common. This includes two related themes. The first is that multiculturalism concentrates too much on cultural diversity and not on what people have in common. Difference and ultimately chaos and violence are seen to be the likely results. An associated problem is that multiculturalism is thought to separate migrants from the mainstream, thus blocking migrant assimilation. Secondly, multiculturalism is thought to celebrate tradition, identity and community for immigrants, but for some Anglo-Australians it means a loss of these. Further, some believe that welfare rights privilege immigrants and discriminate against Anglo-Australians.

Multiculturalism concentrates on difference instead of commonalities

The first position—essentially based on a classical humanism—stresses that multiculturalism emphasises difference rather than articulating what we hold in common. The fear here is that because we live in a multicultural society where everyone is able to express their differences, then we are likely to end up holding very little in common. Thus, we should all be treated equally rather than differently. Further, if all differences and interests can be expressed then this will lead to major conflicts where different interest groups will compete for diminishing resources which can lead to violence. Peter Hollingworth, Anglican Archbishop of Brisbane, elaborates this position:

> Multiculturalism runs the risk of emphasising difference, to the exclusion of what we hold in common. I believe that issue needs to be challenged on the grounds that if we fail to articulate a commonly agreed set of goals and directions, we are likely to move down the path towards further fragmentation and social disintegration. (*Australian* 8 September 1994, p. 19)

His concern is that Australia will follow the path of the USA which he claims is based on an ethos of individualism which has become extremely litigious. His argument rests on a powerful liberal humanist ethic, that we should concentrate on the dignity of the individual yet at the same time focus on what we have in common. What we have in common is usually expressed under the term 'equality', which is part of the dominant ideology in liberal democracies. However, this raises a significant contradiction. On the one hand, all citizens are supposed to be equal before the law, and to be treated equally by the state and other institutions. On the other hand, liberalism, especially in its current guise of economic rationalism, is based on the notion of the naturalness of inequality and therefore legitimates a society stratified on the basis of class, gender, ethnicity, sexuality, etc.

This argument usually comes from those who have difficulties with the idea of 'difference', especially from members of dominant groups who accept Australia's ethnic pluralism (like Hollingworth 1994) but who do not fully consider the effects of unequal power relations on the modern subject. Many who use this argument believe in the possibility of a homogeneous society which can be achieved through a multiculturalism that is as assimilationist (even though they would not use that term) as possible, as the best way of avoiding ethnic conflicts and violence. What is not questioned here is that usually assimilation means that minority groups integrate into the majority culture long before they have the real opportunity to change any fundamental aspects of that culture. To concentrate on what we have in common is as important as to concentrate on difference. But if we *only* concentrate on what we have in common, then that is a sure way of keeping the disadvantaged in their place because it comes back to the universalist liberal argument of all being equal, so that socio-economic disadvantage or political exclusion is seen as the fault of the individual.

The contradictions created by the images of a common humanity under the banner of liberal humanism have been well analysed by feminist, Marxist and other critical theorists. Certainly, many who support feminism and multiculturalism have struggled against the universalising and hence discriminatory aspects of liberal humanism. Pauline Johnson (1994, pp. xi–xii) suggests that:

> An anti-humanist posture, which sees in the norms and ideals of modern humanism only the totalitarian ambitions of a particular, privileged subjectivity committed to the universalisation of its own will and interests, has certainly provided a much needed warning about the ever-present dangers which lurk within humanism's efforts to produce a universal category of humankind which breaks the bonds of traditional, particularising integrations.

Yet humanism needs to be retained, since feminism and multiculturalism are still part of the humanist project of modernity which is committed to the integrity and self-determination of people both as individuals and as members of social groups. Thus Johnson (1994, p. xi) proposes what she calls a 'radical humanist' feminism which 'understands humanism as an historical project born of conscious value choices and the vagaries of critical, social and political movements'. This necessarily entails the emancipatory ideals of modern humanism which we can extend to the individual's need for group belonging and group identity (see Young 1990a). Habermas (1994, p. 113) suggests that individual identity can only be conceived intersubjectively. People can 'become individualized only through a process of socialization'.

Multiculturalism means loss of culture and community for Anglo-Australians

This argument comes from Anglo-Australians who feel a sense of loss of community, of traditions and of a way of life previously seen as homogeneous and comforting. In its most extreme form the argument is that multiculturalism divides the society into a group of tribes and so destroys the national culture. Blainey popularised this view in 1984, with his assertion that 'An immigration system set up originally to serve the nation had been undermined. Now it was the nation that exists to serve the immigrant' (Blainey 1984, p. 100). According to him, 'Sadly, multiculturalism often means: Australians come second' (*Age* 21 September 1984). Clearly, by 'Australians' he meant Anglo-Australians and not the millions of naturalised immigrant Australians who have benefited from the integrative characteristics of multiculturalism. This argument is racist and nationalist and has a strong populist appeal.

In Chapter 2, Castles linked such populist racist discourses with globalisation, economic restructuring and the erosion of popular cultures. Wieviorka (1994, p. 25) suggests that the recent rise in racism in many Western European countries is due to the 'decomposition of national industrial societies'. If people lose their jobs, and find their environment and safety declining, then they often blame migrants for undermining the nation. Racism can help strengthen group and personal identity in a situation of crisis. This explanation can be applied to Anglo-Australians: many believe they have lost a sense of culture and community and say that this is due to multiculturalism. According to them, multiculturalism promotes migrant cultures and communities and ignores Anglo-Australian culture. Anglo-Australianness has been lost.

But what has actually been lost? Many traditions of the 1950s and 1960s have indeed gone. Cultures, including migrant cultures, have gone through significant transformations. Migrants were initially compelled to live in working-class areas, such as the western suburbs of Sydney, in search of jobs and cheaper housing. As migrant communities grew, they fought against racist practices by gradually reshaping what was previously an exclusively Anglo space and place. As a result, cultural diversity saturates the daily life of the urban space: there has been an increase in the rate of intermarriage between Anglo-Australians and people of non-English-speaking background; they share many social services and neighbourhood centres; they shop where languages other than English are spoken; they have a Chamber of Commerce whose membership is multi-ethnic. The everyday life of members of the various ethnic groups who live and work in such areas is closely interwoven. Shops, services and public bodies are run by multi-ethnic personnel. In several Sydney local councils, mayors and many councillors are of non-English-speaking background. In such areas of high migrant density, Anglo-Australians have become one ethnic group among many.

The complaints which come from Anglo-Australians about such

changes range from genuine feelings of dislocation to outright racist discourses. This loss of identity is real for many Anglo-Australians because they feel they have lost their hegemony over the cultural and geographical spaces they once controlled. They feel they have been disempowered by multiculturalism when they see 'multiculturalism', or more specifically 'cultural diversity', confidently on display in the street and in the neighbourhood. This problem has been expressed to me as follows: 'Some Australians feel they have lost their identity and community because of multiculturalism, just as some men feel they have lost their masculinity on account of feminism.' These movements have challenged the identities and cultures of previously secure and dominant groups in Australian society.

Thus, for some, to lose their dominance means a loss of identity, culture and community. Hegemonic identities cannot float freely, they have an institutional base. Indeed, during the period of assimilationism, Anglo-Australian ethnic/national identity was structured *in dominance* over other group identities, including Aboriginality. Many recent arrivals claim this is still the case. But those who lament this loss have resisted changes to their dominant identity. Because a dominant identity suffers from uncertainty and instability, the loss of dominance can mean a sense of loss of identity. In the process of attempts to redress the effects of discrimination and exclusion experienced by migrants and indigenous Australians, many Anglo-Australians claim *they* are now being discriminated against. The point here is that Anglo-Australians have benefited from that dominant Anglo identity, whether they are racist or not. This sense of loss is not in itself racist, but it can often be expressed through racist discourse and practices.

A clearly racist discourse emerges when some people claim that multiculturalism provides migrants with special privileges: the myths range from government housing grants for Vietnamese migrants to government handouts for cars. Other practices are not myths but are distorted to provoke a sense of injustice. For instance, there have been polemics about pensions being sent overseas to Australian pensioners of migrant origin. Anglo-Australians are often surprised to hear that they too can request the same service.

Multiculturalism also elicits unfavourable responses from the Anglo-Australian middle classes. Although there is much truth in the idea that cultural diversity is 'consumed' and enjoyed by the middle-class yuppies of the inner cities and the viewers of SBS, some middle-class people feel disempowered by multiculturalism. For example, 'Australia's unofficial poet laureate', Les Murray, who has received numerous large grants from the Australia Council, also claims to have suffered a sense of loss of identity and culture. In September 1994, he launched the following attack on the Australia Council:

> They are creating an Australia that is exclusive. Multicultural, they call it. But they are discriminatory, they exclude. 'They' are not just the Australia Council; they are the ruling elite of today's Australia: the cultural bureaucrats, the academics, the intellectuals . . . They are excluding people like me from their Australia—the country people, the rednecks, the Anglo-Celts, the farming people—they have turned their backs on us. They act as though they despise us. We don't have a place in this multiculturalism they talk about, because we are the ones they constantly denigrate. They denigrate the majority of Australians who are born in this country, those that have mainly British ancestry . . . We Old Australians, not always Anglo but having no other country but this one, are now mostly caught and silenced between the indigenous and the multicultural . . . (Bennie 1994).

This is a fairly articulate lament from someone who feels he has lost his sense of hegemonic identity within the cultural scene. It is instructive to know that Murray has formed the Australia Council Reform Association with Mark O'Connor who is a leading member of Australians for an Ecologically Sustainable Population, a well-known organisation whose anti-immigration discourse is part of a broader racist rhetoric.

The problem multiculturalism poses for artists of non-English-speaking background is curiously different. Les Murray represents multiculturalism as having such a high status that it is damaging to the position of 'old Australians'. However, artists of migrant background or those who deal with multicultural issues often find that their art ends up being seen as second-rate. The very label of 'multicultural art' means that their works are marginalised from the mainstream (Castles & Kalantzis 1994; see also Gunew & Rizvi 1994). This problem is central to the notion of Australian national culture and identity. If art which arises outside the mainstream of Anglo-Australian culture is stigmatised as intrinsically inferior and not worthy of inclusion in prestigious galleries, theatres, etc, this is a way of maintaining cultural dominance through practices of everyday racism.

Multiculturalism discriminates against immigrants

The following critique comes mostly from migrants who argue that multiculturalism does not deal adequately with many structural and everyday forms of racism. In addition, some migrants believe that multiculturalism blocks assimilation because of its emphasis on ethnicity. As always, contradictions emerge between rhetoric and reality; and around the relationship between multiculturalism and racism.

Multiculturalism is racist

This argument is essentially concerned with the gulf between multiculturalism's anti-racist claims and its actual practice. Multiculturalism emerged at a time when the social movements of the 1960s and 1970s were having significant political effects for many disadvantaged groups. A migrant lobby emerged with strong representation from the left. Gradually 'ethnic professionals' became involved who, along with 'femocrats' from the women's movement, have brought about significant legislative and bureaucratic reforms. For those who had experienced assimilationism, the transition to multiculturalism was seen as positive, despite all the problems. Many who work in the community sector have adopted a policy of criticising the shortcomings of multiculturalism in the public arena, while trying to deal with the contradictions as best they can in their daily work.

Many recently arrived migrants, on the other hand, conclude that multiculturalism has failed them; that it does not live up to its claims, and that it is therefore racist. One argument often comes from skilled migrants and refugees whose qualifications have not been accepted in Australia. Others whose qualifications have been recognised find they still have difficulty finding work in their professions, due to discrimination. The official concept of 'productive diversity' (which originated in the Prime Minister's Department) means that the nation should benefit from the human and cultural capital of our ethnically diverse population. But for many migrants this has become an empty slogan which contrasts sharply with the actual structural and everyday racism they experience in the labour market (see Collins 1991; Iredale 1992).

In the social policy area the contradictions of multiculturalism are most obvious: a wide range of labour market programs, social welfare programs and education programs claim to redress institutional imbalances which affect the socio-economic position of migrants and their children. The 1989 *National Agenda for a Multicultural Australia* went beyond earlier policies in its explicit concern with the removal of 'barriers' to the achievement of equal opportunities for migrants. The subsequent *Access and Equity* strategy was designed to improve bureaucratic responses to cultural difference. Another major goal has been to increase equality of educational and occupational opportunities through skills training, rather than to concentrate on notions of 'cultural deficit' as in the past. Other institutional strategies address racism, such as the work of the Human Rights and Equal Opportunity Commission (and the equivalent state anti-discrimination boards), and the Community Relation Strategy.

The intent and rhetoric of all these policies is anti-racist. However, there is an enormous gap between the stated policies and actual practice. *Access and Equity* is a case in point. Since the late 1980s, all government departments have been required to devise *Access and Equity* plans to improve service delivery to groups with differing needs and situations, and to report regularly on their implementation. Yet in everyday bureaucratic practices, these plans have simply become one task among others which has little impact on actual service design and delivery. The plans are often little more than statements of intent, with no performance indicators or budgets. They have had little measurable effect on the way government relates to minorities. In general it can be said that multicultural social policies have had only a marginal effect, and that their funding is minute compared with the large budgets of the main service-delivery departments concerned with health, social services and education.

This illustrates the analytical importance of distinguishing between the aims and rhetoric of multiculturalism and its actual effects in the context of the pervasive racism which operates through the institutions and in the cultural domain. It is around some of these issues that the British debate on multiculturalism has turned. Black people in England have seen multiculturalism, especially in social work and in education, as a divide-and-rule strategy, which locates black people's disadvantage in cultural dissonance, and 'ethnicises' them into distinct and isolated groups. Instead, they argue that the stress should be on anti-racist education, which locates the problem in white racism. Anti-racist education has a dual task: it is designed to help white children cast off the racism which is an integral part of British culture, while empowering blacks to unite as a people and fight racism (see Troyna 1993).

Another associated problem of multiculturalism raised both in Britain and Australia is that of cooption: that is, the incorporation of ethnic minority leaderships into state agencies and strategies. The contradiction here is that far more is achieved by working within the parameters set by the state than from the outside. However, it also means that people become incorporated into the ideologies of state organisations to the point where they may lose their abilities to even perceive the need for change (see Jakubowicz 1981; Parrella 1993).

Therefore, my suggestion is that we promote a dual strategy. We need to retain and to continue to develop our multicultural social policy and programs, particularly at the levels of planning and delivery. At the same time, we need to construct anti-racist strategies and organisations *outside* the state apparatuses in order to bring about an effective analysis and basis for change. My concern here is that those who call for the end of multiculturalism because it discriminates against migrants or because it has not dealt adequately with racism, run the risk of throwing out the baby with the bath water. We need to pay more attention to racism. It seems to me that multiculturalism cannot work effectively without this dual strategy.

Multiculturalism is divisive and blocks assimilation

A further argument against multiculturalism sometimes raised by recent arrivals is that it relies too heavily on an ethnic group model through which the patriarchs of certain communities can retain control of community activities. This varies from group to group, because in some cases women are very active at the community level and in others they are not. This problem was raised in early debates on multiculturalism (see Jakubowicz et al. 1984) but still persists, especially for those communities which experience numerous fractures based on ethnicity, region, religion and politics. Service delivery is still sometimes organised on an ethno-specific basis, for instance for newly arrived refugee groups, but sometimes also for special-needs categories such as the aged within established communities. In these cases, there may be tendencies towards conservatism and separatism.

Many of us who are active at the community level are fully aware of such contradictions, but we take the position that until we can change the funding structures and structures of representation, the migrant clientele is best served by these ethno-specific services (see Vasta 1993a). One major problem here is that mainstreaming of services is still unable to deal adequately and in a non-discriminatory way with the specific needs of many first-generation migrants.

Multiculturalism has contradictory effects on migrants in different class locations. For example, as a social policy, multiculturalism is usually considered to be a useful mechanism of integration for working-class migrants who require assistance to integrate into the lower socio-economic echelons of the society. For educational and economic reasons, working-class migrants usually need longer to learn English and to cope with different cultural and social practices. Cultural maintenance and group solidarity is vital to help working-class migrants deal with the many discriminatory experiences they encounter. Multiculturalism is essential for them, both as a social policy and as an ideology of cultural pluralism.

For middle-class migrants, the situation is much more ambivalent. Many conservative recent arrivals who have the cultural and economic capital to integrate into the host society fairly rapidly not only see multiculturalism as a patronising hand-out of welfare by the state, but they also believe that an ideology of pluralism hinders them from assimilating into the dominant culture. They do not want to belong to a minority culture or to have a visible minority identity. One major reason for this is that minority cultures are still discriminated against even where multiculturalism officially exists. Unfortunately, racism has not been eradicated by multiculturalism, but many believe it is multiculturalism which contributes to their experiences of discrimination.

On the other hand, many middle-class migrants or children of migrants have benefited directly from multiculturalism. They have been able to use their cultural capital and their control of ethnic cultural symbols to benefit from the jobs and resources made available through multiculturalism. They have gained leadership positions within ethnic communities, or jobs within community associations and welfare services. They have taken on the role of entrepreneurs or professionals serving ethnic communities, or mediating between them and the wider society. Above all, more and more members of the second generation have been able to make use of their educational success in Australia to gain public sector jobs connected with management of cultural diversity.

As a social policy, multiculturalism was originally geared to the needs of the working-class migrants who predominated at least up to the early 1980s. The services which developed out of their needs are still important, and will continue to be so, especially for those who come through the family reunion and refugee categories. But in recent years, entry policy has placed more emphasis on skills and cultural capabilities. The highly skilled, English-speaking migrants who now come from Asia, and even some middle-class refugee groups, seem more interested in socio-economic assimilation than in cultural maintenance. Such shifts may change the balance of migrant support for multiculturalism, and could become a potential source of conflict within migrant communities in the future. In any case, it should be clear that the argument that multiculturalism blocks assimilation is related to the interests of one specific group of migrants, and not to the migrant population as a whole.

Multiculturalism discriminates against immigrant cultures

Within the discourse that multiculturalism discriminates against immigrants there is a third argument, namely that many recent arrivals feel their cultures are undermined and discriminated against because they are not accepted as part of the public culture. Representatives of such groups believe that Australian institutions should find ways to include all languages and important cultural practices.

The term *multiculturalism* can be misleading for recently arrived immigrants who have not experienced its evolution. Long-standing immigrants know that multiculturalism has never meant complete cultural pluralism in the sense that all cultural practices should be allowed equal status before the law. For example with regard to family law, the norms of a liberal democratic Western society are dominant, which exclude cultural practices like bigamy, or superior rights for men in marriage agreements. The majority of immigrants accept the principles of a unitary legal system and accept English as the lingua franca. This has been spelt out clearly in a series of policy statements (see ACPEA 1982; AEAC 1977; ALRC 1992; OMA 1989).

Thus Anglo-Australian institutions and identity are dominant despite multiculturalism. This gives rise to yet another contradiction. As Stratton and Ang (1994, pp. 152–3) suggest, 'The problem with official multiculturalism is that it tends precisely to freeze the fluidity of identity by the very fact that it is concerned with the synthesising of unruly and unpredictable cultural identities and difference into a harmonious unity-in-diversity.' This creates problems for many migrant communities (see Chapter 7). On the other hand, many are comfortable with Australian institutions and cultural practices when they compare these with those from their home countries where there may be a lack of democratic rights, very inefficient bureaucracies, and above all religious and cultural norms which are repressive towards women and other groups. Ultimately, changes to the law and other institutions are likely to occur only through political struggle and negotiation.

Some people who oppose cultural pluralism fear that it might lead to some of the problems associated with the term *political correctness* in the USA. There the movement for multiculturalism has been concerned with changing the dominant understanding of history and culture, which is based on the achievements of, mostly, white men. The roles of women and minority groups have been largely excluded from the curriculum and from dominant views. The conservative reaction to this movement has been based on the slogan of 'political correctness', which is portrayed as an attack on historical accuracy and free speech. Behind the slogan lies a crucial struggle over identity, although it is clear that that concept of multiculturalism is very different from that prevailing in Australia.

Multiculturalism preserves or creates inequalities

The inequalities discussed in this section are not all necessarily racist. Indeed, some arguments refer specifically to the problems created at the intersection of class and ethnicity and gender and ethnicity. Others are more readily defined as racist. Overall, the positions discussed here illustrate the complexities and contradictions inherent in managing cultural diversity.

Multiculturalism preserves the inequalities of traditional cultures

One very important debate around multiculturalism is that, because it is based on the notion of tolerance of other cultures, then we are compelled to accept these cultures without distinction. Researchers and the media have reported problems which emerge in ethnic communities which cling to their traditions. Community workers are usually the ones who deal with many of these issues on a daily basis. For instance, what is considered child abuse in Australian society may be considered good training in Vietnamese culture. Thus, parents beat their children in the belief that family honour must be maintained over and above the needs of the individual. Middle Eastern parents are known to arrange marriages for their 15- or 16-year-old daughters, despite their strong resistance. The media report cases of girls badly bruised or even killed by their parents in order to save family honour. Some reports show more awareness of the complexities than others (see Legge 1994).

Some of the responses to these problems, such as 'send them back home', are racist. Often the entire culture is denigrated and multiculturalism is blamed for promoting tolerance of such bad behaviour. To read multiculturalism as tolerance for *all* social and cultural practices is both problematic and misleading. Just as the myths and facts of the social policy aspect of multiculturalism need clearer public airing, so too does this very significant aspect of multiculturalism. In its study *Multiculturalism and the Law* (ALRC 1992) the Australian

Law Reform Commission has accepted the need for differentiation and removal of cultural biases within a unitary system of law. This may mean amending court rules to take account of cultural difference, just as it may mean accepting that traditional Aboriginal communities should have the right to use traditional forms of justice without recourse to the mainstream legal system.

For migrants, some cultural issues could be negotiable, for example, how to deal with refugee street-frequenting youth who fall foul of the law. These problems usually have to do with unemployment and other structural issues rather than 'ethnic' issues. If their communities can find ways of dealing with these problems outside the legal arena, then clearly such initiatives should be supported. But many of the problems raised around family honour are based on sexist and patriarchal practices which support the unequal and even harmful treatment of women. In Australia, multiculturalism is based on the notion of removing the disadvantages and discrimination experienced by migrants on account of their 'migrantness', on account of their ethnicity. If multiculturalism is anti-racist, then it should also be anti-sexist.

This raises two problems. One is that multiculturalism in Australia is generally seen simply in terms of ethnic difference. As a result, multiculturalism tends to exclude minorities based on lifestyle, sexual preference and the like, thus fragmenting the struggle against discrimination towards all minorities. This makes multiculturalism unnecessarily narrow in scope. For this reason alone some would prefer that 'multiculturalism' be dropped. Usually, the argument which follows about its replacement is both naive and assimilationist. One argument goes that multiculturalism would be unnecessary if social policy for migrants were mainstreamed. But mainstreaming does not always work precisely because there is a lack of sufficient knowledge about migrant needs and a lack of political will to implement the programs in a non-racist way. I would argue that until we find new and better models for responding to the needs of minorities, the term should be retained.

The second problem once again relates to the tension between pluralism and universalism. Should *all* cultural practices be accepted in a culturally plural or multicultural society? Multiculturalism should accept difference but not discrimination. If difference is discriminatory, then it is unacceptable. This means that there are certain human rights which are universal. Certainly this was one of the battles fought at the 1994 World Population Conference in Cairo between feminists and the religious patriarchs of Italy and Iran. From a universal human rights perspective, wife bashing, for example, is unacceptable from any culture. Feminist politics in Australia has established a principle of equality for women which, although still imperfect, has gone a long way to combating many gender discriminatory practices.

However, the process of informing these communities about these issues is totally inadequate and at times racist. For example, there are numerous cases of Anglo-Australian feminists behaving in culturally inappropriate ways in their attempt to remove what they perceive to be discriminatory practices against women in certain migrant communities. These cases usually range from practices of infibulation/circumcision in some communities to other practices which are considered to be abusive by Australian cultural standards. What often happens is that the issue and the process of dealing with it become confused, so that the ethnic community women and the Anglo-Australian feminists end up at loggerheads (Furtie & Donohoue-Clyne 1994). Furthermore, the problem arises that migrant cultures then get blamed for their 'backwardness' and sexism as if Anglo-Australian culture no longer suffers from such problems.

Multiculturalism has done little to improve gender equality for immigrant women

The position of immigrant women in multiculturalism continues to be one of struggle. In many ways immigrant women have benefited from multiculturalism in the same way as other immigrants. However, there are specific problems which require closer attention (see for example Alcorso 1993; Bottomley 1984; de Lepervanche 1989, 1990; Martin 1984, 1991a). Migrant women continue to be placed in a marginal position when it comes to official policy. For example, the *National Agenda* of 1989 hardly refers to women at all. Martin (1991a, p. 123) illustrates how immigrant women, within multiculturalism, are positioned as a 'disadvantaged group' with 'specific interests or problems related to their femaleness'. She states that 'In the ethnicist argument, the first conception is underscored by a tendency to list "migrant women" as one of the many problems afflicting ethnic groups—for example, along with health, children, education, unemployment and so forth.' As a result, there is generally a commitment to a notion of pluralism which basically 'boils down to *ethnic* pluralism' (pp. 123–4):

> For females, this means that the claims of women are always secondary to, or a sub-clause of, the ethnic claims; there is no mention of an equivalent female community . . . the ethnic group represents women, and the family, and is their bridge to public life.

In an important sense, women only achieve the status of a disadvantaged group once this has occurred.

Things have begun to change for immigrant women, many of whom are politically committed to a broader range of issues than simply the politics of ethnicity. This has led to the emergence of Speakout (Immigrant Women's Speakout of New South Wales) and ANESBWA (Association of Non-English Speaking Background Women of Australia) and other immigrant women's organisations. Why immigrant women have set up their own organisations needs to be understood in terms of their specific historical and political experiences of racism and sexism which were either ignored or dealt with inadequately by ethnic organisations and the mainstream women's movement. The relationship between Anglo and NESB women has also been structured in racism (Vasta 1993b) and this has been well documented (see Martin 1991a). Of course, NESB women will also have to pay special attention to issues of class, region, ethnicity and other relationships of power which construct difference.

Coalition politics, which is based on cooperation over issues rather than on identity politics, is seen as the best way forward by many women, and indeed this often works well among women at the community level. Aboriginal, Anglo, NESB and other groups of women need to organise outside the state apparatus (as well as carry on with the work within the state) if any real weight is to be given to the notion of a coalition politics. However, a coalition politics will be difficult to achieve while feminists from the dominant ethnic groups continue to reproduce (consciously or unconsciously) structural racist practices as briefly mentioned in the preceding section. Ultimately, the relationship between gender and ethnicity (and not simply gender) has to be the basis of any political action when dealing with class, sexuality or other forms of women's disadvantages.

Multiculturalism preserves class inequalities

In Australia, the debate around multiculturalism, ethnicity and class began in the early 1980s. Marie de Lepervanche (1980, pp. 34–5) claimed that:

> promotion of ethnicity . . . masks conflicting class interests and the nature of class relations . . . class appears simply as one among many ties and society is defined in terms of a multiplicity of

cross-cutting linkages . . . There are in fact no ethnics; there are only ways of seeing people as ethnics.

This paper was significant because de Lepervanche alerted us to the way in which the hegemonic definition of ethnicity, in the name of cultural differences, ignored issues of class inequality for the majority of migrants. Jakubowicz (1981, p. 4) developed the argument that 'ethnicity as ideology mediates Australian class relations, by reifying the history of peoples into a static category of theoretical labelling'. He argued that theoretical primacy was accorded to ethnicity, as ideology, over class (p. 6). This meant that multiculturalism, due to its discursive primacy over class, became a means of social control of migrants, although at the same time multiculturalism would threaten Anglo-Australian cultural dominance.

This position, while important, tends to ignore the dynamics of culture, identity and agency. Migrants appear to be totally constrained by their class location: a dominant ideology operates in such a way that there is no room for them to construct their own (separate or communal) ethnic identities. But there are always two simultaneous processes at work in the construction of ethnic identities in the migration process. One is based on self-definition in relation to a number of characteristics, such as being an immigrant or being of immigrant background and sharing minority languages and other cultural traditions and histories. This is a political construct as identity is often defined in relation to a dominant national identity. On the other hand, ethnicity is used by a majority group to draw boundaries and marginalise people of minority ethnic cultures. In other words, ethnic identities or ethnicity generally become an issue either when a dominant identity is imposed upon a group or when a group is excluded from a national identity. Thus, ethnicity becomes a site of struggle (Vasta 1993a).

Within the framework suggested by de Lepervanche (1980) and Jakubowicz (1981), ethnicity and gender always appear as secondary relations. How these are constructed together and modified by migrant resistance and struggle is too easily ignored. Nevertheless, in Australia these debates had a central influence in the transformations in multiculturalism which occurred during the 1980s, so that by the late 1980s, multiculturalism was concerned with increasing equality through educational and occupational skills training rather than concentrating on cultural pluralism as it had in the past. Labour market training has become a top priority for many immigrant organisations.

There are similar debates in other countries such as Britain and Sweden (Alund & Schierup 1991).[2] In Britain, for example, some observers suggest that multiculturalism is simply a new way of controlling minorities by emphasising 'cultural difference', and is therefore a form of racism. Instead, they suggest that we should concentrate on socio-economic issues as the central problem. Similar arguments have become highly influential in the Netherlands, which is moving away from a minorities policy with strong multicultural elements, which had been introduced in the early 1980s. This is a very powerful argument because it claims that as long as immigrant minorities are categorised on the basis of their ethnicity, they are likely to remain unskilled and unemployed (see Lutz 1993; Rath 1993). In other words, according to this argument, multiculturalism creates the conditions for discrimination against migrants.

There is, however, a central problem with this position. While it shows how 'ethnicity' has taken on explanatory and political primacy over class issues, it ignores the dynamics of racism. The position implies that the central problem is ethnic/racial categorisation, rather than the actual existence of racist practices. Refusing to name ethnic categories will not make them disappear, if they are constantly being reconstructed by exclusionary practices. Migrants experience racism both structurally and in many everyday practices, simply because of their ethnicity, their migrantness. Again, ethnicity and gender relations are analytically placed as relations secondary to class. But immigrants experience their class and gender relations ethnically, due to the racist practices of the dominant group.

In France, there is a similar discourse on ethnic differentiation as a form of discrimination, but it is also related to the notion of national identity. The 'Republican model' is supposed to integrate immigrants individually as citizens, and to guarantee them equality of rights. Many people reject the very idea of multiculturalism because this signals the image of a plural identity which directly challenges the notion of a unitary French identity and a homogeneous French culture. French national identity is based on the idea of a unified political identity and not on a shared culture (Brubaker 1990, p. 16). In other words, cultural pluralism is anathema to French identity. It is thought that if migrants assimilate, then they are French. This is not dissimilar to the previous Australian model of assimilation. However, the French model ignores the fact that economic, political and socio-cultural discrimination differentiate migrants to the point where assimilation is often untenable.

The paradoxes of the French model were shown in that country by the affair of the *foulard islamique* (the Islamic headscarf) which led to the expulsion from school of a number of young Muslim girls in 1989. In 1994, the issue returned with sensational media reports, and a directive from the Minister of Education forbidding the wearing of religious symbols at school. These often strong reactions show how an assimilationist model blocks understanding of the very real contradictions involved in intercultural relations. A recent sociological study of the symbolic meanings of the headscarf for young Muslim women has shown that some have chosen to wear the scarf as a sign of their resistance to assimilation and their wish to display their bicultural identity. The *foulard* (scarf) has become a sign of resistance both to the discrimination they experience from French society and resistance to the discrimination they experience as girls in their own ethnic culture. The study goes on to argue that the reaction around French national identity has 'created' the *foulard* as an issue of identity conflict. The French reaction was so strong because the *foulard* was (wrongly) seen as a rejection of a secular and superior French national identity (Gaspard & Khosrow-Khavar 1995).

Such international examples are relevant for the Australian debate. The concept and practice of multiculturalism differs from country to country. However, to revert to an assimilationist model, simply because class inequalities and racism have not been adequately dealt with, would be problematic because that reversion has racist tendencies itself. Therefore, it is important for Australia to look at these cases carefully so that we can find a more appropriate way forward.

Conclusions

The relationship between commonalities and difference forms the basis of debates on ethnic and national identities. The idea of ethnic difference implicit in multiculturalism is seen by some to create an unprecedented social fragmentation. Thus the argument that we should start concentrating on commonalities (rather than difference) is a significant one. However, in my view, the basis of the problem has been displaced. If ethnic oppression and disadvantage is still defined as a problem of ethnic difference (or due to the 'problem' migrant, as it was in the early days), then yes, multiculturalism has failed. But if ethnic oppression and disadvantage is understood as a result of class, sexist and racist power relations, then multiculturalism is a useful strategy to combat racism. A valuable suggestion about radical humanism is made by Johnson (1994, p. 135) when she states that:

> allegiance to these universal value ideas neither prevents a deep questioning of the particularistic shape in which these historical

forms appear nor does it prevent augmenting their meaning as new horizons are opened up by a range of contemporary social struggles.

Nevertheless, some might say that multiculturalism creates an atmosphere of passive tolerance. This means that people can hide under the mantle of multiculturalism conveniently believing that its very existence means that racism has disappeared (see Essed 1991). One pertinent example of this is that many people of migrant background have achieved upward mobility through involvement in the development and delivery of multicultural programs and equity programs. But it is also clear that there is a glass ceiling for NESB people and women: they are generally advisers rather than actual policy-makers—a role still mostly filled by Anglo-Australians. Certainly migrant involvement in this area has grown rapidly under multiculturalism (compare the involvement of Greeks, Serbs, Croatians, Italians, etc. during their first ten years in Australia with the same period for the Vietnamese), but these glass ceilings have a lot to do with racist and sexist cultures of our institutions.

Essed warns that 'one of the most problematic consequences of the ideology of tolerance is that this includes *tolerance of racism*' (1991, p. 270). This is especially noticeable in our institutions as well as in the way migrants of Asian background are positioned both at the official and community levels. Stratton and Ang (1994, p. 155) point out that:

> the cultural status of Australians of varieties of Asian descent in 'multicultural Australia' is still a fragile one. While Chinese, Vietnamese, Malaysian, Singaporean and other migrants from the Asian region are now considered an integral part of Australia's mix, these groups are still collectively *racialised* whenever a wave of moral panic about Asian immigration flares up.

In Australia, passive tolerance and explicit racist practices coexist with many anti-racist programs. Thus, we can say that multiculturalism is both racist and anti-racist. On the one hand, there is a level of social control and containment of difference and, on the other hand, multiculturalism includes many anti-racist programs. This contradiction also operates in our drive towards a transformation of national identity. Despite the relentless economic drive towards inclusion in the Asia-Pacific region, it is still a myth to think that Australian national identity is multicultural. It is predominantly Anglo, but also unstable as it is constantly challenged by the realities of multiculturalism. Nevertheless, there is still a dominant ideology of Anglo-ness as well as an official but unrecognised everyday racism as illustrated by the following example.

The state promotes cultural diversity in an attempt to create tolerance of difference, and in an attempt to get Australians to open up to Asia (see Chapter 10) but it does little to inform the public about racist practices—especially those within the state. This ambivalence was clearly evident in Sydney's bid for the 2000 Olympics. In this, Annita Keating, wife of the Prime Minister, was presented as the authentic voice of Australian multiculturalism—she was born overseas, she can speak several languages and she speaks English with an accent. This raised many eyebrows within ethnic communities about the authentic voice of migrants in Australia. Certainly a privileged, middle-class voice is one possible voice but hardly a representative one. Moreover, this was the first time that many Australians had seen Annita Keating publicly in her capacity as an 'ethnic'. It appears that none of the migrants who have helped make multiculturalism what it is today were asked to represent 'multicultural Australia' in the public profile of the bid. This is a good illustration of the practice of 'pulling out an appropriate ethnic' for the appropriate occasion.

Anglo racism, both institutional and interpersonal, is still there, and there is a growing level of everyday racism coming from long-standing migrant communities towards recent arrivals, in particular towards Asians. This is all the more reason, then, for us to understand that:

> racism operates in three domains of conflict: (a) conflict over norms and values, (b) conflict over material and nonmaterial resources, and (c) conflict over definition of the social world. Each of these areas of conflict is maintained through marginalising, problematising, and containment processes, but the specific forms they take on everyday life are locally determined (Essed 1991, p. 291).

In an epoch of globalisation and increasingly complex identities, it is increasingly difficult for nation-states to integrate their populations. Some nation-states are more successful than others, but none has overcome the instability brought about by the dialectics of domination, whatever the broader social and economic changes which have occurred over the past fifty years. Australia has a unique opportunity to work on the issues of identity and integration as we deliberate over our change to a republican state. Clearly, we need more discussion and strategies on how we can improve and extend the basis of multicultural-ism as part of the process of improving political participation and bringing about greater democracy.

The main issue is that we agree on basic principles and values and use them to devise mechanisms, both ideological and practical, which can accommodate the changing processes of difference. This means that we need to embrace the current ambivalences of multiculturalism as mentioned throughout this chapter: we need to take its moderating and emancipatory aspects; its levels of control and participation; its legitimation of the existing order; and its possibility for innovation. We can use these as a basis for a new synthesis for a democratic civil society. This is a crucial issue of political agency, for it favours a set of principles which undermine unequal power relations across class, gender, ethnicity, sexuality etc. In contradiction to Taylor (1992), whose liberal politics of recognition are based on the binary opposition of individual versus group rights, Habermas (1994, p. 113) provides a different perspective when he suggests, 'A correctly understood theory of rights requires a politics of recognition that protects the integrity of the individual in the life contexts in which his or her identity is formed'. In Australia, what could emerge is a new sense of identity, formed out of political struggles and negotiations over the relationship between social justice and difference, as incorporated within the idea of a new Australian republic.

4

The changing political economy of Australian racism

Jock Collins

Racism has been an integral part of Australian society since white invasion more than 200 years ago. But racism is not a static phenomenon. Rather, the processes of racialisation (Miles 1982) of immigrant and indigenous peoples change over time. Economic and political changes in Australia over the past decade have transformed the dynamics of racism in the labour market and in broader society. The recession and economic restructuring have resulted in a dramatic transformation in the nature and availability of work. At the same time, changes in industrial relations policy—including the decentralisation of employer–employee negotiations under the enterprise bargaining framework and the award restructuring process initiated under the Accord—and vocational education reforms have fundamentally changed the organisation and structure of the workplace. These changes have led to complex changes in the size and composition of Australia's immigration policy—most noticeably reflected in the increasing reliance on highly qualified Asian immigrants. Nearly half of all immigrant settlers arriving in Australia over the period 1986 to 1991 came from South and East Asia (Stahl et al. 1993). This is a remarkable change to immigration patterns, since Asians were excluded from entering Australia as the White Australia policy dominated immigration selection from Federation in 1901 to the late 1960s (Collins 1991, pp. 204–11). Similarly, the enactment of the Native Title Act (Rowse 1993), and the establishment of a reconciliation process between Aboriginal and Torres Strait Islanders and non-indigenous Australian society, have changed the processes underlying the racialisation of Australia's indigenous peoples.

73

One of the main dimensions of racism is racial discrimination at work. Racist attitudes, practices and ideologies are produced and reproduced in the labour market as in other spheres of society. In Australia, it has been immigrants from non-English-speaking background (or NESB immigrants) and Australia's indigenous peoples—the Aboriginal and Torres Strait Islanders—who have been the main victims of racial discrimination in the labour market in particular, and society in general. The Australian labour market, like the whole economy, has undergone rapid restructuring in recent decades. Cyclical crises—in the form of the severe economic recession of the 1990s, and structural change stemming from global economic restructuring and domestic policy shifts—have been the major forces behind these changes. At the same time, the Australian government has introduced legislation which prohibits the most overt dimensions of racial discrimination. This article attempts to sketch some of the major aspects of this changing political economy of Australian racism.

There are many manifestations or forms of racial discrimination in the labour market. The first is disproportionately high rates of unemployment experienced by NESB immigrants, Aboriginals and Torres Strait Islanders. This can be explained partly in terms of the racist attitudes and practices of the 'gatekeepers' of the labour market, that is, individual employers or personnel officers, and partly by the more indirect form of institutional racism. Here racism acts to exclude NESB immigrants, Aboriginals and Torres Strait Islanders from participation in wage labour. Another manifestation or form of racial discrimination occurs when NESB immigrants or people of indigenous background are employed, but in jobs below their ability. Here racist attitudes and practices, conscious or unconscious, of individuals and/or institutions are a barrier to the meritocratic recognition of the skills, qualifications and capabilities of NESB immigrants, Aboriginals or Torres Strait Islanders. The result of this form of inclusive racism is that they are disproportionately concentrated in lower-paying, inferior jobs compared to others of equal ability or equal human capital. Patterns of labour market segmentation emerge, marked by gender and ethnic or 'racial' background, with men and women from NESB or Aboriginal background demonstrating different and inferior employment profiles to those of others in the labour market.

Much of this is, of course, heresy to conservative social scientists, who explain such labour market outcomes as meritocratic outcomes for individuals with 'inferior' levels of human capital. Clearly, racism in the labour market and elsewhere in society is an elusive phenomenon to document and demonstrate. This in part stems from an absence of any hard data. There are no statistical series on the incidence of racist decisions by personnel officers or employers, who do not record the number of times per day that they have acted in a racist way. Indeed, one of the features of contemporary racism is denial, because racial discrimination is deemed as an unacceptable—and in Australia's case, unlawful—way to behave. Legislation on anti-discrimination, equal employment opportunity and racial vilification has been introduced by federal and state governments (Foster & Seitz 1993). These laws outlaw the practices of racial discrimination at work and in the community. But despite the existence of these laws—and bodies such as the Human Rights and Equal Opportunity Commission—racial discrimination in Australian society continues in the 1990s, often in an indirect or informal way. A report on racial discrimination which reviewed all aspects of the Australian evidence for the International Labour Office concluded that:

> despite the existence of significant legislation outlawing discrimina-
> tion and the introduction of racial vilification legislation in some
> States, there is ongoing and systemic evidence of discrimination at
> the general workplace level, involving in particular immigrants from
> NES [non-English-speaking] countries (Foster et al. 1991, pp. 110–
> 11).

Australia is not alone in this regard. A major survey of racial discrimination among migrant workers in Western Europe recently reached similar conclusions.

One of the central concerns of this chapter is the way in which various conservative economic and sociological theories attempt to explain—or explain away—racial discrimination in the Australian labour market. This partly stems from the social construction of notions of *race*, *gender*, *skill* and *human capital*. Skill is not an objective category of actual or potential labour market productivity, as conservative economic and sociological theories claim, but is a social cate-
gory, shaped historically by the male-dominated, sexist power structures of Australian society (Burton 1988). As a result, some aspects of the skills of men and women from an NESB or indigenous background—
which can be referred to as cultural capital as distinct from the narrower conservative concept of human capital—have often been unrecognised and unrewarded in the labour market. But even more disturbing is the finding that the very signs that should indicate to potential employers that workers possess cultural skills—an accent, hinting knowledge of at least one other language; cultural knowledge, indicating an ability to deal with a multicultural or multinational market; or knowledge of

Aboriginal culture—trigger negative responses in employers or labour market gatekeepers. Viewed through the ideologies of racism and sexism, these cultural skills are reinterpreted in the eyes of these gatekeepers as 'poor communication skills', 'high training costs', or 'unreliability'. This is an example of indirect racial discrimination, which occurs when employment practices which are in themselves not explicitly discriminatory have discriminatory outcomes.

Indirect racial discrimination also occurs when the level of language proficiency required for jobs is in excess of the level really needed. As the Council of Europe has found, the impact of such language requirements on migrant workers in Europe is discriminatory, since their command of the host country's language is often imperfect (Zegers de Beijl 1990). Since most jobs in the Australian labour market of the 1990s will be linked to vocational education and training, access to vocational training is critical to a worker's ability to achieve upward employment mobility via access to job ladders. The potential for indirect labour market discrimination against immigrant or indigenous workers emerges because of the greater emphasis placed on English-language ability as a criteria for entry into vocational training programs.

At the same time, changes to the institutional framework of industrial relations in Australia have seen centralised wage decisions under national wage cases of the last decade recently replaced with decentralised enterprise bargaining. This has been accompanied by large-scale award restructuring within the Industrial Relations Commission. These awards, which specify a job's scope and the resultant wages and conditions, have been broadened to take in a greater number of job tasks. As a consequence of these changes, weaker sections of the labour movement—such as those with large numbers of NESB men and women workers—will lose out on future wage increases and improved working conditions (Collins 1990). Baker and Wooden (1992) found that the ability to communicate in English has become a critical screening device for entry into the award restructuring processes for women in the Australian communications industry, while Levine et al. (1992) found that in the automobile industry it was more difficult for those workers who have poor English skills to participate in retraining under award restructuring.

Racial discrimination in the labour market, direct or indirect, individual or institutional, has the effect of confining its victims—usually men and women from NESB immigrant or indigenous backgrounds—to unemployment or employment in jobs below their capability. The inferior labour market position of immigrant or indigenous men and women serves to help reproduce negative stereotypes of these people, which is the fabric of the prejudice directed against many NESB immigrants and Aboriginal people in broader society. In this way, ideologies of racism and sexism are produced and reproduced in a changing economy and society. These ideologies help construct NESB immigrants and indigenous peoples as the Other, reinforcing social divisions in Australian society. They also lie behind incidents of racist violence and abuse in the workplace and in the community. In other words, to borrow the slogan from a recent campaign, 'racism sucks' from a humanitarian point of view, given the impact of racism on the lives of the victims. But racism also has a negative impact on the bottom line of business profits and productivity, since the economic potential of the victims of racism remains unfulfilled. This points to the contradictions of racial discrimination in Australia. The benefits for employers in terms of the divide-and-rule effects of racism on the Australian working class may be outweighed by the extent to which racism is a barrier to improved labour productivity. At the same time, racism also stands as a barrier to attempts to internationalise the Australian economy. Anti-Asian attitudes will constrain the ability of Australia to further enmesh with the dynamic Asian region, and limit the potential of industries such as tourism and education to attract Asians to Australia.

This chapter first reviews the evidence relating to racial discrimination in the Australian labour market today. This analysis stresses the importance of understanding the political economy of racism. The next section surveys the labour market profile of NESB immigrants and Aboriginal and Torres Strait Islanders—including unemployment rates and occupational concentration—to present the evidence for inequality in the labour market. Following this, the theoretical debates between conservative and radical scholars over discriminatory versus meritocratic explanations of these unequal labour market outcomes for NESB immigrant and indigenous men and women will be discussed. The chapter then considers the impact of economic restructuring in Australia on the dimensions and dynamics of racial discrimination in Australia in the 1990s. Such an analysis requires a focus on how matters of ethnicity, gender, class and racial background intersect to determine different patterns of racialisation for NESB immigrant and indigenous men and women. Next, some of the contradictions of contemporary Australian racism are discussed before a brief conclusion.

Discrimination in the labour market: the evidence

There is much debate as to the extent and nature of racial discrimination in the Australian labour market. This section looks at the evidence relating to the unequal labour market outcomes for many immigrants and indigenous people in the labour market today in terms of unemployment, labour market programs, labour market segmentation and earnings differentials. There is no doubt that NESB immigrants and indigenous people have much higher rates of unemployment than others. This is the racism of exclusion. Similarly, NESB immigrants and indigenous people appear to earn less than others with similar qualifications, while immigrant workers in particular face problems such as the non-recognition of skills and qualifications gained overseas. These emerge from the racism of inclusion.

Unemployment

NESB immigrants appeared to bear the greatest burden of the 1974–75 and 1982–83 recessions in terms of disproportionately high unemployment rates (Collins 1991, pp. 115–19), and recent studies have confirmed that this was also the case in the 1990s recession. Ackland and Williams (1992, p. 28) conclude that 'In the last three recessions, immigrants from NESBs have fared worse in the labour market than either those from ESBs or those born in Australia.' Jones and McAllister (1991) reviewed the unemployment experience of immigrants up to 1989 to find that Lebanese and Vietnamese unemployment rates were about four times greater than that of the Australian-born. They also found that NESB immigrants who had recently arrived suffered an unemployment rate two to three times higher than immigrants of English-speaking background who arrived during the same period.

These findings are confirmed by the official unemployment rates from the 1991 census (Table 4.1), which clearly show that NESB immigrants do have significantly higher rates of unemployment than the Australian-born. For example, Vietnamese-born women had the highest unemployment rate (44.8 per cent), nearly five times greater than that of Australian-born females (9.5 per cent). Other birthplace groups with female unemployment rates at least twice that of Australian-born females include Turkey (34 per cent), Lebanon (32.9 per cent), Taiwan (27.8 per cent) and Indonesia (19.7 per cent). A similar picture emerges from official male unemployment rates. The Australian-born male unemployment rate (11.5 per cent) was much lower than

Table 4.1 Australian unemployment rates by birthplace and gender, 1991

Country of birth	Unemployment rates (per cent)	
	Males	Females
Australia	11.48	9.54
New Zealand	13.63	11.91
United Kingdom	11.72	8.71
Cyprus	14.92	13.19
Greece	13.49	10.95
Italy	9.99	7.64
Yugoslavia	16.58	14.17
Germany	12.49	9.94
Netherlands	10.95	7.94
Czechoslovakia	15.99	13.20
Hungary	15.56	14.36
Poland	18.33	18.95
Ukraine	13.30	11.85
Lebanon	33.66	32.90
Turkey	29.70	34.00
Egypt	14.39	15.35
Indonesia	17.02	19.72
Malaysia	12.21	11.13
Singapore	12.47	11.39
Vietnam	35.87	44.76
China	14.93	18.40
Hong Kong	13.50	13.91
Japan	4.90	8.60
Korea	14.52	17.58
Taiwan	27.50	27.79
India	12.19	13.89
Sri Lanka	13.07	16.33
Canada	10.74	9.17
USA	9.36	9.14

Source: ABS 1991; *Census of Population and Housing*: special cross tabulation prepared for the Bureau of Immigration Research.

the Vietnamese-born (35.9 per cent), the Lebanese-born (33.7 per cent), the Turkish-born (29.7 per cent) and the Taiwan-born (27.5 per cent). Many other NESB birthplace groups have significantly higher unemployment rates than Australian-born males, while most ESB migrant groups had unemployment rates similar to, or below, Australian-born males.

Aboriginal and Torres Strait Islanders also suffer very high rates of unemployment, particularly youth and women. During the economic boom of the mid-1980s, when the average unemployment rate was about 8.0 per cent, data from the 1986 census revealed that one-half of the teenage Aboriginal labour force was unemployed, as were 40 per cent of Aboriginal 20–24-year-olds. Similarly, in 1986 Aboriginal women were only half as likely to be employed as non-Aboriginal women, and were more than twice as likely to be unemployed (Daly 1991, p. 93). The overall unemployment rate of indigenous people in 1991 was three times the national average (Miller 1991, p. 81).

While these official unemployment rates indicate unambiguously that NESB immigrants and indigenous peoples experience unequal labour market outcomes, they actually underestimate the severity of the extent of unemployment. Official unemployment rates do not include the 'hidden unemployed', that is, those without jobs but who are not counted in official statistics. This occurs partly because of the very narrow definition of *unemployed* used in surveys. A person is counted as unemployed only if they have not worked at all in the week prior to the survey and have actively sought work during the previous month and are available to start work (Norris 1993, p. 207). Because of the very high rates of unemployment during the 1990s Australian recession, job vacancies were scarce. Many unemployed were discouraged from continuing to seek work and stopped looking. While this may be a rational response to labour market realities, the result is that these people disappear from unemployment statistics and are said to have left the labour force. In addition, an unemployed person who is married to an employed person forfeits any right to unemployment benefits. There is thus little incentive to register with the Commonwealth Employment Service as unemployed.

Because of its very nature, it is difficult to measure hidden unemployment. Nevertheless, estimates of the 1974–75 recession suggested that hidden unemployment was so large as to double official unemployment rates, with NESB immigrants reported to be two to three times more likely to be included in the hidden unemployed (Stricker & Sheehan 1981, p. 71). One consequence of this is a reduction in the labour force participation rates—the proportion of those aged between 15 and 65 years of age who either have jobs or are unemployed—of NESB immigrant men and women. Labour force participation rates were also substantially lower for indigenous people, partly due to the discouraged worker effect, indicating high rates of hidden unemployment. As Wooden (1993, p. 41) concluded in a more recent report, 'if discouraged job seekers were included as part of the unemployed . . . 1.8 percentage points would be added to the official unemployment rate for the Australian-born, while the rate for immigrants would be increased by 2.9 percentage points'. Hidden unemployment is an even greater problem for Aboriginal peoples. Miller (1991, p. 81) found that there were 3.7 economically inactive indigenous people to every employed person, compared to the national average of 1.3 economically inactive people to every employed person.

Labour market opportunities are particularly difficult for indigenous people in remote and rural regions. Elliott Johnston QC, head of the *Review of the Training for Aboriginals Program*, reported the existence of:

> [a] particularly intractable employment situation of Aboriginal people living in small multi-racial towns. Regular labour market opportunities in these areas are extremely constrained due to economic conditions, the closed nature of the local labour markets, and the low skill level of many Aboriginal residents (Johnston 1991, p. 87).

Johnston recommended that committees comprised of representatives from local employment promotion committees, Aboriginal groups, local employers, government departments and trade unions be established to help promote Aboriginal employment, particularly in those areas where there was the greatest disparity between Aboriginal and non-Aboriginal unemployment rates.

Part of the inferior position of Aboriginal and Torres Strait Islanders in the Australian labour market is rooted in the poorer educational performance of indigenous people. Only 85 per cent of indigenous children of compulsory schooling age were participating in primary or secondary education, compared to a national participation rate of almost 100 per cent, according to 1986 census data. Less than half indigenous people aged between 15 and 19 years were attending some form of educational institution, when the comparative national rate was around 90 per cent. Indigenous students are also underrepresented in higher education in Australia, with indigenous comprising 0.9 per cent of the higher education students. This figure, however, was 80 per cent higher than five years previously (Miller 1991). As the report *Social Justice for Indigenous Australians 1993–94* (1993, p. 13) concluded, 'The harsh fact nonetheless remains that Aboriginal and Torres Strait Islander people continue to be at severe disadvantage compared with other Australians.' But the inferior position of Aboriginals and Torres Strait Islanders cannot be solely explained by differences in education or human capital. As Miller (1985, p. 92) argued in his *Report of the Committee of Review of Aboriginal Employment and Training Programs*, 'even if we allow for differences in geographic location, education and the age structure of the population, we still find that Aboriginal people are disadvantaged in the labour market'.

Labour market programs

Another arena of labour market discrimination relates to the access of NESB immigrants, Aboriginals and Torres Strait Islanders to programs which are designed to help unemployed people re-enter the labour market. Despite their higher unemployment rates, the evidence suggests that labour market programs have not adequately targeted unemployed NESB or indigenous men and women. The *Review of Migrant and Multicultural Programs and Services* (DIEA 1986, p. 151) concluded:

> the picture that emerges is of the most disadvantaged job seekers being excluded from the very labour market programs under which they are intended to receive preferential treatment because their disadvantage (in this case lack of English) is considered to be too severe for them to achieve success in those programs.

Similarly, indigenous people are underrepresented in labour market programs, despite experiencing unemployment rates three times the average (*Social Justice for Indigenous Australians 1993–94* 1993, p. 12). Jones and McAllister (1991, pp. 71, 86) found that the outcomes from general labour market programs are significantly poorer for Aboriginal people than for any other disadvantaged group in Australia, including those with language difficulties and the long-term unemployed.

Labour market segmentation

I argued in 1978 that the Australian labour market was segmented along the lines of gender, ethnicity and Aboriginality. In other words, there were six segments of the labour market: males born in Australia and the major English-speaking countries (ESB immigrants); NESB males; females born in Australia and the major English-speaking countries; NESB females; Aboriginal men; and Aboriginal women. Each segment was very different, with the workers born in Australia and ESB immigrants over-concentrated in the best, highest-paid jobs in the male and female labour markets. Males born in Australia and the major English-speaking countries dominate what Piore (1980) calls the 'primary' labour market, that is well-paid jobs requiring significant education and training, with good conditions, significant autonomy, and access to career paths. Their female counterparts are usually at the bottom rungs in this primary labour market. In contrast, NESB males and females tend to be over-concentrated in semi-skilled and unskilled jobs in the blue-collar sector or 'secondary' labour market where tasks are routinised, autonomy is non-existent, pay is low, conditions are bad and there is little access to job-ladders. These are the 'factory fodder' jobs that immigrant workers occupy in many countries (Castles & Miller 1993). Aboriginal employment patterns are so different to all others in Australia that Aboriginal labour appears to be a completely different segment, with different dynamics, different barriers and a different profile to the other labour market segments.

Labour market segmentation is not static. Rather, the segment shifts with changes to the employment structure over time. National and international economic restructuring has transformed the structure of the labour market since the 1970s. As a consequence, patterns of labour market segmentation have also changed. Taylor (1992) reviewed 1986 census data to investigate the occupational profiles of Aboriginals and Torres Strait Islanders compared to other Australians. He found that occupational segregation between Aboriginals and Torres Strait Islanders and others in the workforce declined considerably during the 1970s: in 1971 about one-third of indigenous peoples would have had to change their occupation or employment to achieve an occupational profile equivalent to that of other Australians. By 1981 less than one-fifth of indigenous peoples would have had to change occupations. In 1986 he observed growing indigenous employment in skilled occupations, including clerical, administrative, managerial and professional occupations. Nevertheless, indigenous workers were still underrepresented in these groups and overrepresented in the unskilled occupation of labourers and related workers. Exploring the gender dimension of indigenous occupations, Taylor (1992, p. 24) still found in 1986 an 'overwhelming concentration of Aboriginal and Torres Strait Islander females in semi-skilled occupations, compared to the male emphasis on unskilled labouring jobs'.

In 1991, indigenous workers were most underrepresented in the white-collar sector of the labour market: managers and administrators, professionals and clerks, and in personal services and sales occupations. Rough parity between indigenous workers and the national average was evident for the trades and para-professional occupations. Only in the manual, blue-collar occupations of plant and machine operators and labourers and related workers—where indigenous workers were on average twice as likely to be employed in the labourer category as Australian workers—did indigenous workers have a larger relative presence than the national average as a whole.

Economic restructuring is changing the opportunity structures for both new and old migrants. This, together with changes to Australia's immigration program, has had an impact on patterns of labour market segmentation. In the last decade, immigration intakes have been progressively reduced, with entry increasingly limited to those with the highest skills and qualifications. One consequence of this is that many NESB immigrants arriving in Australia in the last decade have been highly skilled and qualified professionals, technicians and managers. This is particularly the case for Asian immigrants, who make up the majority of immigrants entering Australia in the 1990s (Collins 1994). In 1990–91, for example, when eight of the top ten source countries of Australia's migrants were Asian (Inglis 1992, p. 25), one-quarter of Indian-born and 15.7 per cent of all Asian-born settler arrivals were professionals (Awasthi & Chandra 1993, p. 23, Table 15). Many of these immigrants find jobs in the primary labour market, while others move into business ownership. Many immigrant professionals, such as doctors, establish themselves in small businesses. Moreover, in the mid-1970s Australia introduced a 'business migration' category to annual immigration quotas (Collins 1991, pp. 91–2). In the decade following the introduction of the Business Migration Program in 1981, more than 11,000 business migrants and about 50,000 of their dependent family members arrived in Australia (Borowski 1992). A large proportion of recent business migrants have come from Asian countries.

As a result of these changes to immigration intakes and the Australian economy, many Asians have moved into 'primary' sector jobs where hitherto few NESB immigrants were to be found. Hence 1986 census data for New South Wales shows a relatively high concentration of immigrants born in Asian countries such as Malaysia, Hong Kong and India in managerial, professional and technical occupations (Collins 1989), despite continuing problems that many NESB immigrants still face having their qualifications recognised in Australia (Castles et al. 1989). Hence 30 per cent of Japanese-born and Taiwanese-born men were managers or administrators in 1991, compared with 16 per cent of the Australian-born. Those born in Hong Kong, Korea and Malaysia tend to cluster in the finance and business sectors of the economy, while those born in China, Japan and Thailand are concentrated in the personal and recreational services, including the restaurant and tourist industries. In contrast, Indochinese men and women—particularly those from Vietnam who arrived as refugees—are concentrated in low-skilled jobs in the declining manufacturing industry (Khoo et al. 1993, p. 9), with Vietnamese women overrepresented at eight to twelve times the rate of Australian-born women in the declining clothing industry (Castles et al. 1991, pp. 42–52). These changing and uneven patterns of racialisation of Asian immigrants—a response to economic restructuring and corresponding changes in Australian immigration policy—therefore lead to different 'opportunity structures' for more recently arrived NESB immigrants, with a subsequent impact on patterns of labour market segmentation.

Explaining racial discrimination in the Australian workplace

There is much debate as to the nature and extent of racial discrimination in the workplace in Australia. This is because such practices are difficult to detect and prove. As Foster et al. (1991, p. 109) put it, discrimination 'is difficult to define both within and across disciplines'. Moreover, the distinction between discrimination and disadvantage is not clear.

In the absence of such hard data much of the debate on racial discrimination in Australia has centred on the earnings differentials of immigrant workers vis-à-vis their Australian-born counterparts. Most NESB immigrant men and women earn less than others in the Australian labour market (Collins 1991, pp. 156–61). The key debate here is whether these earnings differentials are meritocratic or discriminatory. If they merely reflect differences in the human capital of different immigrant groups in the Australian labour market, this would support the meritocratic view. According to this view, different average earnings merely reflect differences in education levels and qualifications, or different competencies in English language, between NESB immigrants and others. But if NESB immigrants with the same human capital as others earned less, this would indicate discrimination. Econometric studies by sociologists Evans, Jones and Kelley (1988) conclude strongly that there is no evidence of racial discrimination in the labour market.

Foster et al. (1991, p. 61), on the other hand, conclude that the evidence on the labour force status of immigrant workers 'does lend itself to analyses of patterns consistent with discrimination'. A number of studies support this view. Chapman and Miller (1983) concluded that immigrant workers received lower returns for their education and experience than did Australian-born workers (see also Stromback & Williams 1985).

Human capital theory, embodying the meritocratic model, does not work well in accounting for the labour market experience of indigenous people. Jones (1991, p. 42) found that Aboriginal women earn about a dollar less per hour than Anglo-Celtic women average, with only about one-third of the difference due in any way to differences in endowments of human capital, the residual due to 'occupational discrimination, weak attachment to the formal labour market, and poorer educational experiences of Aborigines'. Similarly, Miller (1991, p. 83) controlled for differences in educational attainment in an attempt to explain what he calls the 'widely different degrees of success of Aboriginals and non-Aboriginals in the labour market'. He concluded that variations in human capital cannot explain the degree of inequality between Aboriginals and non-Aboriginals in the labour market:

> the major part of the substantial unemployment rate differential between Aborigines and non-Aborigines cannot be explained by the standard methodology that economists employ, and thus may be attributable to labour market discrimination and/or cultural factors (p. 85).

Given the preceding history of the relationship between immigration history, policy and racism in Australia (Collins 1991, pp. 198–223)— and the persistence of attitudes and practices of prejudice against immigrants (HREOC 1991)—it would be surprising if prejudice does not flow over into the labour market in some way. Perhaps the answer is that it depends who is looking and what they are looking for. The problem with the neo-classical economic theory of racial discrimination is that it presumes that racial discrimination occurs only if white employers are prepared to pay a higher wage to whites to avoid employing blacks or coloured workers (Arrow 1972; Becker 1957). Such employers are said to have exhibited a 'taste' for discrimination. For these economists, racial discrimination is simply a phenomenon of exclusion. The fact that employers might express their taste for discrimination by employing blacks or coloured immigrants—men and women—to work for low pay in bad conditions to maximise profits does not appear to fit into the abstract world of economic rationalism.

In another recent economic rationalist approach to Australian immigration, Lloyd (1993) applied rational public choice theory to the political economy of immigration to argue for the 'rationality' of racism. Lloyd argues that individuals have objective economic and social interests that are affected by immigration in general or by a specific ethnic group of immigrants. Those individuals who suffer real income loss because of immigration—or who think that their real income will fall because of it—are dubbed by Lloyd the economic 'enemies' of immigration. Those who experience or expect that their real income will rise because of immigration are economic 'friends'. These friends or enemies then form coalitions or interest groups to lobby for or against immigration. This behaviour is deemed to be rational, with Lloyd referring to 'natural' friends and 'natural' enemies of immigration in general or of immigrants of a particular type.

The great danger of this approach is that it appears to justify anti-immigration or anti-immigrant actions and attitudes. It is only 'natural', understandable, rational behaviour of individuals attempting to maximise their actual or perceived living standards. Those who think that they will be worse off because of immigration are rational to actively oppose it or the particular immigrant group that they consider responsible for worsening their income. Although it is impossible to work out, objectively, who gains and who loses from immigration in general, or specific components of the immigration intake in particular (Collins 1991, pp. 105–7), Lloyd proceeds as if this can be objectively determined. For example, he quotes Spindler (1987, p.49) to argue that 'immigration of unskilled labour should be strongly opposed by resident unskilled workers [but] strongly supported by skilled labour'. No evidence is given to support this argument, ignoring research (Junankar & Pope 1990; Pope & Withers 1990) that suggests that resident workers gain from immigration with a net increase in jobs. Since Lloyd's analysis rests on individual perceptions of the impact of immigration, some understanding of how prejudice influences such behaviour is required. But Lloyd admits that he has ignored these factors in his analysis. At a time when ethnic conflict and racist violence are dominating world headlines, any analysis that attempts to rationalise racist attitudes and actions against immigrants—no matter how ineptly—is dangerous in a society still struggling to overcome racism and social conflict.

Changing dimensions of racial discrimination in the Australian labour market

There have been many anecdotal accounts by immigrants of their experience of racism in the workplace (Foster et al. 1991, pp. 100–7). These experiences, though widespread, are dismissed by some quantitative sociologists as soft evidence at odds with the world of econometric models or the narrow definition of racial discrimination that constrains the vision of conservative economics and sociology. This blinkered approach to the study of racism leads to the impact of racial discrimination being reduced to just one aspect: earnings differentials. But racial discrimination occurs in many guises. As we have seen, higher unemployment rates, and occupational concentration in low-status jobs, can also be linked to racism. Moreover, indirect racial discrimination can occur when immigrant or Aboriginal men and women are excluded from jobs and vocational education because of a view that these workers have inherent problems of communication and training. Institutional racism may lead to the non-recognition of overseas-obtained qualifications. We need to explore these dimensions of racism if we are to fully understand the complex nature of racial discrimination in the Australian labour market.

One immigrant response to racism in the workplace has been to leave paid employment to enter small business as self-employed or as an employer (Collins & Castles 1992). Kidd (1991) has recognised the need for the study of racial discrimination in the workplace to include the fact that many immigrants choose self-employment to avoid facing discrimination. Studies of ethnic small business in Australia support this view, and point to racism as one factor blocking the mobility of immigrants in the workforce and leading to the disproportionately high rate of immigrant small businesses (Castles et al. 1991). The European evidence also supports the link between the growth of ethnic small business and racial discrimination (de Beijl 1990, p. 46).

A number of studies of the experience of NESB immigrant women in the workplace point to many instances of racist attitudes and practices on the part of employers, supervisors or trade union officials (Nord 1984; Storer 1976). Outworkers appear to be particularly vulnerable in this regard (Centre for Urban Research & Action 1978; Centre for Working Women's Co-operative Limited 1986). More indirectly, immigrant women appear to bear the greatest burden of the costs that are accompanying the restructuring of the Australian economy and the changes to institutional arrangements in the workplace that have occurred in the last decade. NESB immigrant women are the greatest losers in the move away from centralised wage decisions to decentralised enterprise bargaining (Collins 1990). They also appear to bear the greatest burden of economic restructuring in Australia, exacerbated by federal government policy to reduce levels of protection to the clothing, footwear and textiles industries where the majority of workers are NESB immigrant women. Immigrant women are the most likely to be pushed out of wage-labour into the informal world of outwork because of this economic restructuring (Alcorso 1991). But even those immigrant women who remain in jobs covered by awards appear to be further marginalised by the changes to date under the award restructuring agenda (Yeatman 1992).

Another aspect of institutional racism relates to the way in which institutions in the Australian labour market respond to overseas-obtained vocational qualifications. The irony is that while high levels of qualifications are often required to get entry into immigration intakes, many NESB immigrants do not have their qualifications and skills recognised (Castles et al. 1989). This prevents them from fully utilising their human capital in Australia, despite the fact that these qualifications are 'cost-free', having been paid for by some other government. NESB immigrants are much more likely than ESB immigrants to have their qualifications rejected by Australian professional organisations (Collins 1991, p. 97). Chapman and Iredale (1990) found that only 39 per cent of formally skilled immigrants subjected their overseas qualifications to official assessment and of these, only 42 per cent had them recognised as being equivalent to Australian qualifications. Chapman and Iredale note that earnings studies showed that those immigrant workers who had their qualifications recognised did not subsequently earn more than those whose qualifications remained unrecognised, and that employers appeared to treat all immigrants— qualified or not—as homogeneous.

Recent restructuring of the economy, combined with changes to the skill and ethnic profile of the immigration intake in the last decade, has had an impact on patterns of labour market segmentation. Many of the Southern and Eastern European immigrant groups who arrived in Australia in the 1950s and 1960s are today being discarded from the manufacturing sector and thrust into the ranks of the unemployed (Ackland & Williams 1992). Australia's largest Asian birthplace group, the Vietnamese, are the latest wave of NESB immigrants destined to be factory fodder. But such jobs were hardest hit by the 1990s recession and the more permanent economic restructuring of the economy. The Vietnamese-born have rates of unemployment four to five times the average, and are the worst hit by 1990s unemployment (Viviani et al. 1993). On the other hand, we have seen that many new Asian immigrants are highly qualified and find employment in well-paid white-collar jobs, often in the professional and managerial and administrative occupations. While patterns of labour market segmentation have exhibited these changes, it is strongly apparent that many NESB immigrant men and women are still employed in jobs below their ability, or are without jobs at all. This disadvantage cannot be fully accounted for by 'meritocratic' factors such as English-language ability or education. Racial discrimination of the indirect or direct kind clearly plays an important, if elusive, role.

The potential for indirect racial discrimination is clear following the recent developments in vocational education and training in Australia. Following three major reports by Mayer (1992), Finn (1991) and Carmichael (1992), there has been a move to a nationally uniform, competency-based approach to education and to a restructuring of the vocational education system. A new Vocational Education Certificate system will be the credential-base for these changes which reflect the critical link between work and education and training that has accompanied economic restructuring. These changes mesh with movements to the multi-skilling of workers as industrial relations awards are also restructured.

It is clear that in this new Australian workplace environment, as in most Western economies (Thurow 1975), an applicant's chance of getting a job is linked to the employer's perception as to the applicant's suitability for training. Similarly, in the choice of existing employees to take part in new training opportunities—with the key to opening the doors to newly established career paths—the issue of training suitability will become increasingly important. This problem is exacerbated by the emphasis in the new workplaces on communication skills and teamwork. English is the language of training, with English proficiency seen as a necessary qualification to enter training.

The danger here is that conscious or unconscious racism and prejudice create negative stereotypes of a job applicant of NESB or indigenous background. Despite the fact that an immigrant with an accent might be a great communicator, great in teamwork, possess multilingual abilities and speak English well, an accent hints to many employers that there are potential costs, not potential benefits, in employing this person. Hence an accent or physical appearance may lead employers—or in larger public and private corporations their gatekeepers, such as personnel officers—to reject these applicants on the ground that they might cost too much to train and/or might not be able to benefit from training. Similiar views restrict the access of indigenous people to the labour market. In this example, rational behaviour, defined in the manner of conservative economic theory as taking actions that on the basis of probability maximise profits, will discriminate against NESB and indigenous workers if employers or personnel officers hold racial stereotypes which view all NESB migrants as having communication problems and all indigenous people as being 'unreliable'.

The same argument applies to female skills and stereotyped attributes. If employers believe that, on the balance of probabilities, female workers will be unreliable or short-term employees—they will leave to have babies or take excessive time off work because of their children's illnesses—it is rational not to hire them or, if employed, to pay them less than equivalently skilled males who do not carry the burden of the same stereotypes. In the case of women from NESB or indigenous backgrounds, racism and sexism intersect, creating barriers to their employment or their promotion within employment. Even when workers are judged on the competencies that they can demonstrate, the social and cultural construction of skills and qualifications perpetuates discrimination on a gender and racial basis (de Lepervanche & Bottomley 1988). These are skills which non-immigrants generally do not have. Yet the contradiction is that the very worker attributes of accent, gender and skin colour that should indicate the possession of cultural capital by prospective employees generally trigger off precisely the opposite response: images of high training costs, communication problems, low productivity and unreliability.

There is considerable evidence of such discrimination. Baker and Wooden (1992) studied immigrant women in the communication industry—which includes such major public sector employers as Australia Post, Telstra and OTC—to see if they had a similar experience of industry restructuring to non-immigrant women in the industry. The study found that ability to communicate in English—perceived or real—had become an important screening device for job selection in the first instance, and for entry to award restructuring processes, including training. Similarly, Levine et al. (1992) studied the automobile industry and found that it was more difficult for those workers who have poor English skills to participate in retraining under award restructuring. A study of the impact of award restructuring on the clothing industry (Yeatman 1992, p. 70) also found that '"immigrant women" are at high risk of the intensification of their already low labour market status'.

One innovation that accompanies the vocational education change to competency-based standards is recognition of prior learning. Workers who demonstrate that they can do the job, receive a Vocational Education Certificate. Recognition of prior learning holds the potential to redress some of the entrenched racial and gender imbalance in the labour market that has resulted from the social construction of what constitutes human capital and from the non-recognition of skills acquired overseas. In fact, the experience to date suggests that past inequalities will be further entrenched. As Kalantzis (1992, p. 6) has argued:

> In fact, the influence of the competencies on curriculum is, more than anything else, going to be testing driven. In their nature, moreover, these tests will invariably put a greater premium on written and spoken communication. This means, however, that students and workers of non-English speaking backgrounds, for

example, will appear not to be competent. Competency training and assessment will actually, albeit perhaps inadvertently, test linguistic performance more than what people can or cannot do.

Despite Australia's culturally diverse labour force, cultural factors are not adequately recognised or rewarded in the labour market. Culture was excluded from Mayer's list of the seven competencies that workers were required to demonstrate (Mayer, 1992). But there is a strong argument that cultural capital is an important part of a worker's skill, and should be included as the eighth (Kalantzis 1994). In a culturally diverse society and workforce, cultural knowledge is important.

The economic, social and political contradictions of racism

While it is important to study the historical origins of racism in capitalist societies such as Australia, Canada and New Zealand—and link them to the needs of colonial and capitalist growth, expansion and political dominance—it is critical to focus on the contradictions that racism carries with it. As Bolaria and Li (1988, p. 39) put it, 'racism can be socially counter-productive in creating excessive social tensions'. Four recent examples from Australia—and one from the USA—illustrate this point.

The first is the 1988 bicentennial immigration debate, triggered by John Howard, then leader of the Liberal–National coalition (Collins 1991, pp. 301–6). Howard, desperate to win an election against Labor Prime Minister, Bob Hawke, and requiring only a few percentage points swing his way, played the 'prejudice' card by turning immigration and multiculturalism into a political issue. He declared that as Prime Minister he would reduce Asian immigration 'if necessary' and abandon multiculturalism in favour of a policy of 'One Nation'. Howard was clearly attempting to attract those Labor voters who, because of attitudes of racism and prejudice, opposed Asians and multiculturalism. While the extent of opposition to Asian immigration is debatable—Victorian RSL President Bruce Ruxton claimed that as many as 80 per cent of the population were opposed to it—a large number of Australians do still hold strong attitudes of racial prejudice. Surely the task of convincing a small percentage of Labor voters to swing to Howard on this issue would be easy.

But Howard's political masterstroke backfired. The decisive blow came from his traditional constituency—big business in Australia. Corporate Australian capital viewed the dynamism of the Asian region with eager eyes. Australia's economic future lay with improved economic and political relations with Asia. Howard's stance on Asian immigration was criticised widely in the Asian media as a return of the White Australia policy. Clearly, the initial appeal of Howard's attempt to gain from the politics of prejudice had backfired, with continued anti-Asian racism a barrier to improved Australian–Asian relations. The first words that his replacement, Andrew Peacock, uttered to the press conference announcing the change of leadership were that the coalition would return to a bipartisan immigration policy, including acceptance of multiculturalism and abandonment of any suggestion that Asian immigration would be treated any different to immigration from other regions.

A second contradiction is the way in which racial prejudice and racial discrimination of individuals and institutions limits the economic contribution of immigrants and Aboriginal people. According to neo-classical economic theory, a person is paid a wage in relation to their marginal productivity. Investment in human capital—education, training—can increase this productivity and hence a person's income (Norris 1993). However, racial discrimination—conscious or unconscious—can lead to an under-utilisation of the human capital of immigrants and Aboriginal people. The New South Wales Minister for Ethnic Affairs, Michael Photios, recently estimated that the cost to that state of not recognising the skills and qualifications—the human capital—of immigrants was $250 million per year. This problem is exacerbated by the way in which the skills which constitute human capital are socially constructed. Many female skills are thereby undervalued and under-utilised (Burton 1988), while we have seen that immigrants and Aboriginals are hampered by a monocultural, monolinguistic valuing of skills in the education system and labour market. As a recent report put it, 'Without competence in Cultural Understandings, counterproductive inequities and prejudice can arise. Discrimination in the workplace leads to inefficiency, absenteeism, inflexible work practices and lower productivity' (NLLIA Centre for Workplace Communication & Culture 1994, p. 9).

A third example, developing the previous points, relates to the attempt by Australia to increase economic ties with Asia following the *Garnaut Report* (Garnaut 1989). A recent report (Department of Foreign Affairs & Trade 1992) on the success of Australian businesses in penetrating the South-East Asian market found that few if any corporations had employed Asian-Australians in this task. This is despite the importance of cultural traditions in business negotiations and partnerships. The report (pp. 237, 240) found that 'there is a prominence of ethnic Chinese in the [South-East Asian] business community' but laments that the cultural skills needed—and available in Australia—for negotiations with these ethnic Chinese, are not utilised, are a largely 'untapped resource':

> Australia has a valuable asset in its citizens of Asian origin who understand the cultures and languages of the region and maintain close links through family and other personal networks. Very few firms in Australia appear to draw on this pool of skills to any great extent when dealing with the region . . . Developing personal relationships is of critical importance in establishing links with the South-East Asian business people.

A fourth example relates to the recent success in having Sydney chosen as the venue for the Olympic 2000 Games. Australia has been championing human rights abroad: the Minister for Foreign Affairs, Gareth Evans, recently announced that aid to Papua New Guinea would be tied to improvements in human rights. While this approach is laudable, the contradiction is that this focuses attention on Australian human rights. In this way, the deplorable Third World conditions of health, education, employment and living standards of Aboriginal and Torres Strait Islander peoples—a legacy of 205 years of racism and prejudice—are an international embarrassment for the Australian government.

Finally, there is a link between racism and social conflict in contemporary societies, as the recent events in Europe and the USA vividly testify. Some would argue that ethnic diversity itself leads to social conflict and undermines social cohesion. The 'race riots' in Los Angeles in 1992 have been widely interpreted as proof of the inevitable link between ethnic diversity and social conflict. However, a closer study of the factors underlying the Los Angeles riots suggests that it is the racism and prejudice that shape the lives of ethnic minorities—and the resulting socio-economic disadvantage and political disenfranchisement of the black and Latino people in the USA—that is to blame for these conflicts (Collins 1993). The USA does not have programs and services of multiculturalism and biculturalism that attempt to create the conditions for equality of all, regardless of racial or ethnic background. There is no safety net of Medicare or unemployment or welfare benefits that prevents people falling far below the standards of society as a whole. The lesson from the Los Angeles riots is that ethnic diversity will lead to social conflict unless every attempt is made to ensure the indigenous and immigrant minorities are given equal opportunity and equal access to the society's economic, social, political and cultural resources. Racism is, of course, a barrier to such access and equity, and hence a precondition for social conflict in ethnically diverse societies such as Australia, Canada and New Zealand.

Conclusion

Racism and prejudice have been persistent features in white Australian society. The labour market has not escaped from racial discrimination: it both reflects and reproduces racist social relations. NESB immigrants, Aboriginals and Torres Strait Islanders suffer from disproportionately high unemployment, are overlooked in labour market programs, and are employed in jobs below their abilities. It is not plausible to explain these unequal outcomes in the labour market in solely meritocratic terms, although conservative economists and sociologists put much effort into this task. But the issues are complex and subtle. The processes of racialisation in the labour market and in broader society change over time and are often contradictory. The main forces for these changes are the international and national processes of economic restructuring, corresponding changes to Australian immigration policy and intakes, changes in the industrial relations and education systems, and the contradictions of racism themselves. When private and public sector institutions respond to these changes and new opportunities emerge to help overturn discriminatory outcomes, new racist practices and possibilities arise.

Racial discrimination is strongly entrenched in individual prejudice (Markus 1988) and in negative stereotypes which justify discriminatory outcomes for the victims, as well as in institutional practices in the labour market. Often racism takes an indirect and unintentional form. Clearly, there is still much debate about, and an urgent need for further research on, the many facets of racial discrimination. As yet there have been no studies of the influence of racist prejudice on employment selection procedures, on promotion prospects, or on decisions as to who should be fired when economic downturn leads to retrenchments. New research, investigating the complex nature of racial discrimination in Australia, is urgently required. Critical here is the way in which sexist and racist ideology (Vasta 1991; Yuval-Davis & Anthias 1989) has shaped the social construction of what constitutes human capital and led to unequal labour market outcomes, particularly for men and women from NESBs and indigenous backgrounds. In addition, recent cyclical and structural economic changes have thrown the labour market and related institutions into a state of flux hitherto unseen in post-war Australian society. These changes throw up many opportunities to overcome discriminatory labour market outcomes, yet the evidence to date is not encouraging. At stake is not only the continued inequality and individual hardship for the victims of racism and the threat to social cohesion that racism poses. At issue also is the under-utilisation of the ability of NESB immigrants, Aboriginals and Torres Strait Islanders and the corresponding diminution of Australia's economic potential in an increasingly internationalised economy and society.

5

Mis/taken identity

Wendy Holland

I'm gasping for breath in my own struggle and am not too sure where to turn. My life abounds in incongruities. I can't return whence I came, yet I dare not and cannot forget, for I am reminded by the pain and passion of what it means to be Aboriginal in this country—not just by my past and my ongoing experiences, but by those of the Aboriginal community as a whole (Holt 1993, p. 176).

Like Lillian and other murris I know only too well what it is like to grow up aboriginal in australia and to experience racism. The racism directed toward murris in this society has been a constant reminder to me that I belong to a black family. Yet growing up blonde, blue-eyed, and fair-skinned, I certainly cannot deny my english and irish heritages. Nor can I deny the opportunities I have been afforded as a result of my whiteness and being mis/taken as white in this racist society.[1]

Living in a white body and identifying as a murri[2] means that my experience of racism has always been different to that of a murri living in a black body. Only recently have I been able to identify and deal with the various ways racism has affected my own life and that of my family. In learning to deal with the patterns of behaviour that I have developed over the years as a result of my own internalised racism, I am much more aware of the various ways we, as murris, perpetuate the racism within our own communities. Essentialist notions of aboriginality that exist within many murri communities reinforce racism. For example, some murris take the position that being born aboriginal makes one an expert on all matters related to aboriginal people. While it is important to recognise that essentialist positions do have strategic political value at times, essentialist notions of aboriginality often restrict us from acknowledging and celebrating the diversity within our own families and communities. It also denies the differences that many of us embody within ourselves.

Growing up for the most part of my life in an inner-city, working-class and culturally diverse neighbourhood I, like my family, have come to know a lot about difference. In recent years I have also come to appreciate more fully that many individuals and groups now living in this country are also affected by racism. The collapsing of the binary opposition—through which many of us have come to view the relationship between murri and non-murri people as simply a relationship between black and white australians—is necessary in order to facilitate a broader understanding of racism.

Given the recent high court *Mabo*[3] decision and subsequent negotiations, plus the federal government's aboriginal reconciliation plans and discussions in relation to republicanism, I believe that all australians are witnessing a critical moment in the history of this country. It is a time when the authenticity of *the* aboriginal identity is being fiercely contested among murris as well as between murris and other australians. The identity of 'who is a *real* australian' is being subjected to much debate and it is time for those of us who often live on the margins of this society to put forward our positions and refuse to be silenced.

In order to explore these issues further in this chapter, I have chosen to reflect on my own experiences growing up and living in a racist society. This exploration is therefore intensely personal and grounded in a subjective experience. It has been written with a number of audiences in mind. I hope that this chapter is useful to people from a variety of social and educational backgrounds who are interested in working against racism. Of utmost importance has been my desire to communicate in a way that is accessible and meaningful for a broad readership.

Re/membering

The british invasion of this country brought with it a culture which had a long history of racism. We can instance the british attitude toward the irish, whose country they first colonised in the thirteenth century. Taking over people's lives and land, as the british did in africa, india, north america and then australia, has been justified on the grounds of moral, social and cultural superiority when the underlying reason was really political and economic expediency.

The creation of the legal fiction *terra nullius*, meaning empty land, by the british deemed aboriginal people to be less than human. It provided the basis for the decimation, dispossession, displacement, institutionalisation and exploitation of aboriginal people.[4] The process of constructing 'aborigines' as *Other* enabled the british to justify their invasion and colonisation of this land and its first peoples. There were no treaties made between the aboriginal peoples of this land and the invaders. Reynolds (1995) suggests that this legal fiction, which had been developed in britain, had no credibility amongst the invaders or the invaded at the time.

While indigenous people suffered this insult first, racism was soon extended to other groups. Murris and many others within australia have subsequently suffered from the racism of a dominant white australian culture born of a british invasion. It manifested itself against the chinese and afghan immigrants in the nineteenth century. Later waves of european immigrants became known as 'wogs', 'balts', 'dagos', etc. while more recently the 'lebs', the 'boat people' and the 'slopes' have suffered from the racism of the dominant culture. For many of these people there has been some hope for improvement in their position as a new wave of immigration brought a new set of victims. In contrast, many murris have remained at the bottom of the pile.

Now I am not saying that all white australians *are* racist, or for that matter all non-white australians *aren't* racist. It is understandable, but not justifiable, that many post-1788 'new australians' have absorbed unquestioningly the racism of the dominant white australian culture and have learned to act out the racism toward murris in this society. I am not saying either that murris can't be racist toward others: of course we can! However, I am saying that racism is about power and that there are very few murris in this country who have managed to have power over their own lives, let alone power in relation to the affairs of this nation.

Re/membering is a form of resistance; it is a life-affirming and self-defining act. Re/membering is a cry of defiance in the face of that which would steal our past, predetermine our future, cut short our present, challenge our humanity, render our lives meaningless, and make us invisible. It is our refusal to be silent, our rejection of oppression (Featherston 1994, p. v).

Re/membering the past is important because the past has shaped our present. Often murris are accused of dwelling on the past. A lot of australians, in particular white australians, would be happy if we just forgot the past. What is to follow is my story, a story about difference and some stories about my own past and experiences of racism.

My earliest re/membering of my own cultural difference and that of other australians was when I was five years of age. Sophia and I were in the same class at school. She was greek australian. We used to be friends until my family moved to a different suburb.

The other kids at school used to harass Sophia because they considered her to be different from themselves. They'd call her a 'wog' and pick on her for no reason. They would tell her to go back to her own country, which didn't make much sense to me because I knew she had been born in australia and that made her greek-australian as far as I was concerned. I just didn't understand it because I thought Sophia was okay, she was my friend. I used to get really angry with those other kids. I didn't understand at the time that those kids were being racist toward Sophia.

I didn't understand too much about my own difference either, despite the fact that I was experiencing it through the racism directed toward Sophia. It has only been in the last few years that I have been able to make sense of myself, my own family difference, and that time with Sophia.

Sophia and her family were just like the people who had lived next door to me when I was living with my mother's family. They too were greek-australian, and my experience of them was that they were good neighbours. They never seemed to worry about the fact that some of my family were fair-skinned while others were black.

I never had much to do with my father's family, who were white. It seemed that some of them didn't think too much of my mother's mob because all they could see was our blackness. It was *their* racism that got in the way of us ever really getting to know one another as a family. Their racism was also a constant reminder to me that I belonged to a black family. My father seemed to be able to mediate his way through the situation quite well, although he himself had more to do with my mother's family than his own and I am certain that at times it must have been difficult for him. It was always my mother who would remind me that I was as much my father's child as hers and that I should show respect to his family.

The family that I grew up with didn't think of themselves as different from anyone else in the neighbourhood. We didn't have a need to go around naming ourselves 'aboriginal' or for that matter 'black' because it wasn't necessary, nor was it an issue within my family. Now that's not to say that we were ashamed of being murri, it's just that it didn't matter. It only mattered when we moved outside the safety of our own home and immediate community.

Where we lived, people knew that most of my family were murri and they generally accepted us for who we were. This was because of the culturally diverse nature of that neighbourhood. Besides, my family were respectable—quiet and hard-working people who mostly kept to themselves. Looking back I suspect that my family behaved and lived the way they did because they were very much aware of the racism and their position as blacks in the broader community. They were trying to be 'cleaner than clean, better than best'. They were obviously determined not to let racism beat them.

The decision on the part of my family to conceal their identity as aboriginal can be viewed as a creative strategy in dealing with racism. It wasn't a matter of my family 'selling out' on their aboriginality or that they thought they were better than other murris. It was simply one strategy they adopted for survival reasons!

School was the place where I first re/member experiencing racism. It was also the place where I re/member learning about my own family difference via racism. My schooling offered little in the way of providing an understanding of aboriginality and the reality of murri life in the 1960s and 1970s. I will never forget the brief moments in which *'the australian aborigines'* featured in our lessons at school. It was in my early years at primary school that 'aborigines' got their first mention. They were typecast as black, naked and unintelligent, and were portrayed as nuisances to the european explorers.

The last mention of 'aborigines' was when I was in my final year of primary school. I clearly remember the one page that had been dedicated to *'the australian aborigines'* in our *Effective Social Studies* text. 'Aborigines' and their society (note singular usage, as if 'aborigines' were monocultural, which was clearly not the case) were depicted as simplistic, childlike and heathen. Aboriginal women didn't even get a mention, it was as if women didn't exist. 'Aborigines' were presented as if they were transfixed in time. There was no reference, let alone any discussion, in relation to the british invasion and colonisation of this land and its impact on indigenous people. The one and only illustration on the page of the text was of a naked black man standing on top of a rock with one leg up on the other, poised holding a spear as he gazed into the distance . . . ah, the timeless 'noble savage'!

When I explained in class that some of my mother's family were aboriginal and that we did not live like the murris depicted in the textbook, I re/member feeling really embarrassed and confused when the teacher dismissed my family as not *real* 'aborigines'. It was in that moment that I re/member recognising the complexities and contradictions inherent in naming my own identity, or rather multiple identities. I can re/member feeling confused for a long time.

It was when I left home to go to teachers' college in rural new south wales that I became acutely aware of racism, my own difference and the politics of difference. At that particular point I re/member being really angry and defiant in the face of racism. I re/member how I refused to be named by others and would name myself aboriginal, which created a problem for some of my peers on campus. It also created a problem for me from time to time, because I often felt a sense of isolation. This experience of isolation was often the result of the *covert*, as much as the *overt*, racism operating among the student body.

The issue of addressing racism in society was very much on the agenda for the college for a number of reasons. Firstly, the college was located in a town where there was a significant murri population and it considered it had a responsibility to that particular part of the community. Secondly, through its affirmative action program the college was attempting to open its doors to murris who wanted to become teachers. Thirdly, the college recognised the importance of educating *all* australians in the area of 'race' relations. A one-semester *Race Relations* course had been introduced as a compulsory part of our teacher training.

It was an extremely exciting and challenging time for myself and many other students. In *Race Relations* lectures there was often heated debate. It was hard not to show my anger with some of my peers for example, when some of them spoke out about their complete dislike for blacks because of what they had experienced in their own home towns. I also re/member the debates which attempted to discredit and deny aboriginality to us fair-skinned murris. They were intense times, and I was often affronted by the level of ignorance and fear of difference among my peers. What was of real concern to me was that these students were in training to be teachers and that one day they would be out in schools teaching. It was frightening to think what some of them might be like in a classroom where there were aboriginal kids, or kids from other culturally different backgrounds for that matter.

One particular *Race Relations* episode I will never forget was the experience orchestrated by a couple of students and a lecturer around the issue of difference. This experience really heightened my awareness of difference and what happens to people who fear differences in others. I have titled this story . . .
.

The Robed as Other

Over a period of about a month, two students dressed up in robes (their whole bodies completely covered) appeared at different times and in different locations on campus. They had been briefed by the lecturer not to speak to anyone. What they were required to do was to observe people's reactions to their presence, especially when they remained stationary for any lengthy period. No-one at this stage knew their identity except for the lecturer.

When these fully robed bodies appeared in different parts of the campus, the initial response from people was usually one of curiosity and interest. Some people attempted to ask questions of the robed bodies, but information was never forthcoming. Most students just went about their campus life without making too much fuss about the robed bodies, until one day when one of the robed bodies was attacked by a group of male third-year students.

It actually got a bit scary when this 'gang' started to harass one of the robed bodies. They barricaded one into a corner, shouting abuse. A few other students tried to intervene to stop people from getting hurt. It became obvious that the time had come to call a halt to the exercise.

A few days later, the robed bodies appeared behind the lecturer in front of the two hundred-odd students. As they slowly made their way toward the lecturer, she began to reveal the purpose of the exercise and the real identities of the robed players. Tension and anger from some of the students, in particular those students involved in the harassment episode, began to mount.

The two students spoke about their experiences during the exercise. Of course they talked about the curiosity expressed by some, but they also revealed some really disturbing experiences. The lecturer then took the opportunity to expand on the issue of difference and to reinforce the seriousness of the consequences of fear of difference. It was an unforgettable experience for many students in the course.

I will always respect this particular lecturer for orchestrating such a powerful experience, which I am sure prompted many students to confront their own racism in a very immediate way. However, the exercise operated in a framework that was confined to notions of external appearance. While it recognised the oppression of people who looked different, the oppression of those of us who did not embody the physical aspects of being black was ignored. For those of us murris who were fair-skinned, our aboriginality went unrecognised; this reinforced racism in the silencing of what we had to contribute to the discussion. The experience of being murri goes far beyond surface physical appearances.

I am still reminded of *The Robed as Other* experience and of my own difference living in this society. Post-war immigration opened up this country significantly in terms of 'race' relations. The referendum of 1967 giving murris citizenship was a milestone in australian black–white relations, and the demise of the white australia policy[5] in 1972 meant australia began to come to terms with its own racist past. However, the racism of the dominant white culture toward murris is still deeply embedded within the australian psyche.

To name or not to name

Before 1788, those of my ancestors who were indigenous to this country would not have considered themselves aboriginal or, for that matter, black. The indigenous people of this country only became 'aborigines'/blacks as a result of invasion and colonisation by the british who, ironically, came to be australians. The use of the term *aboriginal* is problematic, in that it carries so many different meanings and it is one of the most disputed terms in this country. According to aboriginal anthropologist Marcia Langton (1993, pp. 28–9), it has been noted that there are at least sixty-seven definitions of aboriginal people, which, she says, reflect:

> not only Anglo-Australian legal and administrative obsession, even fixation, with Aboriginal people, but also the uncertainty, confusion and constant search for the appropriate characterisation: 'full-blood', 'half-caste', 'quadroon', 'octoroon', 'such and such an admixture of blood', 'a native of Australia', 'a native of an admixture of blood not less than half Aboriginal' and so on. In one legal case, whether or not an Aboriginal person lived in a 'native's camp' became an important issue of definition.

Langton goes on to say that:

> This fixation on classification reflects the extraordinary intensification of colonial administration of Aboriginal affairs since 1788 to the present. Elaborate systems of control aimed, until recently, at exterminating one kind of 'Aboriginality' and replacing it with a sanitised version acceptable to the Anglo invaders and immigrants. Perhaps Aboriginal affairs is the longest 'race' experiment in history?

For many murris, cultural hybridity is an extremely sensitive issue. It stands to reason, given Langton's reflections and the legacies of past racist government policies, that there is such strong resistance by many murris to recognising any 'dilution' of aboriginality. It just doesn't make sense to speak of oneself as 'full-blood', 'part-aboriginal', 'half-caste' or 'quarter-caste', etc. Besides, you would never hear a white australian speaking of themselves as being 'full-blood celt'! Identity is not about hierarchies. No one experience of being 'aboriginal' in this country is more real than or superior to another. It is racism that has taught us to think in this way. So it is not uncommon to hear comments from one murri to another, or to someone who might be struggling to come to terms with their aboriginal identity, like 'You better make up your mind whether you're aboriginal or you ain't!', or 'You're aboriginal and that's all there is to it!' While this all-or-nothing stand is a good example of the strategic political nature of identity, it can in turn lead to essentialism.

Essentialism within murri communities only works to reinforce the racism of the dominant culture. It is evident in the way some murris say that only aboriginal people can speak on aboriginal matters. It is also evident in the way some murris make out that all whites are bad. Essentialism is evident in the way some murris want to romanticise the so-called *traditional* aboriginal society and write off the society we live in today. As Langton (1993, p. 27) says in reference to aboriginal people and film-making:

> There is a naive belief that Aboriginal people will make 'better' representations of us, simply because being Aboriginal gives 'greater' understanding. This belief is based on an ancient and universal feature of racism: the assumption of the undifferentiated Other. More specifically, the assumption is that all Aborigines are alike and equally understand each other, without regard to cultural variation, history, gender, sexual preference and so on. It is a demand for censorship: there is a 'right' way to be Aboriginal, and any Aboriginal film or video producer will necessarily make a 'true' representation of 'Aboriginality'.

Stuart Hall (1992a, p. 310) challenges the notion of essentialism when he refers to us as now living complex, fragmented lives as post-modern subjects, without fixed or permanent identities.

> Everywhere, cultural identities are emerging which are not fixed, but poised, in transition, between different positions; which draw on different cultural traditions at the same time; and which are the

product of those complicated cross-overs and cultural mixes which are increasingly common in a globalised world.

Essentialism within many murri communities is about the denial of difference that has always existed and continues to exist within our communities. These days I never assume that other murris are necessarily prepared to work against racism in the broader community, let alone sexism, class oppression or homophobia.

Interrupting the gaze

This next story is set in the early 1980s. It is a story about addressing the issue of racism in the classroom and the cultural politics of identity. I had been appointed to a year six class where there was a range of abilities and skills. Apart from one student who identified as 'aboriginal' and three or four other students who had southern european australian heritages, the rest of the students were mainly white australian. It was a rather difficult and unruly class. As a new teacher to the school I had a lot to deal with. Although I was well placed to address any matters of racism within the classroom and/or staffroom, choosing the right time was crucial.

At the beginning of second term my grade supervisor advised me that I was to teach the themes *'australian government'* and *'australia's natural resources'*. For a number of reasons I knew that teaching these themes just wouldn't work with my class, so I planned a series of lessons about *australia and what it meant to be australian*.

In opening up the discussion I asked the students what they had learnt about *australia and being australian*. As there was little response, I tried asking them what they knew about aboriginal people. Using present tense, I asked them, 'Who are the first australians?' and of course their response was 'The abos, miss!' My immediate reaction was to make it clear to them that I would not tolerate derogatory labels such as *abos* in the classroom. I then explained why the term was offensive to murris. There was general agreement not to use such a term again.

Once we were over that hurdle I persisted with wanting to know what they knew or had learned about 'aboriginal' people. They responded with comments like: they're 'black' 'lazy', 'uneducated', 'smell a lot', 'ladies don't do their housework', 'eat witchetty grubs', they 'go walkabout', 'don't work', 'want land rights' and that 'the people living in their neighbourhood were more civilised than those aboriginal people living in the northern territory', etc. Their negative stereotypes far outweighed the positive aspects of murri lifestyles and cultures, which was not so surprising given how deeply embedded the racism is within this society.

My immediate reaction was to challenge their stereotypes in order to point out that what they had told me didn't fit with my experience of being an aboriginal australian. Until that moment the students had assumed that I was white and were quite shocked when I revealed to them my family background and history. In naming myself aboriginal I was aware of the problems inherent in describing my identity in this way. At the time I was conscious of the very powerful position I was in as a teacher when challenging the students' perceptions of what it means to be aboriginal in the 1980s.

In discussing my identity with the students, I became aware of my own use of 'australian' in describing my english and irish heritages. What I had done was to equate my whiteness with being australian, ignoring the fact that many post-1788 'new australians' were not necessarily white. I took the opportunity to then discuss the issue of 'who is an australian' with the students. I made a point of talking through the fact that a number of people who had immigrated from various places and for different reasons who were now living in australia were not white and that they were as much australian as white australians. The few southern european students in the class obviously felt acknowledged and supported by my stance because they were able to express their annoyance at the way they were considered not australian.

The next day in class we discussed at length the previous day's session. We defined and explored the issues of 'stereotyping', 'generalising', and 'ethnocentrism'. When I made the point to the students that what they had done the day before was to stereotype murris, it was interesting to hear their response. It was quite obvious that many of the students had discussed the issue of intermarriage with their families the night before in an effort to understand what I had told them about my family.

One student proceeded to explain how it was wrong and unfair to stereotype groups of people as the class had done in relation to aboriginal people. The student compared this experience with that of his own in growing up in a western suburbs housing commission estate. He discussed how he hated the way outsiders to their community often stereotyped them as 'housos', 'westies' and 'dole bludgers'. Other students joined in the discussion by talking about their own experience and what it was like for them to be labelled in derogatory ways, for example, as 'wogs' and 'lebs'. Some of the female students raised the issue of being put down on the basis of their gender.

In the midst of all of this, it came to my attention that some members of staff didn't really know how to deal with my difference. I re/member one day, when I was in the middle of teaching, I happened to notice the principal gazing at me from the back of the room. His gaze was penetrating. To interrupt his gaze, I looked at him and smiled. Without saying anything, he just turned and walked out of my classroom. He looked so perplexed, I knew he didn't know what to make of me. In the course of a conversation not long after this particular incident, the principal said to me, 'You know Wendy you're obviously more intelligent than most blacks.' I was so surprised by his comment that I didn't know what to say in response. I re/member feeling really angry and confronted by his racism. I also re/member thinking to myself at the time, 'What, because of my whiteness I'm more acceptable than, say, my sisters who look more like my mother!' and deciding not to react in the situation. As a relatively new teacher to the school, I recognised that the principal had more power than I did in the situation.

In the context of my own classroom, I recognised that I was in a position of power to be able to challenge the students' racism and understanding of aboriginality. I also recognised the importance of being open to what students had to say and the need for real dialogue in order to further develop their understanding of identity and that of aboriginality. My relationship with the students changed dramatically as a result of that moment in the classroom. The students' relationships with each other also changed.

As Langton (1993, p. 33) says:

> 'Aboriginality', therefore, is a field of intersubjectivity in that it is remade over and over again in a process of dialogue, imagination, representation and interpretation. Both Aboriginal and non-Aboriginal people create 'Aboriginalities', so that in the infinite array of intercultural experiences, there might be said to be three broad categories of cultural and textual construction of 'Aboriginality'.

Langton continues by explaining these three broad categories. She identifies the first category as the experience of aboriginal people interacting socially with one another largely within an aboriginal cultural context. The second is the stereotyping, iconising and mythologising of aboriginal people by white people who have never had any real first-hand experience of aboriginal people. The third is those constructions which are generated when aboriginal and non-aboriginal people engage in actual dialogue, where individuals test and adapt imagined models of each other in order to find some satisfactory way of comprehending the other.

By providing a substantial overview of the various constructions of aboriginal identity, Langton is not at all reactive or defensive in her approach. She encourages an opening up of the identity debate in this country, not just in relation to what it means to be aboriginal, but what it means to be australian in the context of post-colonialism. 'Rather than making prescriptions, I am trying to move boundaries and undo the restrictions which make it so difficult for any of us to speak' (Langton 1993, p. 7).

Despite Langton's efforts to provide a substantial overview of the various constructions of aboriginal identity, I am still reluctant to use the word *aboriginal* in describing my own identity. By my very being, I disrupt essentialist notions of aboriginality and no longer find it useful to identify in a way that denies a part of myself or any part of my family. These days I find it much more useful and liberating to be able to speak of myself as having multiple identities and to recognise that in different contexts and at different times I assume different identities. As Hall (1992, p. 277) so eloquently puts it:

> Identity becomes a 'moveable feast': formed and transformed continuously in relation to the ways we are represented or addressed in the cultural systems which surround us. It is historically, not biologically defined. The subject assumes different identities at different times, identities which are not unified around a coherent 'self'. Within us are contradictory identities, pulling in different directions, so that our identifications are continuously being shifted about.

To illustrate my point, I tell one last story. I have titled it . . .

Too much police rescue

I was making my way home through the back streets of an inner-city suburb one night when I happened to notice two police officers standing over a black youth. They had the youth pinned against a wall, with a torch shining in his face. As I drove by I felt really uncomfortable about the situation and wasn't sure what to do. By the time I had driven around the block, I had made up my mind that I would idle my car so that the headlights were shining right on the police.

Less than a minute after I turned up, the police officers turned off the torch, and a couple of minutes later, they let the youth go. It was obvious that they started to get a bit nervous about being watched. I continued to sit in my car while the youth walked away. I made a point of watching the police as well, and they knew it too. While I am not quite sure what the youth had been up to for the police to take the action that they did, I was convinced that he didn't deserve the treatment that he received.

Now what was interesting was what went through my mind at the time of the incident. I re/member feeling really angry and ready to jump out of my car in order to take on the police in relation to the way they were treating the youth. However, I knew that if I did, I probably would have ended up being abusive toward the police . . . creating even more trouble. I also recognised that it was safer to be in my car, rather than on the street, given my gender. At the same time I distinctly re/member recognising the power I had in the situation as I sat within my car.

Looking white was to my advantage in this particular situation, and I knew it! I also knew that if I were questioned by the police I could use my position within my workplace as well as support from other members of staff to challenge such racism. This is not the first time that I have been placed in such a situation and it probably won't be my last. Racism is alive and well in australia today, and I know only too well what it is like to be on the receiving end of it.

Conclusion

Writing this chapter has been a challenge in that it represents a significant shift in the way I have come to speak more recently about my own identity. I have become extremely aware of the complexities and contradictions inherent in the process of naming one's identity and have only just begun to confront this issue myself. The process of re/membering some of my own, and some of my mother's people's experiences of racism has been painful. It has also been difficult to recognise and to name some of the ways in which many of us, as murris, have internalised the racism of the dominant australian culture and developed essentialist notions of aboriginality reinforcing racism.

My own experience of racism has always been different to that of a murri living in a black body. I am constantly aware of the way that others gaze at me, both literally and metaphorically speaking, when I identify with my blackness as much as my whiteness. I often find myself being aware of the literal gaze and my constant internalising of that gaze and how it translates in an internal sense according to the shifting positions I find myself in. I am also constantly gazing outwards in an attempt to make sense of the cultural systems that surround me.

There is a certain silencing that happens around a discourse informed by both historical and contemporary essentialist notions of 'race'. In writing this chapter, like Marcia Langton I am attempting to open up dialogue in order to move boundaries and undo the restrictions that make it difficult to speak. Subjectivity is dependent on coming into language in a way that enables us to identify ourselves. It is through dialogue with each other that we will come to understand the differences and complexities involved in living in a post-colonial context.

6

Aboriginal Rural Education Program:
A case study in anti-racist strategies

Carol Reid and Wendy Holland

At the 1991 census, indigenous educational outcomes in New South Wales were unequal to those of the rest of the community. Only 15 per cent of Aboriginals[1] and Torres Strait Islanders over the age of 16 were at school, compared to 30 per cent for the general population. In terms of qualifications, only 2.5 per cent of indigenous people had tertiary qualifications, compared to 13 per cent of the general population. As well, the proportion of unskilled indigenous people was almost 20 per cent higher than for non-indigenous people. In all fields Aboriginals and Torres Strait Islanders were underrepresented. (All figures are from Australian Bureau of Statistics, Census 1991 Data.) These unequal educational outcomes lead to reduced employment opportunities in the labour market in particular, and help explain the general socio-economic disadvantage of New South Wales indigenous people.

More than a decade has passed since the Federal Government, on the advice of the National Aboriginal Education Committee, determined that access to tertiary education, in particular teacher education, was critical if Aboriginal educational outcomes were to improve. Racist assumptions regarding Aboriginal student ability, lack of access to education at all levels, and the cultural insensitivity of educators were seen by the committee as contributing to these inequitable outcomes. Multi-institutional racism, in the form of inadequate basic infrastructure in many communities, created conditions that made education peripheral to the daily life of Australian indigenous peoples. Educational institutions reinforced this distance between indigenous[2] and non-indigenous Australians' educational outcomes through institutional practices, curricula and teaching methods. Effective strategies and educational practices are critical if social justice is to be achieved by Australian indigenous peoples.

This chapter will outline the way in which one initiative—the Aboriginal Rural Education Program (AREP), at the University of Western Sydney (UWS) Macarthur—has attempted to challenge the practices that marginalise and exclude indigenous students in tertiary education in New South Wales. The promotion of indigenous participation at tertiary level is an anti-racist strategy if the process moves beyond just enrolling more indigenous students. It is anti-racist if it gives control of subjects and courses—indigenous and non-indigenous content—to indigenous people. Whatman (1995) sees a progression from enclave to teaching/research centre to faculty as a way of redressing assimilationist histories. This anti-racist strategy is occurring at UWS and is a product of indigenous activism from within the university as well as a product of astute benevolence on the part of UWS management.

We will argue that coalitions of indigenous and non-indigenous people are crucial to the development of anti-racist processes and practices within the wider university. Firstly, we will give an overview of the development of the AREP courses situated in the socio-political context of 1970s Aboriginal activism and anti-racist struggle. A necessary consequence of developing programs in the AREP mode has been the challenge to dominant myths of 'blackness' and 'whiteness'. In these sections we will challenge the notion that *different* means *less than* in terms of curricula and language (knowledge). This is explored through a discussion of the strategies that have been designed to create indigenous educational experiences that are more culturally appropriate and personally and politically empowering.

The site

As an institution, the UWS is a product of the reforms to higher education introduced by Labor Education Minister Dawkins in the late 1980s. It is also a response to an increasingly diverse population in Western Sydney. In some ways it is poised at the cutting edge; geographically, UWS sits among migrant, working-class and indigenous communities sharing the outer suburbs of a burgeoning Sydney. In fact, the western and south-western regions of metropolitan Sydney have the largest concentrations of indigenous people in Australia in terms of actual numbers. Instinctively, UWS has known that its path would have to be different to that of the established inner-city universities because of its youth; spatial factors such as access to resources; and its clientele. This is a bonus on one hand, for UWS Macarthur and its network members (UWS Nepean, UWS Hawkesbury) are not constrained by tradition in the way in which older universities are, yet remain caught in the same trap of standards and norms that these universities dictate. However, global changes, such as the increasing internationalisation of education and a shift to competency-based education, potentially enable UWS to develop a niche, focusing on the development of new cultural competencies such as those suggested by Kalantzis (1994). The university's response to this challenge will determine its future direction and success.

Perhaps we can best understand the general issues that confront any institution hoping to embrace cultural diversity, and the specific issue of anti-racist educational strategies, by looking at the development of AREP at UWS Macarthur. While UWS Macarthur became a federated network member as recently as late 1989, its history of delivering courses to Aboriginal students goes back to 1983 (Aboriginal Rural Education Program Review Document 1994) when it began offering courses in the Schools of Education and Community and Welfare Studies. These programs grew out of federal initiatives and indigenous activism to improve the access of indigenous students to tertiary institutions. In particular, there was a need for welfare workers who were skilled and culturally sensitive to work in their own communities, where the legacy of two hundred years of paternalism and continuing racial discrimination was evident in high levels of unemployment, substance abuse, and family breakdown. Indigenous involvement in education at all levels was seen as important due to systemic failure to provide indigenous students with appropriate educational opportunities. Furthermore racism, manifest in the exclusion of Aboriginal students from schools and universities and in classroom practices (such as discipline codes), has a long history in Australian education (Bridges 1994; Fletcher 1989; *Weekend Australian* 1992). The National Aboriginal Education Committee, which was formed in 1977, recommended a policy that would improve Aboriginal access to institutions, provide support to students, and increase Aboriginal input to the content of curricula and to decision-making at all levels where Aboriginal students were involved.

The Aboriginal Rural Education Program

The AREP is a part-time mode of study carried out over five two-week residentials a year. Students come from all over New South Wales and are accommodated in nearby motels funded by the Department of Employment, Education and Training. Typically, a full-time three-year degree will be completed in five years in the AREP mode. Recently, the Centre for Indigenous Australian Cultural Studies has taken over the first phase which covers the initial two years. Students may leave at this stage and obtain a Diploma in Indigenous Community Studies. Previously, if students were unable to complete their full degree, they received no award.

The particular historical junctures that gave birth to the AREP have their genesis in the 1967 referendum which gave Aboriginal Australians citizenship rights. From this point, government programs moved from a policy of assimilation towards a policy of self-determination. During this period and throughout the 1970s, struggles over equity issues in relation to immigrants, women and Aboriginal Australians took on new forms that sought to recognise the dimensions of exclusion such as language, culture and issues of knowledge and power. In this context, issues of racism and sexism were seen to 'devalue particular resources of individuals and so deny them the benefits and opportunities available to others' (Lynch 1990, p. 7).

The formation of the National Aboriginal Education Committee in 1977 provided a voice for Aboriginal people. Its rationale, aims and objectives published in 1980 stressed Aboriginal involvement at all levels of policy-making, funding and administration of programs (Sherwood 1982). This stance was reaffirmed in 1991 with the publication of the *National Report* of the Royal Commission into Aboriginal Deaths in Custody and the Human Rights and Equal Opportunity Commission's *Report of the National Inquiry into Racist Violence in Australia*. The National Inquiry into Racist Violence found that schools and campuses may be accused of perpetuating institutional racism in terms of their educational philosophies and in their roles as workplaces. Migrant and Aboriginal peoples found 'their own experiences [were] largely absent from curriculum material or represented in ways that offend[ed] them and also reproduce[d] racism in the wider community' (HREOC 1991, pp. 346, 353). The report's recommendations went beyond simply increasing the presence of women, migrants and indigenous people in education institutions. They stressed the importance of change to the culture of these institutions, including the content of curricula, teaching methods and decision-making processes.

Initially, UWS Macarthur was constrained by funding processes which were largely piecemeal, short-term and aimed heavily at student support. Annual changes to models of funding and the range of bodies

(Department of Aboriginal Affairs, Commonwealth Tertiary Education Commission, Commonwealth Department of Education, Department of Employment, Education and Training) distributing funds created a reactive rather than proactive environment for the development of programs (McConnochie 1990, p. 1). The patterns of funding also concealed inequities in funds distribution within the academy—favouring established disciplines—as well as preventing any long-term development of philosophies and goals. Given these funding constraints, UWS Macarthur did well to continue with the AREP considering the expenses individual faculties incurred. Beyond funding, many issues had to be confronted; they ranged from program delivery to curriculum content, control over indigenous content, and development of staff. We will explore some of these issues in greater detail.

Prior to the development of the AREP courses, there was considerable struggle over creating space in the academy for alternative modes of delivery and over challenging dominant myths regarding 'Aboriginality'. The following comment from a committee member of the Education Sub-Committee of Council, Macarthur Institute of Higher Education, demonstrates these earlier obstacles:

> it was a waste of time investing huge sums of money in Aboriginal education because it was generally well known by psychologists that Aboriginal people were not capable of working at the higher levels of cognition required to satisfy tertiary education (quoted in Lynch 1990, p. 42).

Given this argument, based on scientifically racist[3] assumptions, it is not surprising that one proposed strategy, to increase indigenous participation at tertiary level, was the establishment of *enclaves*. The development of enclaves was both deliberate and astute, since an enclave is a territory which has very clear boundaries and is protected within another territory. In practice, this meant the establishment of an Aboriginal centre—the Macarthur Aboriginal Liaison Unit—staffed by indigenous and non-indigenous people with appropriate experience, at the university. Such a centre would provide a safe haven for students to withdraw to, and to develop strength through, so that they could come to terms with the unknown and frightening experience of tertiary education which, paradoxically, was both liberating and threatening to identity. The enclave then, can be seen as an anti-racist strategy which developed out of the need for cultural support and cultural maintenance, a central tenet of multiculturalism. The need for separate structures to provide this was a recognition of the fact that university culture was culturally supportive of—and reflected—dominant social groups in society. There was little space for minority cultures. However, the notion of enclaves met with some ambivalence:

> Certainly the centre was given to us a fait accompli . . . there was no real debate about whether we would have one, but rather we have got one, it's being imposed, and you will work within the framework (Dean, Participating Academic School, quoted in Lynch 1990, p. 43).

The Macarthur Aboriginal Liaison Unit was established in 1983 to support indigenous students. In addition, courses in social welfare and teacher education were delivered to indigenous students separately from full-time students—often called 'mainstream'—in what has become. known as the AREP mode. Essentially this turned out to be twenty-six weeks of study squashed into ten weeks each year. The proposal for separate centres, courses and subjects was supported by some in the hierarchy—particularly those with experience with indigenous communities—and treated with suspicion by others, who criticised the proposal as being separatist.

But what are the limitations of the enclave approach? Such an approach has contradictions. How can you effect change to the dominant culture of the academy if programs are separate? Certainly, one of the key issues for senior management at UWS Macarthur was that courses would not be 'watered-down' and that 'the course must be equivalent to the standards in the general diploma' (Lynch 1990, p. 45). Here is the familiar intersection of different identity and ability in the social construction of 'Aboriginality'. On the other hand, bridging programs were intended to provide 'compensatory educational support [but] within their curriculum offer cultural support' (Lynch 1990, p. 17). This approach often resulted in an emphasis on Aboriginality situated within a remedial program. The concentration solely on acquiring the skills of the academy meant that lecturers approached the teaching of Aboriginal students in terms of their deficiencies. For indigenous students, this approach devalued their potential contribution and their cultural difference. In this compensatory model, difference once again intersects with ability.

One way in which the culture of the institution has been slow to respond is in terms of structural processes such as timetabling, accommodation and staffing. University structures have been unable to accommodate the different rhythms of the AREP mode and needs of the AREP student body. In this way the dominance of the culture of the institution has prevailed and the discourse of difference has become equated with deficit. Frequent calls to leave residentials due to the deaths of relatives, family illness or family business are the legacy of racist policies of segregation and assimilation and continuing racism manifest in high unemployment. The success of students is often linked to the flexibility and assistance of individuals rather than the university providing a program tailored to a section of the community. A different program is an anti-racist strategy because it recognises the different social realities of different groups of people. This extract from a university committee meeting shows the way in which this discourse of difference model is highly racialised:

> One of the things it was agreed was that in no way would standards be dropped for the Aboriginals. Macarthur was never going to be accused of having a black pass or a red pass as it's known in Canada where certain tertiary institutions in their desire to assist indigenous groups drop standards. That was firmly hammered out on the committee (Lynch 1990, p. 51).

The continuities in the racialisation of indigenous people here and overseas are no accident. Colonisation is alive and well in the discourse of difference in countries such as Canada, New Zealand and the USA. It occurs in the way in which we define 'normal' and 'standards' and the ensuing assessment procedures. Teaching is essentially an evaluative process (Johnston 1990) whereby approximation to a norm forms the basis of assessment. The norm being assessed—whether it is behavioural or cognitive, for example—is never questioned. Shifting the academy's construction of standards means conceptualising knowledge and skills as embedded with *cultural understandings* (Kalantzis 1994). Shifting the gaze from the students to the culture of the academy has been the task of committed indigenous and non-indigenous lecturers, indigenous student activists and indigenous education groups at all levels of policy. This struggle is, of course, situated within a wider struggle in the community over difference and the ways in which institutions privilege certain knowledge and skills, thus maintaining current relations of power.

While multiculturalism has provided space for voices of the Other and a celebration and maintenance of culture, it needs to be extended to embrace anti-racist strategies which call into question the fundamentally racialised processes and discourses of the academy. Multicultural education policies have legitimated the continuation of this discourse in the construction of cultures as 'fixed' and homogeneous (Rizvi 1987). However, it is important to acknowledge that multicultural policies and their impact upon indigenous education have been a step forward from assimilationist policies because hitherto marginalised groups have been able to establish enclaves within the academy and challenge the very practices that continue to exclude them. The next section of this chapter will attempt to look at the possibilities by examining current initiatives in course development while reflecting on the past decade.

Challenging myths

> And as those who have been completely marginalised are so radically transformed, they are no longer willing to be mere objects, responding to changes occurring around them; they are more likely to decide to take upon themselves the struggle to change the structures of society which until now have served to oppress them (Shaull in Freire 1972, p. 13).

Freire conceptualised education for oppressed groups as a process of *conscientisation*. Central to this process is an understanding that education is not neutral and serves particular purposes, somewhat in the same vein as Kalantzis (1994) has argued about the embeddedness of cultural understandings in the Mayer Committee's Key Competencies.[4] In specific courses and subjects that have been developed through the Centre for Indigenous Australian Cultural Studies[5] at UWS Macarthur, AREP students are becoming aware of the processes that have shaped their lives and continue to marginalise them in Australian society. The subjects are designed to build on students' knowledge and experience while providing access to the dominant cultural forms of expression, and knowledge of processes and discourses that disempower. The history of governance in relation to indigenous people is a particular focus through community studies giving macro and micro understandings of the manifestations of racism. Such subjects are designed to situate indigenous experience within a social and historical context, rather than concentrating on the pathology of the individual which is the dominant approach to psychology-based disciplines such as education and health.

While there is no doubt the AREP program has been successful over the past ten years, with over 150 graduates from both the Faculty of Education and the Faculty of Arts and Social Sciences, students have often experienced racism once they are working in their chosen professions. They have been unprepared for the isolation and cultural difficulties that are experienced as an indigenous person caught between institutional practices and people who totalise Aboriginal culture around negative myths on the one hand, and their own communities who also totalise 'white' society. There have been painful examples of this—

suicides, resignations and opting out of courses and careers after these experiences. Curricula that take account of these experiences are an anti-racist strategy through the acknowledgment of different historical realities. While based on notions of race and thus open to criticism of continuing racialisation through *different* curricula, we prefer to see the response as a consequence of the opposition to the concrete reality of a racially structured society. This *politics of difference* is a theory and practice which is produced in opposition through a critique of practice (McLaren 1995). It is found in language, folklore, and in the social and economic realities of contemporary life.

In 1995 there are approximately 150 teachers employed within the New South Wales Department of School Education (NSWDSE) who identify as Aboriginal. A number of these teachers are graduates from UWS Macarthur's AREP as well as from full-time studies. While there has been an increase in the number of Aboriginal teachers employed in the public school system, many Aboriginal teachers still face problems similar to those experienced by Aboriginal teachers in the early 1980s. This is despite the fact that significant work has been done to raise awareness of *all* teachers in relation to indigenous Australian issues over the last decade. We first reflect on the way in which negative constructions of Aboriginality impact upon our AREP graduates by citing the experience of one of us, Wendy Holland, an Aboriginal, formerly a teacher and now Head of the Centre for Indigenous Australian Cultural Studies.

Out there in the workplace

As a young teacher employed by the NSWDSE in the early 1980s it became important for me to be able to meet and network with other Aboriginal teachers. Identifying and being identified as an Aboriginal teacher (because of priority employment) was not easy. It was difficult being in the position of having to justify the NSWDSE's affirmative action strategy of *priority employment* for Aboriginal teacher graduates to other people on staff. It was also difficult having to deal with the subtle and not so subtle racism that existed in the workplace. The opportunity to network with other Koori teachers occurred in 1984 when I was seconded from the classroom to the NSWDSE's Equal Employment Opportunity Unit to work as the Aboriginal Teacher Liaison Officer.

In this role I liaised with the 38 other Koori teachers employed in public schools across the state and facilitated the first Equal Employment Opportunity Career Development Workshop for Aboriginal teachers. Meeting with each of the teachers was both personally and professionally very rewarding. It was tremendous being in a position to facilitate an opportunity for the teachers to come together, and to share experiences as well as ideas. The opportunity to meet one another alleviated some of the isolation that many of the teachers had been experiencing as, in most cases, the only Aboriginal person on staff.

At the workshop there was much discussion in relation to the issue of racism. Several teachers identified incidents of racism that they had experienced or had observed in their own schools. For example, the issue of *priority employment* and the racist backlash that many of the teachers experienced because they had accepted employment under the NSWDSE's affirmative action strategy were discussed at length. There was general agreement between the teachers that it was difficult enough adjusting to teaching without having the added pressure of dealing with racism in the workplace. Workshop sessions were facilitated to assist the teachers in developing strategies to deal with such racism. Recommendations were made to the Equal Employment Opportunity Unit in relation to the in-service training of all NSWDSE employees. Another example discussed by the teachers was the concern about inherent racism in the questioning of their formal qualifications.

There was also much discussion between the teachers about how they perceived their role in implementing the NSWDSE's 1982 mandatory Aboriginal Education Policy. While some teachers expressed feelings of inadequacy in relation to implementing Aboriginal studies and perspectives in their own classroom or school, there were others who indicated that they were very much involved in this work. The teachers talked at length about the complexities and contradictions involved in each situation. There was general agreement among the teachers on the need for an intercultural communication subject with an emphasis on Aboriginal studies in all pre-service teacher training.

It was interesting that the teachers were able to acknowledge that, just because they had grown up Aboriginal in this society, it did not make them experts on all matters relating to Aboriginal people, cultures and issues. They rejected notions of being seen as 'experts' in the area of Aboriginal Studies. They wanted to be better equipped to challenge stereotypes of Aboriginality and the racism directed toward Aboriginal people. They wanted the opportunity to further their own understanding in this area of study. They understood that to be able to effectively implement Aboriginal studies and perspectives within their own classrooms it would require further learning on their part. They supported the view that *all* teachers should be responsible for the implementation of the NSWDSE's mandatory Aboriginal Education Policy, not just Aboriginal teachers. The teachers also viewed the countering of racism in schools as being the responsibility of *all* teachers and not something that should be left up to the Aboriginal teacher.

In my capacity as the Equal Employment Opportunity Aboriginal Teacher Liaison Officer I was also responsible for checking on each Aboriginal teacher's employment status within the NSWDSE. The outcome of this investigation revealed that the majority of female Aboriginal teachers had been employed on a temporary basis, as compared to their male counterparts who were mostly permanently employed with the NSWDSE. This had serious repercussions for the female teachers in terms of their work conditions and career prospects. This situation was similar to that experienced by all other female employees within the NSWDSE at that time.

The discussions that took place at the workshop revealed that many of the teachers were also facing challenges from the local community where they were teaching. While a number of teachers experienced a great deal of support from their local community, there were others who indicated that they were coming under a lot of pressure and criticism. During the mid-1980s a few non-Aboriginal people withdrew their children from the local school on the basis that they didn't want them taught by Aboriginal teachers. Their argument was that these particular teachers weren't as qualified as other teachers, simply because they were Aboriginal. What they were unwilling to accept because of their racism was that these teachers were just as qualified as any other tertiary-trained teacher. Dealing with overt racism is one thing, whereas for many Aboriginal teachers their experiences of racism have been much more subtle and covert. No less difficult to deal with, just different.

A number of Aboriginal teachers also revealed that they had not only experienced criticism and, in some instances, racism from some non-Aboriginal people, but that from time to time they had copped criticism from other Aboriginal people. Derogatory labels such as 'flash black' or 'uptown' were used to put teachers down if they didn't comply with what was expected of them. Some Aboriginal teachers came under more criticism than others because of their supposed lack of involvement in Aboriginal community activities. They were being discredited and labelled as teachers who just happen to be Aboriginal as compared to others labelled as real Aboriginal teachers. Criticism of this kind reveals the way in which colonisation is alive and well in Australia still and continues to affect Aboriginal Australians. It also reveals how the racism of the dominant society has been internalised by some

Aboriginal people to the point where they often act it out against one another.

To be a teacher is difficult enough; to be an Aboriginal teacher can be twice as difficult because of the racism in society toward Aboriginal people. Aboriginal teachers have not been exempt from the racism in the community. My next story is a sad one and I will never forget it. I remember meeting with one teacher who shared the story about her cousin who took his own life. As an Aboriginal teacher working in a small country town he was quite isolated. He apparently lacked support in the workplace as well as from the local Aboriginal community.

In a recent conversation with another Aboriginal educator, I was not surprised to learn that many Aboriginal teachers today continue to experience similar pressures to those experienced by Aboriginal teachers ten years ago. The training and appointment of Aboriginal teachers is an important strategy in redressing past discrimination. However, if Aboriginal teachers are to be successful then they need support and encouragement. They do not need racism to further hinder them from becoming effective teachers of both Aboriginal and non-Aboriginal students alike.

Myths of 'blackness'

Schools and teacher education establishments are concerned with the production of knowledge. There is no question that education serves a purpose for the state by preparing people for the workforce. We need only to consider the controversy around the tertiary entrance rank to see that the competitive academic curriculum still prevails (Connell 1993; Marginson 1993). Shifting a monolithic structure such as an education bureaucracy is a daunting task. However, there have been some recent interesting debates regarding the need to be explicit about how texts work and what their purpose is, as well as a shift to broadening the acceptance of a variety of linguistic variations of English—oral and written—(Cope & Kalantzis 1993; Eades 1981). The latter trend is significant for AREP students and clearly more oppositional and politically empowering because it challenges orthodoxy around central issues of culture—that is language, specifically as a vehicle for cultural transmission.

One of the challenges in AREP teacher education programs is to deal effectively with issues related to language, expectations and racist assumptions. When a student's practicum report contains comments such as 'the student is reliable and always on time' (we are talking about mature-age students), what does this tell us about underlying understandings of Aboriginality? In schools where students have been attending practicums, why are there complaints about dropped 'h's and 'g's rather than comments about the clever use of humour and metaphor. As Eades (1995, p. 9) recently put it: 'Standard Australian English speakers find French speakers "seductive" when they drop their aitches—but not when Aborigines do.' Complaints have also been made about how indigenous students respond to social control; silence, for instance, is often read by teachers as indifference or insolence. Aboriginal English, with all of its nuances and associated meanings, is not accepted as a functional linguistic system and a vehicle for the transmission of culture. Rather, it is largely seen as 'bad' or 'sub-standard' or 'working-class' English (Eades 1981).

What are the consequences for teacher education where Aboriginal teachers are expected simultaneously to be role models—read 'standard' role models; to solve all literacy and numeracy issues in the school because they happen to be 'black'; and also to change the system—while learning just to do their job effectively?

Why is it that these 'myths of blackness' continue within a multicultural society? According to a recent study of racism, ethnicity and the media, Aboriginality 'provides the sharpest sense of "race" and social difference' (Jakubowicz et al. 1994, p. 40) in terms of images in the media in Australia. Compounded by the spatial marginalisation of Aboriginal people in rural areas—where our students largely come from—these images reinforce the physical and cultural differences of the Other. When academics are confronted with the experiences of students whose lives are thus circumscribed, they invariably call upon stereotypes of Aboriginality as an explanation for responses that may or may not be similar to non-Aboriginal students. Therefore, one important anti-racist strategy is to provide development of academics regarding culturally appropriate pedagogy that includes an understanding of their own 'whiteness' as opposed to focusing on the Other (Solomos & Back 1994). Questions about their expectations, responses, the knowledge they privilege, and the forms that give expression to that knowledge, are more likely to provide insights to the mechanisms by which power relations are maintained through pedagogy.

But what has multiculturalism got to do with these dilemmas? Rizvi (1987, p. 22) argues that the ideology of multiculturalism in education 'is so broadly used that it accommodates many competing and often irreconcilable political positions'. We think this is a significant factor operating within the academy and schools because multiculturalism can conceal many interpretations and practices which may still be inherently assimilationist. For example, a prevalent interpretation of multiculturalism is the 'celebration' model whereby cultural differences such as dance, diet, dialect and dress (Daniels 1986) are seen as the only real manifestations of difference. Power does not get a mention because central to this model is the ethos of containment of differences to maintain cohesion. Through celebration we pat them on the head for being different (Kalantzis et al. 1990, p. 22) without attending to issues of social justice.

Giroux (1992, p. 113) has argued that 'race and ethnicity have been generally reduced to a discourse of the Other, a discourse that, regardless of its emancipatory or reactionary intent, often essentialised and reproduced the distance between the centres and the margins of power'. In the academy, the AREP program is already operating in a space at the margins or borders. As we said earlier, timetables, staffing and university-wide structures have not been tailored for the AREP mode. Between residentials there is little or no contact, classes usually get leftover rooms with a shortage of specialist facilities, and staff often teach classes in addition to their normal timetable. Because we have had to deal with being structurally marginalised we have formed coalitions of people within the university from various disciplines and attempted to give AREP a higher profile within the university by having students on campus almost continuously across three programs. In this anti-racist strategy we challenge myths of blackness which would site the students' Aboriginality, rather than the inadequate delivery of courses, as the basis for any problems.

In challenging myths of blackness we do not forget that in Aboriginal communities, cultural workers in schools are often isolated because they have no-one with whom to engage in meaningful dialogue without relying upon myths of blackness inherent in the discourse of difference associated with reified notions of Aboriginality. For safety, cultural workers have fallen back on essentialism—claims to spirituality and knowledge based on 'birthright', 'blood', 'race', 'culture'—because the language they use to express their location is often not accepted because of its so-called emotional, personal and de-centred nature. Dominant discourse around Aboriginal identity tends to remain focused on a fixed notion of culture; thus any 'hybridity' is seen as lacking purity and consequently, authority (McConaghy 1994). The discourse of the Other is so firmly entrenched in notions of 'race' that authenticity—how real one is in terms of the dominant social construction—is brought into question if this approach is abandoned. Although 'whiteness' is at the centre of this paradigm, it continues to be invisible (Giroux 1992, p. 117).

The Royal Commissioner enquiring into Aboriginal Deaths in Custody, Justice Johnston, commented:

> I had no conception of the degree of pin-pricking domination, abuse of personal power, utter paternalism, open contempt and total indifference with which so many Aboriginal people were visited on a day to day basis (*Social Justice for Indigenous Australians 1993–94* 1994, p. 21).

How then, do we begin to challenge practices that continue to oppress and circumscribe indigenous lives? One important aspect of the recently developed AREP Indigenous Community Studies Diploma has been the recognition that indigenous students bring knowledge and skills to the academy. Within subjects taught by the Centre for Indigenous Australian Cultural Studies there has been a move to include popular culture as a focus for exploring identity. In this way, various texts are studied to develop knowledge about the process of representation. Texts then are seen to include aural, visual and printed signifiers in analysing social identities (Giroux 1994, p. 129). History (oral and printed) of local communities—indigenous or non-indigenous—allows for the exploration of patterns in society that give meaning and expression to social practice. 'Fashion and prescription' (McConaghy 1994) then, in the construction of indigenous identities, are seen to be historical and contextual.

Indeed, students who have completed the centre's subjects have begun to challenge the quality of teaching and aspects of course delivery offered within the academy. Group solidarity, maintained through the enclave mode and defended strongly by the student body, ensures that transgressions of cultural norms are no longer tolerated. We are not talking about stereotypical Aboriginality in any way. Rather, the students are acutely aware of paternalism and resent having to endure its manifestations during their educational experience. The AREP student body is different in terms of Aboriginality and its concomitant histories: moreover, the students are invariably mature-aged with children often in attendance, they have full-time employment in Aboriginal-related industries or positions and they are considered the fortunate ones in their communities, thus carrying a heavy load in terms of social commitments. Quality assurance, in terms of AREP, is about culturally sensitive teaching that does not negate the student's Aboriginality nor construct it in any homogeneous or reified manner. As Wendy Holland argues in the next section, 'myths of whiteness' also affect the quality of the teaching/learning situation.

Myths of 'whiteness'

> Racism, colourist and interracial hostility and violence are too often fuelled and perpetuated by a lack of communication and unwilling- ness to listen to others and the single-minded pursuit of one's own goals and needs at the expense of other people's needs and welfare. In combating these behaviours, dialogue and a willingness to listen and trust are essential (Manyarrows 1994, p. 77).

The experience of living with racism on a daily basis affects not only the lives of Aboriginal people but also the relationship we have with others. While 'myths of blackness' continue within this multicultural society, so too do the 'myths of whiteness'. The effect that racism has on our lives as Aboriginal people is reflected in the way many of us act out the hurt on ourselves and others most like us—that is, other Aboriginal people. Drug and alcohol abuse, violence, isolation, mistrust and criticism of other Aboriginal people are just some of the behaviours that stem from the way we have internalised racism and the 'myths of blackness'.

The experience of day-to-day racism has also led many of us to be suspicious of 'whites'. Now I am not saying that 'non-white' Austra- lians can't be racist toward Aboriginal people. Many of them have, in fact, absorbed unquestioningly the racism of the dominant culture toward Aboriginal people. It's just that 'whitefellas' represent power and authority in this country and that too often means trouble for many indigenous Australians. 'Myths of whiteness'—for example, all 'whites' are racist and are not to be trusted, all 'whites' are bad, and 'whites' have all the knowledge—will exist as long as racism continues to be directed at indigenous people and their communities. But how do 'myths of whiteness' manifest themselves in AREP?

Teaching in AREP can be rewarding, yet at the same time it can be extremely challenging. It can be challenging for the Aboriginal lecturers as much as for the non-Aboriginal lecturers, given the baggage that both students and lecturers carry with them into the classroom. This is not denying the importance of Aboriginal lecturers as role models for AREP students. However, the myth or assumption that being Aboriginal gives greater understanding in relation to all 'things' Aboriginal and that Aboriginal lecturers make better teachers in AREP is naive.

> This belief is based on an ancient and universal feature of racism: the assumption of the undifferentiated Other. More specifically, the assumption is that all Aborigines are alike and equally understand each other, without regard to cultural variation, history, gender,

sexual preference and so on. It is a demand for censorship: [that] there is a 'right' way to be Aboriginal . . . (Langton 1993, p. 27).

The myth that 'whitefellas' have all the knowledge is common, particularly among first-year AREP students. They often set the 'white' lecturer up as the 'expert' and as a result they are unable to recognise their own worth, let alone what they have to offer the university. They are often surprised to learn that they have a lot to offer each other, the lecturer and the university. It is therefore critical for the lecturer to dialogue with students and to build on what each student brings to the classroom.

The myth or assumption that 'white' lecturers are racist if they fail a student is also naive. There have been instances when students have failed a subject and they have accused the 'white' lecturer of racism. This sort of myth-making is not only unfair for the lecturer, but it is to no advantage for the student. Such situations have been complex and have required mediation on the part of the AREP academic coordinator.

If we are to challenge and unlearn our 'myths of whiteness/blackness' then it is crucial that we enter into dialogue with one another. There must be a willingness to listen to one another. To listen to the meaning behind each other's words.

Conclusion

Giroux (1992) talks about 'crossing over' as a way of creating dialogue between cultural workers in education. Crossing over is about shifting from a safe position reliant upon essentialist notions of identity in order to enable the creation of another safe 'space' where meaningful dialogue can take place. Working in interdisciplinary coalitions meant we weren't as reliant upon comfortable paradigms. McConaghy (1994, p. 82) comments that 'it is the process of "mediation" which creates the potential for misunderstanding, myth-making and the construction of racial stereotypes'. Our comfortable paradigms are seen in this light to inhibit liberation for those who have had their lives constrained by the discourse of 'race'.

In this chapter we have argued that myths of the Other permeate relations between indigenous and non-indigenous people, particularly within institutions where practice is constrained by structures and discourses which are exclusionary. Historical narratives, anthropological in nature, have shaped the dominant cultural perception of indigenous Australians. As objects of this history, indigenous Australians have created their own myths in order to survive an oppressive system. Governmentality is central to this process, and self-determination is the only way out.

This chapter has discussed different types of anti-racist strategies occurring at UWS Macarthur in relation to indigenous students. Structural changes are slower but a move from special student intakes to the development of the Centre for Indigenous Australian Cultural Studies is an anti-racist strategy addressing the need for power and representation. Other strategies have included the development of a curriculum that is inclusive and empowering in terms of its explicitness about social relations. We have argued that *different* does not mean *less than*, and we see different curricula as an anti-racist strategy.

Finally, we would like to reiterate what was said in the introduction, that an anti-racist strategy is one which involves indigenous and non-indigenous people in direct dialogue. We have not arrived at this point in the history of AREP by ourselves. The struggle has been ongoing and has always involved committed indigenous and non-indigenous people, often engaged in conflict, as it will in the future. To argue that one has to be of a particular 'race' or 'culture' to engage in anti-racist and anti-colonialist practices is a contradiction in terms.

7

Liberal multiculturalism's 'NESB women': A South Asian post-colonial feminist perspective on the liberal impoverishment of 'difference'

Kalpana Ram

> In the life histories of women caught between the obligations imposed by tradition and the promises of modernity which often fail—one produces oneself as a subject by the reflexive awareness of *being subjugated to* the tyranny of stories in which one owes little allegiance, but which become the public face that the person presents to the world (Das 1994, p. 61, emphasis in original).

Veena Das is describing biographical stories told by women from among the labouring poor in New Delhi, India. Yet she could just as well be describing the structural dilemmas of South Asian immigrant women in Western liberal democracies. For when women emigrate from post-colonial India to liberal democracies such as Australia, the 'obligations imposed by tradition' and the deceptive 'promises of modernity' still accompany them. Indeed, the obligations of tradition re-emerge with even greater force, among women who now inhabit the status of a minority group. This is due precisely to the shift in the meaning of 'modernity' that occurs with migration. Whereas in India, modernity is a term that has its own indigenous meanings, in the immigrant context, modernity is reappropriated as an attribute of the dominant Anglo-European population.[1]

I dedicate this chapter to arguing for recognition of the continuities of female experience across the divide of 'post-colonialism' and 'immigration'. This insistence becomes necessary in the face of constant pressure from Western scholarship and politics in liberal democracies like Australia, to split up immigrant female experiences, such as my own, into two fragments: the 'here' of Australia, and the exotic 'there' of India. The former element of experience is admitted into debates on multiculturalism, on Australian identity, and on feminism and racism. The latter is admissible only in more rarefied academic circles dedicated ostensibly to the pure and disinterested investigation of the non-European Other, such as anthropology and 'area studies'.

Does such a split in fact help immigrant women combat the frequently described pincer grip of the movement between racism and sexism? Are the politics of multiculturalism, liberalism, or even an anti-racism or feminism which accepts 'the West' as its boundaries, adequate to the complexity of dilemmas faced by immigrant women from post-colonial societies?

I will here mainly utilise a perspective that can be developed on the basis of taking up different ingredients in Indian immigrant women's experiences, and viewing these in the light of the particular conjunction that has developed in India between feminist theory and post-colonial theory. I utilise that perspective in order to argue for the imperative importance of breaking down the national borders which continue to surround debates about racism and multiculturalism, despite the globalisation of immigrant labour (see Chapter 2). I will deliberately concentrate my efforts on what appears to be the most benign of all the political philosophies currently embodied in Western states, namely the philosophy of liberalism. In its commitment to recognising diversity and promoting equality, liberal multiculturalism appears a bulwark against racism. But how does it appear from the perspective of immigrant women?

Arranged marriage and liberal Western law

It is 1982, and I run into a white feminist friend with whom I shared a collective household in the late seventies. In the meantime, I have married, and the first pressure I feel is to explain myself in terms of a feminism which would judge this decision to involve consent to an oppressive and exploitative institution. 'I had to get married', I tell her. An immediate look of concern comes over her face as she sharply interrogates me: '*Had* to?' I now face a fresh set of pressures: I stand in front of her as the 'traditional' Indian immigrant woman, overwhelmed by the collective unfreedoms of clan, kin and community. There is quite simply no language available to express the simultaneous pleasures *and* pressures of having a more collective sense of one's identity within a diasporically scattered but nevertheless functioning kin group, whose acceptance I desire even as I violate its boundaries by marriage to an Anglo-Australian.

Consider the dilemma of an immigrant woman who wishes to utilise Western law—an important locus for the discourse of liberalism—in order to resist entering into an arranged marriage.

In an overview of such cases—one of the few attempts in Australia to critically examine the intersection of multicultural and feminist legal issues—Raman (1993) finds that the women have to submit to alien frameworks of understanding, all of which are not only inappropriate, but also distort the woman's identity in unacceptably polarised ways. The legal understanding of 'consent' in relation to marriage rests on the liberal notion of individuals contracting with one another. There is no incorporation of any more collectivist understandings of marriage, nor indeed any sense of the collectivist immigrant context in which the woman may experience the pressure to enter into the arranged marriage as all but overwhelming. In one of the cases Raman examines—the only case to occur in Australia—a sixteen-year-old girl of Egyptian origin entered into the marriage because of her parents' pressure, as well as the girl's fears that her younger sister would become ineligible for marriage if she earned a notorious reputation. The marriage was not consummated, and in this case, the petition to annul the marriage was supported by her parents. The judgement gave her the annulment on the basis of upholding the right of the child to self-sovereignty (Raman 1993, p. 17). The other two cases involve Sikh and Pakistani women in Britain. In all these cases, the women came up against the obverse side of the same liberal misunderstanding of collectivities. Collective pressure was regarded as insufficient to grant annulment:

> [In the] three reported cases where a nullity was granted, parental or cultural pressure was not itself sufficient to establish duress. In [the] *Hirani* [case], the Court expanded the notion of economic duress, and, as in *In the Marriage of S*, the primary emphasis was placed on the age of the applicant and therefore their lack of options. *Mahmood* contends that fear of parental or community disapproval is insufficient to constitute duress (Raman 1993, p. 19).

Within these legal terms, then, the woman is either a completely free agent in relation to marriage, in a manner indistinguishable from a person entering any other kind of contract—or, she must establish the most extreme forms of duress and coercion in order to win a legal verdict of annulment. The description of collective pressure as 'duress' does not necessarily do justice to the immigrant woman's experience of her parents' hopes and aspirations. Neither does the experience of dissonance between her aspirations and theirs thereby turn her into the 'individual' of liberal theory.

Consider further the representations of 'arranged marriage' that the immigrant woman is likely to receive from parents and community. These representations further polarise the divisions which must be mediated by the subjectivity of the immigrant woman. If the woman is Indian, she may be given to understand that notions of consent are irrelevant to marriage: that marriage is not a contract but a sacrament in which she becomes incorporated not only into her husband, but equally importantly, into her husband's clan and family. 'Tradition' comes into play in the immigrant context as a homogeneous and internally unified force, making 'India' the repository of an unbroken and continuous identity. Issues surrounding female sexuality, such as marriage, nurture a special capacity to coalesce and galvanise such representations into actions. These representations appear to have the backing and authority of a 'tradition' that emerges larger than life itself.

Arranged marriages therefore highlight dramatically the kinds of dilemmas in which immigrant women are placed by the nature of the dominant discourses at play. They can go along with arranged marriages, and feel they have complied with the powerful authority of what they are assured is 'the cultural tradition'. In the process they may do violence to other aspirations they themselves have nursed. They may well find that their female kin in India are entering into more experimental relations with marriage and the culture in general. And they will almost certainly run the risk of being adjudged to be 'oppressed' within the assumptions of the dominant culture. Raman gives the example of a submission made to the Australian Law Reform Commission in its report *Multiculturalism and the Law* (1992), requiring a woman whose marriage is to be arranged to attend confidential Family Court counselling where she would be informed of her right under Australian law to choose her partner. 'The submission further contends that if the woman is hesitant the marriage ought not to be authorised' (Raman 1993, pp. 32–3).

Multiculturalism's 'culture' and liberalism's 'limits of tolerance'

Would a more faithful interpretation of multiculturalist policies be helpful to the immigrant woman confronting the perplexing predicament I have outlined above?

There are certainly wide variations within liberalism's willingness to accommodate notions of cultural difference. The Australian legal system, for example, is not prepared to make significant concessions in this direction, even in the process of reviewing itself. Raman (1993, p. 31) notes that *Multiculturalism and the Law* is not prepared to concede the principle of cultural difference within the law:

> The Commission explicitly states that separate laws for particular ethnic groups are unacceptable. It prefers legal flexibility to accommodate 'individual preferences'; arguing that special laws may be discriminatory for individuals within a group.

As against this, we have a liberal theorist such as Taylor arguing for a distinction between the defence of certain fundamental rights, and other rights which can be weighted against 'judgements in which the integrity of cultures has an important place' (1994, p. 61). I will consider Taylor's position later in the chapter.

What recurs in all of the variety of liberal formulations, however, are two central features:

- the notion of limits to cultural tolerance, regardless of divergent adjudications of just where these limits are to be placed; and
- the conceptualisation of 'multiculturalism' as a matter of managing the contact between cultures, each of which is understood to be a coherent entity in itself.

The two concepts come together in the formulation of Australian government policies pertaining both to citizenship and to multiculturalism. The Parliamentary Joint Standing Committee on Migration's report entitled *Australians All: Enhancing Australian Citizenship* (1994, p. 97) incorporates principles earlier enunciated in the *National Agenda for a Multicultural Australia* (OMA 1988) in declaring: 'the right of all Australians, within carefully defined limits, to express and share their individual cultural heritage, including their language and religion'. These rights of citizens are subjected to the stricture of 'limits', which are conceptualised in this document (p. 97) in terms of 'the nation' and 'its interests': 'the obligation that all Australians should have an overriding and unifying commitment to Australia, to its interests and future first and foremost'.

I will go back at this point to the immigrant woman facing the issues surrounding an arranged marriage. How does this document, with its invocation of 'difference' as well as of an 'overriding and unifying' identity with the Australian nation, potentially understand her situation? The arranged marriage itself will appear as an index of a larger cultural difference: the immigrant woman is understood to be situated securely within a cultural unity of language, religion, and cultural heritage. As a member of a multicultural Australia, she is invited to participate in public life as a member of this cultural enclave. Overarching this and other similar enclaves of cultural difference is the Australian nation, which transcends or denies the relevance of differences of language, religion and cultural heritage.

But what of the immigrant woman who, by not wishing to enter into the arranged marriage, presents an implicit challenge to this neat and hierarchical arrangement of 'the nation' which supervises the relation between its subsidiary enclaves of difference? The language of multiculturalism only reinforces the previously noted lack of a public discourse for this woman to enunciate the complexity of her position. Instead, it understands her *either* as member of cultural enclave *or* as taking her identity from a larger Australian identity, thus reinforcing her dilemma. The dominant understanding offered to her of 'her culture' is as a static and tightly integrated bundle of customs, language and religion. This reinforces the reified interpretation of her 'tradition' recreated within the immigrant context by 'her community'. The larger nation, with 'its' interests, is by definition something other than this enclave of 'tradition' which she inhabits. Her desires, insofar as they are disruptive of the wishes of the enclave, must then necessarily be understood to be located in the discourses of 'Australianness', which in legal terms, involves invoking notions of individual sovereignty.

Although multiculturalism claims only to 'recognise' a difference which pre-exists itself, it is in fact a site which actively *produces* a certain version of difference. It is instructive to note in this context that the concepts of 'culture' and 'ethnicity' have been argued by many to have been incorporated into a new kind of racism, integrated with ideas of nation, and national belonging (Balibar 1991a; Gilroy 1992). Donald and Rattansi (1992, pp. 2–3) give the example of the parents who in 1987 withdrew their children from a school in the Yorkshire town of Dewsbury because the majority of pupils were of South Asian origin. The father insisted that this was done on the basis of culture, not race.

Yet we would be wrong in assuming that this linking of racism and 'culture' is a historical development of the late twentieth century. Instead, multiculturalism's 'culture' absorbs, without contestation or even awareness, historically older Western understandings of 'other cultures'. Colonial ethnology classified the subject populations of its domain as self-enclosed and discrete 'castes' and 'tribes', whose customs and ritual practices were enumerated in compendious census operations.[2] It is worth remembering too, that the founders of the 'multinational state' of the Soviet Union took this path, making language the criterion for carving up territorial republics, and, in the process, separating languages from their cultural heartlands, exaggerating differences between languages, and creating monolingual states out of bilingual populations (Bedford 1985). In the Stalinist definitions of the 'nation' and its 'autonomy'—'milked of substance', with 'any sign of life bound to be misunderstood' (Bedford 1985, p. 80)—we begin to see, if in an extreme form, some of the startling precedents for an understanding of 'culture' which is intent on a form of 'domestication'.

Anthropologists and contemporary theorists of culture working from the diverse locations of 'identity politics' have repeatedly objected to the reification implicit in notions of ethnicity, race, and even multiculturalism.[3] Fewer have questioned the careful distinctions liberalism draws between 'core values' and the periphery where difference is permitted. In the next section I wish to scrutinise the emergence of this distinction in one of the more nuanced texts on liberal multiculturalism.

Taylor's liberal multiculturalism

Taylor's essay, *Multiculturalism: Examining the Politics of Recognition*, was written in 1992. Since then, as the editor of a recent expanded edition tells us (Gutmann 1994, p. ix), it has appeared in Italian, French and German, with Habermas adding an extended commentary to the German edition. One may well regard it therefore as one of the more influential attempts by a proponent of liberalism to reflect on the politics of difference. I focus in particular on a distinction which he draws in the course of it. The distinction is central to his attempt to make liberalism respond to the challenges from varied proponents of the politics of difference, namely blacks, women, and advocates of multiculturalism. Keeping each of these sets of claims quite distinct and separate, he sets out to deal only with multiculturalism.

Taylor distinguishes between two variants of liberalism. A liberalism which advocates an equality of rights accorded to citizens can and *should* be modified, according to Taylor, insofar as it (a) insists on uniform application of the rules defining these rights, without exception, and (b) is suspicious of collective goals (1994, pp. 60–1). We can recognise in this description the liberalism of the Australian Law Reform Commission's report on *Multiculturalism and the Law*, which argues that 'the law should apply in general terms without specifying groups' (cited in Raman 1993, p. 31). (See also discussion of this report in Chapter 3.)

Taylor endorses those who would criticise such a liberalism for being unable to accommodate the collective goals of members of different cultures who wish to survive within the same society. He concedes that such goals 'inevitably will call for some variations in the kinds of law we deem permissible from óne cultural context to another' (1994, p. 61).

In its stead, Taylor advocates a liberalism which distinguishes between inviolable core rights, and other rights in which the integrity of cultures has an important place. The difference between existing practices of Australian multiculturalism and Taylor's multiculturalism is only a matter of degree, therefore. Both formulations preserve the distinction between core and periphery. Yet Taylor perceives his version as a fundamental departure, capable of preserving liberalism from the 'cruellest and most upsetting [attack] of all':

> The claim is that the supposedly neutral site of difference-blind principles of the politics of equal dignity is in fact a reflection of one hegemonic culture. As it turns out, then, only the minority or suppressed cultures are being forced to take alien form (1994, p. 43).

In fact, however, Taylor submits his favoured model of liberalism only to the simplest version of such a critique—namely to the argument, presumably that of a member of a minority 'culture', who demands that 'actual judgements of equal worth [be] applied to the customs and creations of these different cultures' (p. 68). This is the demand which Taylor goes on to find 'very wrong', a version of 'self-immurement within ethnocentric standards' (p. 72).

The demand he objects to is already a heavily oversimplified version of 'the politics of difference'. Such simplifications do exist in political demands, of course, but they are challenged in practice by other, more complex forms of political reasoning which take into account the real-life intermeshing of cultural difference with differences and inequalities of gender, class and colonialism. Taylor's essay mentions other kinds of 'difference', such as gender difference, but they are kept sealed off in tidy fashion from issues of 'multiculturalism'. It is entirely characteristic that in discussing the Salman Rushdie affair, for example, Taylor sees only two camps: mainstream Islam and Western liberalism, the latter treated as an outgrowth of Christianity in terms of earlier separations of church from state (1994, p. 62). Certainly, these were the two dominant discursive camps. But it is symptomatic that even in a liberalism dedicated to recognising 'difference', only these two binary identities are allowed recognition. Other, more complex forms of the politics of difference that also arose in response to the Rushdie affair are ignored.

The perspective of minority feminisms is once again exemplary in its capacity (not necessarily always realised) to disrupt and question reductionist visions such as Taylor's scenario of a 'West' (characterised by liberalism) confronting an 'East' (characterised by Islamic fundamentalism). The organisation Women Against Fundamentalism was initiated precisely in response to the inability of feminists from minority 'ethnic' groups in the UK to locate themselves in either of these two camps. I will let the editors of its journal describe its politics:

> WAF has always emphasized the need to take into account the complex connections between racism and fundamentalism. We insisted, for instance, that the defence of Salman Rushdie should not be in terms of the cultural superiority of the west against a simplistic and monolithic notion of Islam, but equally we opposed capitulation to the mullahs and religious authoritarianism in the name of multiculturalism posing as antiracism (WAF Editorial Group 1994, p. 1).

Is it mere oversight that such a politics fails to appear in Taylor's overview of the issues? I suggest not. I suggest that its appearance would make it impossible for Taylor to sustain his commitment to the two interrelated but opposed identities which begin to surface in the text, slowly but with all the inexorable force of that history which Taylor's vision of multiculturalism represses:

> The awkwardness arises from the fact that there are substantial numbers of people who are citizens and also belong to the culture that calls into question *our philosophical boundaries*. The challenge is to deal with *their sense of marginalization* without compromising *our basic political principles* (1994, p. 63, emphasis added).

In this scenario, immigrants and indigenous peoples in settler colonies meet the 'we' who inhabit liberal democracies as already formed, internally homogenous identities. 'Basic political principles' and 'philosophical boundaries' function in this instance as the basis of demarcating a Western cultural identity.

Taylor would not advocate taking children out of schools that cannot provide an education based on Western traditions and values. Yet his model of liberalism, which rests on such a unperturbed separation of Western cultural identity from others, provides no safeguards against such racist politics. Nor does it offer the discursive space for coming up with formulations adequate to the political concerns of immigrant women who are not simply encountering 'the West' for the first time, as it were, but are coming to Western liberal democracies from societies which have been reshaped by prior experiences of Western colonialism.

In what follows, I will argue that minority feminisms need the tools of post-colonial theory in order to respond critically to the binary oppositions between 'West' and 'non-West' erected not only by Western political theory but also by minority nationalisms themselves. I use the example of the construction of South Asian immigrants as people of 'non-English-speaking background'. I will go on to argue that minority post-colonial feminisms in turn can function to cast a critical perspective on post-colonial theory.

Post-colonial theory and the place of English in British and in Indian identity

Debates on multiculturalism and racism have been slow to interact with the burgeoning scholarship on colonialism and post-colonialism. Colonialism is fleetingly acknowledged in Taylor's examination of liberalism and multiculturalism, for example. He admits—if only as one consideration among many—that the colonial past of the West makes it 'seem crude and insensitive' to reply 'this is how we do things here' (1994, p. 63). However, this is to locate the problem in the past, and to see the legacy in the present as one of social etiquette across cultures.

Colonialism and racism are brought together for the most part only where the nexus is devastatingly obvious. In Europe, the overlap between the category of immigrant and the category of the hitherto colonised brings the connections to the foreground. In settler colonies such as Australia, the link between colonialism and racism seems obvious only in relation to the indigenous Aboriginal population. It is much harder for Asian immigrants to Australia who come from post-colonial societies such as India, Vietnam, Malaysia, Bangladesh, Hong Kong and Fiji, to explore the relevance of histories of colonialism to debates on multiculturalism and racism in Australia.[4]

Yet this history is vital if we are to understand that the recognition of 'cultural difference' does not mark a break with the politics of colonialism. Nor does an attitude of tolerance or even of respect act as a solid point of demarcation. Both respect and denigration have been moments in colonial constructions of the Western self in an integral relationship to the colonised other. Furthermore, the achievements which the liberal nation-state seeks to celebrate as a solid core for the construction of a self-sufficient Western identity have been fashioned in a colonial relationship to the very people who are now required to pledge their allegiance to these achievements as part of citizenship.

Post-colonial theory explores ways in which both coloniser and colonised bear the stamp of this prior relationship. We need to bring this insight to bear on fundamentally modifying the notion of 'cultural difference' operative in multiculturalism, as well as in Western and in minority nationalisms.

Rather than attempt a representative overview of the theory, I will illustrate its applicability in problematising the category of 'non-English-speaking background' in the construction of the post-colonial immigrant. On the one hand, we have English and English literature celebrated as the language of British and, increasingly, of Western identity. On the other hand, post-colonial immigrants are fashioned in opposition to knowledge of English, their primary identification derived from a 'background' as *non*-English speakers.

The work of Viswanathan (1989, 1992) resituates the development of 'English literature' as an academic discourse in the context of British colonialism in India. As with much of this work on colonialism, there is a nuanced exploration of the colonial state's various shifts in policy, in which it is made clear that there is no one unified 'colonial discourse'. Instead, there is a range of attitudes towards 'cultural difference' that it was possible to adopt within the framework of direct colonialism. Early phases of eighteenth-century British rule were characterised by Orientalism, an attempt to train British administrators in Indian culture in order to rule the country more efficiently, as well as to restore to Indians the true glories of their own past which had become inaccessible through a progressive degeneration of native life.[5] Since the pioneering work on Orientalism by Said (1978), it has become unnecessary to belabour the point that colonialism need not rest on a simple suppression and denigration of the Other. Viswanathan traces the introduction of English literature to a shift in colonial policy, where a balance had to be struck between morally and intellectually 'improving' the people, while avoiding the direct interference in local religion represented by the Christian missions. The power of English literature to improve the mind of the native was perceived to lie in literature's demonstration of the capacity of the individual to observe closely the empirical world, to think and to reason—'an activity deemed wholly foreign to Oriental religions and literatures' (Viswanathan 1992, p. 165). Viswanathan argues (p. 168) that a humanistic program of enlightenment blurred the Englishman's 'material reality as a subjugator and alien ruler . . . the English literary text functioned as a surrogate Englishman in his highest and most perfect state'.

The return to the colonial scene on the part of theorists contains implications which are equally radical for the politics of an *anti*-colonial nationalism. At their mildest, enquiries into colonial discourses require us to re-examine anti-colonial discourses as particular political responses to colonialism, rather than as revelations of 'cultural difference' in all its purity. At their most extreme, there is a complete denial of the existence of any notion of cultural integrity or authenticity in favour of the politics of hybridity.

The paradox for anti-colonial nationalism is that many of *its* claims for a pristine cultural identity are, in turn, deduced from the very terms given by colonial discourses. Claims for Indian identity are forged in intimate relationship with colonially derived antinomies between Indian collectivity and Western individualism, Indian spirituality and Western materialism, Indian tradition and the Western ability to reflect and innovate critically. These contradictory principles have particularly stark consequences for Indian immigrants, particularly if they wish to experiment, or even simply to use cultural resources as a source of critical strategies (Ram 1995).

The mutual interdependencies of colonial and anti-colonial identity formation embody a paradox which has caused much recent scholarly reflection. It has prompted historian Chatterjee (1986) to describe Indian nationalism as a 'derivative discourse'. Others such as Bhabha (1994a) go further and describe both colonial and 'native' identity as radically 'hybrid', as produced in the unstable and uncontrollable exercise of colonial power. In introducing the Word of God and the Word of Man—Christianity and the English language respectively—colonialism encounters not only an alien cultural tradition, but also 'the uncertain and threatening process of cultural transformation' (Bhabha 1994a, p. 33).

We begin to glimpse in the light of the above historiographical arguments, the absurdity of the category of 'non-English-speaking background' to describe Indian and South Asian middle-class professional immigrants. The depth of the Indian elite's engagement with 'the word of Man', namely with English language and English literature, accounts for the astonishment and derision with which South Asian elites who migrate to Australia greet this construction of the immigrant.

Yet to be versed in English, or even in English literature, is not to erase the politics of colonial inequality. Here we come to the theoretical tightrope that post-colonial theory has to walk. Theories that attempt to demonstrate the radical intermingling of identities must at the same time risk the emergence of a new kind of apolitical universalism of hybridity. The tightrope has been walked with varying degrees of success, and using different strategies.

For most post-colonial theory emphasis on interdependencies of identity is combined with an insistence on resistance on the part of the colonised. It is a necessary insistence, given that otherwise the question of inequality, let alone of cultural difference, would be theorised out of existence. Thus for Chatterjee (1986), anti-colonial nationalism may be derivative, but it still labours under the imperative of reworking the premises of colonial discourse in order to arrive at diametrically opposite political conclusions—namely, the need for national autonomy. For Bhabha, non-elite Indians put the project of missionary conversion 'in an impossible position' by demanding a hybrid Indianised Gospel (1994b, p. 118). In contemporary times also, Bhabha argues, hybridity opens up new political possibilities. Notions of cultural totalities and synthesis, operative in the politics of the left as well as of the right, are now open to having their authority questioned and undermined (1994a, p. 35).[6]

The question of what kind of new anti-racist, anti-colonial politics can emerge out of the denial of cultural wholes is still a matter wide open to conceptualisation. Theorists such as Gilroy have begun to explore, in their latest work (1993), the possibilities of using transnational interchanges between black diasporas as a way of reconfiguring the history and politics of modernity. What interests me in this chapter is the question of how the politics of minority and immigrant feminisms can be refigured by a productive interchange with post-colonial theory.

Linking post-colonial and immigrant feminist perspectives

Let me return at this point in the argument to the case of the immigrant woman unwilling to enter into arranged marriage. I have already outlined the way in which she is confronted by two equally unacceptable and polarised discourses which counterpose Western individualism and 'freedom' to representations of ethnic 'tradition' which may well be shared by both dominant and minority communities. An immigrant feminism wishing to fashion a resistant discourse will find to hand, in post-colonial theory, useful arguments with which to disrupt these polarities, and potentially, to create new discursive spaces for women located in this highly invidious position. If we continue with the Indian examples, it is extremely useful for Indian immigrant feminism to be able to exploit the fact that the legal system in India itself is not shaped by any pristine Hindu notions of marriage. Instead, it encompasses what is, at this stage of the argument, a recognisably 'post-colonial' set of contradictions and hybridities.

I cannot do more than gesture towards the complex history of social reform movements since the nineteenth century which have brought in legal changes in marriage law. The history begins as early as the 1850s and results in the first raising of the 'age of consent' in 1891, and the Child Marriage Restraint Act in 1929 (Forbes 1979). Legal interventions in social practices of suttee, of widow remarriage, of polygamy, etc., culminated in the controversial passage of the Hindu Marriage Act in 1955.

I will here utilise the insightful examination by Uberoi (1995 forthcoming) of contemporary judicial decisions based on Marriage Law. Uberoi cites commentators who remark that with the amendments of 1964 and 1976, there is nothing specifically 'Hindu' left in the Hindu marriage law. She points out that a number of provisions of the Hindu Marriage Act (1955) and of the Special Marriage Act (1955) are modelled on the English Matrimonial Causes Act (1950–73). Marriages are treated as contractual insofar as physical and mental incompetence for the obligations entailed, or fraudulently obtained consent, are grounds for voiding or terminating a marriage. However, Uberoi notes that, unlike any other contract, the Special Marriage Act treats unsoundness of mind as making marriage merely *voidable*, not immediately void.

On the other hand, the Indian judiciary repeatedly slides away from marriage as contract, reinvoking marriage as sacrament, and declaring its reluctance to open the doors to peculiarly 'Western' pathologies of family and marriage as its reasons for doing so (Uberoi 1995 forthcoming).

As post-colonial theory is increasingly quick to point out, there is a 'hybridity' here which defeats the erection of cultural compartments: Indian law incorporates Western assumptions and principles, while at the same time invoking principles of cultural difference. The judiciary seem prime candidates for the description of Indian post-colonial elite discussed by Prakash (1992, p. 154): internally split, formed by the binary structure of rationality/religion, but 'neither blinded by "superstition" nor endowed with a scientific gaze but with another sight'.

Yet if post-colonial theory can help immigrant feminism combat oppressive binary oppositions, by demonstrating the hybridity within both 'tradition' and 'modernity', immigrant feminism in turn reveals certain doubts, or, at the very least, critical blind spots on the part of a masculinist post-colonial theory. An immigrant South Asian feminist casting her eye on the literature on marriage law on either side of the post-colonial/immigrant divide does not merely see an ever-proliferating hybridity, nor does she find a process exclusively characterised by internal differentiation. For what emerges equally from such an examination is the existence of larger unities that transcend the colonial divide, continuities which coalesce around the oppression of women. Thus the adoption of Western liberal law in India has left Indian women exposed to the same patriarchal inability (characteristic of liberalism in general) to bring itself to treat marriage as a contract like any other. Instead, marriages in India as well as in the West are treated as only partially contractual. As we have seen, they resemble other contracts insofar as physical and mental incompetence for the obligations entailed, or consent which is obtained fraudulently, are all grounds for voiding or terminating a marriage. The resemblance breaks down, however, when we note that unsoundness of mind is insufficient grounds for annulment of the so-called 'contract'.

But it is not only liberal versions of patriarchy which criss-cross the East–West divide. Principles invoked by the Indian judiciary which are claimed to be based on peculiarly 'Indian' notions of marriage reveal nothing that a feminist located within 'the West' will not find herself already familiar with. In her discussion of judicial decisions regarding annulment, Uberoi finds:

> the subtext of judicial decisions bases [the marital relation] in sexuality, constructed as the natural and legitimate desire of the husband for the possession and use of his wife's body, and the legitimate desire of the wife for a sexual relation geared neither to possession nor to pleasure, but to motherhood (forthcoming 1995).

Whether marriage is conceived as contract or as 'Hindu' sacrament, whether as 'Western' liberalism or as peculiarly 'Indian', all take a common orientation from a naturalising of sexual inequality, and from constructions of gender, sexuality and maternity which are shared across cultural borders of difference.

Bringing issues of post-colonialism and racism into feminist theory has made it impossible to return to the notions of a 'universal patriarchy' with which we began second-wave feminism. However, there remains, from a feminist perspective, something profoundly dissatisfying and unconvincing about the adequacy of an exclusive emphasis on difference and the localisms born of difference.[7] There are so many shared commonalities of gender ideology and discourse across divisions of East–West, colonised Third World and colonising West; there are so many interlocking structures of female oppression. Immigrant feminism's specificity cannot help but illuminate more commonly shared female predicaments.

8

Signs of the time: Race, sex and media representations

Jeannie Martin

This chapter is about the languages of social differentiation and social ranking in mass media representations in Australia. The study of mass media representations of racial/ethnic difference and their link to systems of social domination is obviously germane to multiculturalism, and to the development of anti-racism in Australia. For example, there is already a 'politics of representation' around derogatory mass media representations of racial and ethnic minority groups in Australia, as evidenced in the activities of groups such as the Media Sub-Committee of the NSW Ethnic Affairs Commission, the National Indigenous Media Association, and the Arab Australian Association. These politics link to a widespread public view that the mass media has an inordinate capacity to influence our images of ourselves, our images of others, and the place of both in relation to each, in the general scheme of things in a society.[1]

The following discussion is concerned with the way in which languages of sexism and racism intersect in media representations in Australia. While there has been considerable work on media representations of women and sexism in the media, and a lesser amount on racial/ethnic representation and racism, there has been little study of the way in which the mass media represents the intersection of each system of domination. In this chapter I shall look briefly at the way in which racial (or ethnic) signifiers intersect with, and transform, signifiers of sex (and vice versa) in media languages of social differentiation and social rank in Australia.

The substance of the discussion is focused on one medium, namely television, and the majority of examples will be taken from one genre, namely advertisements. I have made no attempt to cover the totality of media products as they vary too greatly by medium (electronic, print, etc.), by genre (news, soap, sport, etc.) and by origin (local, Europe, North America, etc.).

NESB Australians and Australian television

There have been surprisingly few studies of the representation of Australians of non-English-speaking background (NESB) in the Australian mass media. Apart from the work of White and White (1978) and Rowe (1984), those studies that do exist are of recent origin, and often turn around a single event. For example, the media coverage of the Gulf War generated a spate of articles looking at derogatory representations of Arabic and Islamic peoples in the Australian media. Most of this work analysed media representations of Arabic populations in terms of (a) the construction of the Arab as the Other of Western thought, and (b) the consequent increase in acts of violence against Australian Arabic and Islamic populations (Committee of Arab Australians 1990; HREOC 1991).

Another example, although less widely analysed, was the 'Asian immigration debate'. From the early 1980s, in an orgy of irresponsibility, the Australian mass media redefined a 'lunar right', racist, 'anti-Asian immigration' position as a 'public concern', and periodically ran with this as entertainment.[2] Despite the ostensibly anti-racist stance taken by the majority of the Australian mass media, they nonetheless succeeded in representing 'Asians': as alien; as an invading horde; as dangerous; as numerically excessive; as a drain on the resources and tolerances of 'Australians'; and as sources of riot. In fact, until eclipsed by the spectre of Islam in the early 1990s, the net effect of the media obsession was to resurrect the 'Asian' as the Other of the Anglo-Australian imaginary, those 'collectively held images' (Hamilton 1990) whose circulation through various media simultaneously reaffirmed the cultural hegemony of Anglo-Australia.

There have been three large-scale enquiries into the representation of NESB Australians in the Australian media from the late 1980s. These are: the National Inquiry into Racist Violence (HREOC 1991), two reports to the Office of Multicultural Affairs (Bell 1992b; Goodall et al. 1990) and the work of Jakubowicz and his colleagues at the University of Technology, Sydney (Jakubowicz et al. 1994). The findings of all the enquiries have been consistent. All argue that insofar as NESB populations are represented in Australian television as *Austra-*

lians, they are represented variously as: foreign; invasive; exotic; criminal; violent; comical; sexual; or they are not represented at all.

NESB Australian women and television

There has been virtually no work looking at the representation of NESB Australian women on Australian television in studies of sexism and the media, or in studies of racism and the media (Cox & Laura 1992; Jakubowicz et al. 1994; Martin 1991b). The most recent substantial enquiry into sexism in the media in Australia, carried out by the Office of the Status of Women in 1992, only mentions NESB women in passing, drawing on scant existing research (OSW 1993).

One major problem evident in existing research is that NESB women are *either* subsumed to the general category 'women' in contrast to the general category 'male' (OSW 1993) *or* subsumed to the general category 'ethnic minority' in contrast to the general category 'dominant culture' (in Australia, Anglo).[3] In both cases the complexity of becoming an NESB woman, or of being positioned as such, is compromised by a conceptual apparatus informing research that emphasises fixed categories of domination and subordination at the expense of an account of process that heeds differences in the construction of gender, a plethora of interests, politics and practices and so forth (Connell 1987).

Situating the question: racism and the representation of NESB women in television advertisements

The question 'How are NESB Australian women represented in television advertisements?' needs to be separated first into three questions which are pertinent to all questions about racism and the mass media. These are:

- How are NESB Australian women represented *as Australians* in television ads?
- Who are the Australian women represented in television ads?
- How are NESB women in general represented in television ads?

The reasons for these questions are as follows: not all ads are Australian made and produced, or have 'Australian' characters and scenes; racism and ethnocentrism may as easily be read by *absences*. Absenting populations from public images and texts is often a powerful statement about, for example, ethnic preferences and prejudices; messages about ethnic differences and ranks can easily be read from images and texts that are not Australia-specific, for example via an implicit global ranking of cultures that positions persons of different backgrounds in a particular way in Australia.

Television advertisements

Advertisements are designed to sell products, hence they work through a process of commodification, that is they constitute symbolic material as commodities (Bourdieu 1984, 1991; Thompson 1990). To this end, advertisements in television make use of a number of well-documented devices: repetition, hyperbole, metaphor, allusion, irony, joke, commonplace moral tales attached to the spectacular; particular uses of sound and colour; the elision of 'rational' temporalities and spatialities; substitution, paradox, the juxtaposition of inappropriates, and so forth (Poster 1990; Sontag 1988; Williamson 1978). Advertisements also make extensive use of sexual symbolism, and try to harness desire (in its most extended sense) to the purchase of a commodity. Advertisements are primarily *rhetorical* in nature (Coward 1987; Durand 1983; Sontag 1988). This means ads are *not* about the real. Ads do not pretend to 'mirror reality'. They are not literal, but mainly figurative, although they may claim to move between the literal and figurative (because they are rhetorical).

Much contemporary television advertising uses these devices to sell products by dreams and fantasies, by personalities and lifestyles, linking the products to desire. When authors refer to the fantastic quality of many television ads, they are referring to the deployment of the preceding strategies to this end. Ads are important because they come into our lives as mundane elements of everyday life, despite the limitation of their commodified form and despite the particular semiotics of their content. Racism is also an element in daily life. In many respects, ads share the same terrain as racism, which is why they should be dealt with in media studies of ethnic minority representations.

Representation and audience

Contemporary audience research makes the obvious point that meanings are not given in media products but are produced in the interaction between audience/reader and media product, regardless of the intention of the media producer. Audience research makes the further point that these meanings vary according to the social position of the reader, e.g., class, sex, ethnic background, rural/urban, age.[4] In addition, as Bourdieu's and Thompson's work makes clear, audiences value symbolic forms differently, once again depending on the cultures of their class and other social locations (Bourdieu 1984; Thompson 1990).

This is another way of saying that the reception of media products is obviously more complicated than suggested by a mechanical, top-down view of social reproduction. There is obviously an element of uncertainty in how audiences read media products, and what they do with them, which means that social reproduction is never certain nor complete. To a large extent this is because media events are events in the trajectories of daily life, in which trajectories occupy a different temporality and spatiality to institutions and institutional arrangements (Bourdieu 1984; de Certeau 1988; Murphy 1972; Silverstone 1988).

Reading television ads

How are NESB Australian women represented as Australians?

Overall, NESB Australian women are virtually absent from television ads featuring Australians. Aboriginal women are not represented at all. There are a number of exceptions. For example, in 1992 Sard Wonder Soap featured an Indian woman in an interview segment; a Palmolive soap ad in 1991 starred an 'Asian' woman; and a 1994 ad for lean lamb features a fairly obviously non-Anglo-Australian woman. Likewise, there are exceptions in ads oriented to a specific market, such as Telecom overseas ads—which use extensive, sympathetic, albeit stereotyped, non-Anglo characters (Italian, Maori, etc.: see, for example, the 1994 SBS send-up of one of these). Other examples are ads for 'ethnic food' products such as pasta, and fast food ads. For example, a Red Rooster ad screened in 1992 hailed obviously dark ethnically diverse persons as 'Australian', and foregrounded an 'Asian' child.

Most commonly, non-Anglo-Australian women are represented in servant roles, or as fat, comical, earth-mommas serving their marginal 'families'. This is seen in the Pro Hart ads for carpet cleaner and in some of the older spaghetti ads. In a recent reversal of this type of ad, the services provided for her husband by an Italian momma are replaced by an Australian meat pie.

An exception concerns young women (aged approximately 15–25). Ads directed towards a young audience use a range of images of women—dark, fair, black, although there is often a preference for Afro blacks. Examples are Bacardi, GBs, Jeans West, and Off Limits. Clearly black sexuality and the sexual aspect of the 'exotic' are directed at a young, 'carefree', adventurous audience at a time when the 'mystery of the orient and of Africa'—i.e., *the romance of colonisation*—is enjoying a comeback in some aesthetic circles (Martin 1990). I will return to this in the discussion of non-Anglo men below.[5]

Note, however, that even these were not typical. The typical ads addressed to young people were markedly biased towards blondes, especially when directed to an upmarket audience, or when using a nostalgic, mainly 1950s, setting (i.e. before multiculturalism, before feminism). The inclusion of ethnically diverse images of young people is in fact a variation on a norm which is blonde (Goodall et al. 1990; OSW 1993).

Who is the Australian woman represented in television ads?

Most ads representing Australians (or Australia) call up a 'typical Aussie' or, in the case of women, a 'typical Aussie woman'. These images are densely coded to stand for 'Australia' and to invoke the spirit (or essence) of 'Australianness'. Images of typical Aussie women are deployed to this end. However, there is no single typical Aussie woman. Rather, there are typical Aussie women whose images vary according to: their age; their marital status; their professional status; hair colour; activities; and context (with children, at work, with lovers, in the family, travelling, with friends, doing 'female' things, etc.). Hence there is a variety of images of a typical Aussie woman, doing a range of activities in a range of situations.

There is a class of ads that states bluntly the centrality of Anglo-ness. These ads resolve the diversity of Australian womanhood into a single image, a domestic image of an Australian woman, of a *mother* located at the centre of the Australian home. The domestic products that fall into this class are primarily *staples* (shelter, food, cleanliness, finance, health, education) for family consumption. The staple domestic unit of ordinary life is assumed to be 'the family', and the ads pitch their appeal and content in these terms in prime family viewing time. To this end, this class of ads simulates (in a highly stylised way) the everyday domestic life of typical Australians who stand for Australia and the 'Australian way of life', which is stridently and unashamedly Anglo-Australian.

Aussie-mums have a particular position in the family units portrayed in these ads. We know from feminist studies that mothers go together with the product in most family ads. However, if we start from enquiries about racism, then the sexism of the ads is inflected by racism, or more appositely by dense ethnic coding and messages. If we start from a question about racism, then what we see is an *Aussie*-mum, an image and a character certainly described in sexist terms, but also densely coded as an ethnic character and image. From this perspective the 'Aussie' is as interesting as the 'mum'.

One curious aspect of this class of ads is the way in which a metaphor of blondeness stands for the Anglo-ness of the Australian family, and therefor for the Anglo-ness of Australia as a whole. In most cases this metaphor is feminised then played across the family. It is captured in the figure of a blonde Aussie-mum, pressing home the picture of the normal Aussie family, and pressing home the Anglo core of the 'Australian way of life'.

Blonde Aussie-mums are always represented with their families. On the rare occasion when the Aussie-mum is not blonde, then she is either without her family, or the metaphor of blondeness is passed to the child. In contrast to the representation of 'ethnic' mums, blonde Aussie-mums are always thin and quiet (see above re Italian mommas), and speak differently to Anglo males, whose speech ('un'-accented, deep, confident, general) signifies authority. Non-authoritative speech—high, tentative, accented, particular—ranks women, then non-English speakers, in relation to an Anglo male. In recent years blonde Aussie-mums have given ground slightly to brunette Aussie-mums, but these are still visibly Anglo and remain thin and moderate.

Woman–family–nation

When both terms—Aussie and mum—are considered, what happens in these ads is that diverse images of the female are resolved into the identity of the domestic and the ethnic, or rather of the primacy of the family and its identity with the nation. In some ads in this genre the identity of Anglo-Aussie mum–family–nation is underscored by historical nostalgia (either staged or old footage). Blonde Aussie families roll through history to the present, filling the totality of Australian history, and exhausting the essence of 'Australia', and of 'home'. In fact the ads seem to have primordial content, based on kinship themes, that goes a long way to understanding their force, and the irrelevance of a literal image (Liebes & Katz 1988; Martin 1991b).

A blonde Aussie-mum is not a literal mum (or even blonde), any more than her family is. She is not mum as a mum—your mum, my mum. And the family is not a concrete family *qua* family. Rather blonde

Aussie-mums and their families seem to represent what is at the heart of Australian life: timeless and unvarying Anglo traditions which include a particular sexual division of labour, and class position. In other words, blondeness signals an exclusive and undifferentiated ethnicity caught up in the mystique of the family, and rewritten as the soul of the nation. Blonde Aussie-mums are therefore also ethnic figures, and symbols of ethnic control. The ads make it clear that Aussie-mums are central to social control, even though this function has female oppression as a main effect.

What we have in these images of Aussie-mums is a process of symbolic exclusion in all the main areas of Australian life. Non-Anglo women are emphatically not Aussie-mums: they do not stand for 'typical Australia' and cannot embody Australia's essence. Non-Anglo women—non-Anglo-ness—are peripheral to the core of Australian life, peripheral to the family and peripheral to the nation.

How are non-Anglo women represented in television ads?

Non-Anglo women frequently appear as *foreign* women. Representations of non-Anglo women as foreign, as external to Australia, outweigh their representation as Australians, even in the most limited proportional sense. Overall, non-Anglo foreign women are represented in television ads either as features of an exotic setting, or as exotic imported features of the local scene. In ads, the exotic is always a commodity, *ergo* foreign women themselves are represented as exotic commodities.

Unsurprisingly then, non-Anglo foreign women appear mainly in tourist ads, or in ads for products with a foreign flavour. Some examples of the former are airline ads, such as Lufthansa, Air Pacific, Malaysian Airlines, Singapore Airlines. Examples of the latter are Fabergé, Yoplait, some Sara Lee ads and some car ads. In these ads the foreignness of the women either gives them a sophisticated 'sexiness' or relegates them to servant (or surrogate wife) positions. In a few cases a raw, unsophisticated, natural, sexual availability is linked to the servant/serving role (Goodall et al. 1990).

The ads appear to be addressed to Anglo men, offering them sex and service, and to Anglo women, offering release from like duties. In fact, the ads release Anglo women from nature, from culture, from the static, into civilisation, society and progress; they reposition the alignment of the Aussie home accordingly. Read this way, Aussie-mums and

Aussie families escape nature/culture, and are realigned as the bedrock of society.[6]

The ads suggest the following in relation to the position of non-Anglo-Australian women in Australia:

• All non-Anglo women are foreign. Local Anglo prejudices and exclusions are reinforced through these ads.

• Local class divisions are re-presented as foreign, given from the outside, and are therefore not intrinsic to the inside.

• Non-Anglo women in Australia are never married to Anglo men. Endogamy, marrying inside the group, the ethnic group in this case, is represented as the prevailing marriage rule.[7]

However, *degrees* of foreignness intrude in images of foreign women so that there is a rough fit between the relative privileges enjoyed by some non-Anglo-Australian women in Australia, and the minimal privileges of others. So, for example, from the perspective of the inside, the most foreign women are also among the most internally marginal, the least privileged, enjoying only a tenuous relation to the work process, or relegated to the least desirable work (e.g., Vietnamese, Lebanese, Latin American, Greek, compared with more privileged Northern and Western European non-Anglo women, e.g. German, Scandinavian).

The one exception concerns Afro-American and Asian-American populations who are often represented in contrast to these rules. One reason is that these are probably preferred ethnic images from US advertising, and the ads show the impact of US ownership patterns.

The representation of non-Anglo-Australian men

The positioning of non-Anglo men in Australian television ads blurs the woman–man distinction implicit in the above account. If a male–female opposition is taken, then overall non-Anglo men, particularly those from locally disfavoured groups, are feminised *vis-à-vis* Anglo men (and often Anglo women) in domestic roles such as cooking, serving and waiting. Some examples are pasta ads, travel ads and meat ads. In one ad with a twist, screened in 1991, the 'ethnic' chef is revealed in mufti as an Anglo male faking an ethnic. For his feminine chef role he affects a 'foreign' accent.

A male–female opposition is not limited to showing groups of men with 'female' characteristics, or men in predominantly female roles. If the male–female opposition is taken to also be a culture–nature opposition (or a culture–society opposition) then the majority of ads feminise non-Anglo men in relation to Anglo men, including those ads that represent non-Anglo men as physically strong, as sexpots, and as entertainers. Much the same holds for portrayals of non-Anglo men as violent and brutal, corresponding to a natural 'bestial' side as opposed to the civilised. They are always positioned thus from the perspective of an Anglo male, and in relation to him, whether he be in the frame or not.

What this means is that the signs for female and male are not necessarily attached to sexed bodies, especially if the signs function as prime organising signs for relations of domination and subordination. I have argued in a previous paper that it is possible to read some forms of display as placing all black men under a female sign, while white women move under a male sign (Martin 1990). It seemed here that women (in an almost metaphorical sense) were positioned on the dividing line between black and white (or, them and us), as sites of boundary and transgression, and all other contrasts shifted accordingly. The reason seemed to be the way in which a dialectic of sex and sexuality was written across other delineations, and moved these within fixed contrasts. In fact, as with the images of Aussie families, the displays viewed seemed to have some primordial content and structure around themes of kinship and transgression central to mythic thought. Some similar conventions (possibly aesthetic conventions) seem to hold for this type of television ad.

For example, many tourist ads for Asia and the Pacific place Asian and Pacific males and females under a female sign (as servants, in relation to sex, etc.), while Anglo males and females (released from the previous) occupy the male sign. In other ads, white women and black men fall together under a female sign in relation to white men who exhaust the male sign. For example, in some female product ads shown in 1991–92 (e.g., ads for Panadol, Hickory), singing, dancing or muscular black men were backgrounded to white female models or speakers, presumably to signify some affinity, by implication, to female products. In other cases, the affinity between black male and white female is signalled by a glance, or by an implied mutual sexuality. This separates the black male and white female out from the white male, who is usually also present in the frame, often with the white woman, for example. One curious feature of these ads is that they rarely occur with Asian men, or for that matter, with Australian male Aboriginals.

Often these types of ads, which play on forbidden sexuality, seem to be about the desire of a white male. They have a voyeuristic component—like seen with like—that is not present in the occasional ad linking white men to Asian or black women. Perhaps this is because the 'servant' component, and the implied sexual right of white men to servants, keeps each side in its own unlike categories.

Black or foreign women are rarely present when an affinity is shown between black or foreign men and Anglo or white women. When both sexes are present then the boundary is drawn along racial or ethnic lines, spoken as male/female, as in the Air Pacific and Singapore Airline ads.

There are, of course, occasions when foreign men are shown in control in much the same way as Anglo men. Almost without exception, these men are middle-class men from Western and Northern Europe holding positions of power and responsibility. Once again these images are coded in terms of global and local Australian social hierarchies. The oddity here concerns Japanese men. They are usually portrayed in a combination of the above, i.e. in power and powerful, but also feminised—no doubt this is a fairly accurate metaphor for Australia's troubled relation with the Asian region, and the rising economic power of various Asian economies.[8]

Conclusions

Intersections

The processes of ethnic exclusion, and the processes of constituting ethnic subjects and ethnically based social hierarchies, are very obvious if representations of NESB Australian women in television ads in Australia are considered. Overall, NESB Australian women are virtually absent from ads representing Australia: ads that do include them seem to have the effect (not intention) of emphasising their marginality as 'ethnic Australia'. If one looks at images of Australian women, it is clear that representations of Australian women do much more than spell out male–female relations, or female subordination. The representations are coded by ethnicity as well as sex. This muddies a simple men-versus-women approach, as evidenced in Australian mums and Australian family ads.

NESB women are most frequently represented as 'foreign women', in ads. In these ads the 'foreignness' of NESB women is signalled in their positioning as servants or sexual commodities, and in their accent, colouring, speech, locale, etc. The effect is to position NESB Australian women as foreign to Australia.

If representations of non-Anglo men are considered, in relation to

Anglo women and to Anglo men, it is clear that the signifiers contrasting and ranking male and female are not necessarily attached to sexed bodies. Non-Anglo men and Anglo women often both fall under a female sign in relation to Anglo men, or Anglo women move under a male sign and non-Anglo men fill the female sign, but this is not always the case. In some instances Anglo and non-Anglo males both fall under a male sign in relation to all women along a particular dimension of contrast. These shifts seem to be a function of the way in which cross-ethnic representations are pervaded by sexuality (or its absence), such that actual women sit at the dividing line of ethnic and racial distinctions, as both the symbol of a bound ethnicity, and of its indeterminateness.

Clearly, then, the processes of producing and reproducing ethnic subjects and hierarchies on the one hand, and sexed subjects and hierarchies on the other, intersect and form each other in a complex, context-defined, and rather slippery way. Television ads reproduce and re-present the ideologies and discourse of sex and race/ethnicity central to these processes, in part through the deployment of aesthetic conventions of contrast, so that the same actual persons can be fixed in quite different positions depending on the relevant dimensions and delineations stressed (by the ad, by the audience position). It is obvious that sexuality is implicated in these processes, perhaps much more so than in other discourses and ideologies of ranking, which needs much further analysis. As with the family images, these ads appear to have a primordial, almost mythic, content, independent of their ideological component, that suggests the need for further study of the themes of kinship–sexuality–transgression in ads playing on the ethnic, be they exclusive or comparative (Martin 1990).

Audiences

The question of audience is important here. I argued above that the meaning of an ad is not given in the ad, but is constructed between the image and its audience. Audiences occupying different positions in a social system bring different meanings to ads, so that the actual way an ad is read is always uncertain. However, this doesn't mean that 'anything goes'. For example, there is considerable evidence that ads have derogatory or exclusive images of NESB populations *often enough*, and that these have negative effects on the self-esteem of ethnic minority populations, particularly in the case of children (Berry & Mitchell-Kernan 1982). The rise of ethnic media monitoring groups in Australia is testament to these processes, as is research looking at the negative attitudes and actions of the mainstream towards ethnic minority groups as a result of media representations (Committee of Arab Australians 1990; HREOC 1991). There is no reason to believe that this won't also hold for representations of NESB women, and the way these throw light on the processes of media constitution of marginalised ethnic subjects in general.

Representation, domination and interest

On a final conceptual note, the question of interest—whose interests are served through the (re)production of ethnic/racial and sexual ideologies—is implicit to all discussions in the area, and seems obvious at two levels. First, ads themselves serve the interests of the producers of commodities: this interest is self-evident; there would be no ads otherwise. Secondly, in most ads, middle-class Anglo maleness is the privileged point of reference and authority. It is not surprising, therefore, that ethnic minority group and feminist politics assert that ideologies of ethnic/racial and sexual superiority serve the interests of white Anglo males. Such a claim is also a commonplace in any politics of representation.

Nonetheless, the processes of media representation outlined above suggest a more mobile process in the formation of interests. Perhaps these representations do serve male interests, but their dimensions slip continually. In fact, what comes through is more like a shifting coalition of interests, on all sides, defined through the processes of constituting and reconstituting differently ranked populations. It seems that the processes involved are sufficiently mobile that they could falter at any point, so that some coalition comes together (actively political, or structurally in terms of effects) as an interest-based force. These may be either a force of domination, *vis-à-vis* consenting or resisting populations, or a force of resistance. For example, Anglo men and women may actively constitute an interest-based force through demanding representation that furthers Anglo cultural hegemony, or they may constitute a structural force as an effect of their monopolisation of positive representations (the other side is derogatory representations, absenting, marginalisation, and low self-esteem of non-Anglo populations). Or these interests may coalesce elsewhere, for example in a coalition between non-Anglos and Anglo women against Anglo male hegemony. The point is that interest-based coalitions may persist over time (and space) but they are not fixed, and are certainly not given in a category of actual people *qua* people.

Any media analysis of the representation of NESB Australians is already part of an existing politics of representation that, from the point of view of very diverse ethnic minority groups and interests, comes together in an attempt to challenge forms of cultural domination in the sphere of representation. The foregoing analysis of television ads suggests the importance of including feminist analyses of media representation, and of feminist analyses including the ethnic, without assuming any given or unitary interest. In particular, such analyses should: heed the organising function of sexuality in representations of ethnic and gender-based social differences and subordinations; and separate mythic and primordial components from the strictly ideological and interest bound.

Afterword

Ownership, employment, rights of representation

NESB Australians are underrepresented in ownership and in employment in mass media institutions in Australia (Jakubowicz 1989; Jakubowicz et al. 1994). All major mass media, including advertising organisations, are owned by Anglo-Australians or North Americans. In addition, there is substantial evidence that employment practices are heavily biased towards Anglo-Australians, including the practices of acting and modelling agencies that supply personnel. There have been further complaints that local professional and aesthetic conventions exclude NESB Australians, are often ethnocentric and racist, and are resistant to changes toward a more multicultural perspective (Jakubowicz 1989; Jakubowicz et al. 1994). In media politics all these issues are summed up in the debate about 'rights of representation', i.e., who has control over and the right to represent whom.

A politics of representation would make *independent* interventions in each of these spheres. The interventions must be independent because there is no particular reason why greater minority group representation in one sphere should bring about positive changes in another. For example, greater NESB (or female) representation in ownership and employment does not necessarily entail 'better representation of ethnic minorities and/or women'. Control over representation and the nature of the representation are separate questions. On the other hand, there is some evidence, particularly from film, that greater minority group control over the means of representation does produce less derogatory representation, if only because of a shift in the social location of key production personnel (Martin 1993). Hence the importance of interventions on all of these fronts.

Strategies and representations

Until recently, strategies to counter derogatory and marginalising representations of ethnic minorities and women have relied on a stereotype analysis. There are a number of problems with such an analysis. These are: the assumption that representations are literal; the assumption that negative characteristics are inherently negative, rather than relative to a social relation of power; a lack of clarity about positive stereotypes; a welfare approach which is inappropriate to aesthetic products, and deathly as entertainment. Another problem is a moralistic mainstream bias against the political appropriation of 'derogatory' stereotypes by minority groups (e.g., black gangs) and, locally, the appropriation of Effie from 'Acropolis Now' as an empowering image for young, Greek, female Australians (Jakubowicz et al. 1994; Martin 1991c).

More recently, black activists have viewed stereotypes as rhetorical devices, and tried to alter their context of meaning. These groups have used a variety of techniques (e.g., hyperbole, irony, appropriation of the derogatory image) as strategies aimed at undermining the mainstream morality, and the derogatory representation. Some examples are: the comedy of Lenny Henry; SBS send-ups of Telstra ads; the stage version of 'Wogs out of Work', and so forth. Such strategies are more open to creative work, especially around the intersection of diverse systems of domination such as sex and race. They complement well other strategies such as: product boycott; demonstration; education of media personnel (on the job and in the tertiary sector), and audiences; and the use of existing government instrumentalities to counter derogatory representations.

9
Police racism: Experiences and reforms

Janet Chan

Police racism has received widespread attention in Australia in recent years, following the publication of the *Report of the National Inquiry into Racist Violence* (HREOC 1991) and the broadcasting of a television documentary in 1992 depicting the apparently routine and unrestrained use of racist language by police officers in New South Wales ('Cop It Sweet'). Complaints of racial prejudice and discrimination by police officers are, of course, not a uniquely Australian experience. Police 'race relations' in countries such as Great Britain, the USA and Canada are similarly problematic: in some instances conflicts between police and ethnic minorities have even escalated into open violence and urban riots.[1]

This chapter examines police racism critically in the Australian context. The first section describes the ways in which racism is manifested in police work. These include officers' assumptions about the criminality of certain ethnic communities, their reluctance to use professional language interpreters, over-policing or harassing of minorities, and abuses of police powers. The second section discusses the effectiveness of government reforms aimed at addressing these problems: strategies such as the adoption of non-discriminatory policies, recruitment of officers from ethnic communities, training of police officers in 'cross-cultural awareness', and various 'community policing' programs. In the final section, the persistence of police racism is discussed in relation to dominant theoretical perspectives on policing. It is suggested that successful reforms must take into account the reality of operational police work and the nature of police organisations. Change can be brought about only through a combination of internal reforms, officers' participation, external pressure, and community feedback.

Experiences of police racism

Although 'police racism' is a convenient label for many of the problems ethnic minorities experience in their contact with the police, it is in fact an imprecise and emotive term which can at times confuse rather than clarify the nature of the problems. If we adopt the definition of racism put forward by Castles (1993, p. 1), then 'police racism' refers to the process whereby police authorities stigmatise, harass, criminalise or otherwise discriminate against certain social groups 'on the basis of phenotypical or cultural markers, or national origin' through the use of their special powers. Like other forms of racism, police racism is not a static or simple phenomenon: 'it arises in differing situations, takes many forms and varies in intensity according to time and place' (Castles 1993, p. 1).

Manifestations of police racism can range from prejudicial attitudes, discriminatory law enforcement practices, to the illegal use of violence against members of minority groups. 'Over-policing' has been the subject of a great majority of research studies and enquiries into the treatment of Aborigines in Australia. Among immigrants and Australians of non-English-speaking background (NESB), however, a major issue concerns police officers' reluctance to use professional language interpreters. For those with little or no facility in English, the presence of communication barriers amounts to a denial of equal access to justice, an obvious form of discrimination.

It should be mentioned at the outset that the depth and extent of discriminatory treatment suffered historically by Australia's indigenous people make it inappropriate to equate the experiences of Aborigines with those of other NESB Australians. Certainly, the legal system, until recently, accommodated the dispossession of Aborigines of their own land, as it was impotent in stopping the murder of 20 000 Aborigines in the course of European occupation (Reynolds 1987b, pp. 1–5). Moreover, the historical role of the police in the suppression of Aboriginal resistance to European settlement and the 'protection' of Aborigines (Foley 1984) means that contemporary relations between police and Aborigines cannot be studied in isolation. However, it can be argued that the treatment of other ethnic minorities is in some ways an extension of Australia's treatment of Aborigines. There are undeniable differences between Aborigines and other ethnic minorities in their social conditions and experiences with the legal system. There may even be identifiable differences in experience between NESB groups. In Britain, for example, a survey by Jefferson and Walker (1992) in Leeds found that Asians (from the Indian sub-continent) reported less negative experience and more favourable attitudes towards police than did Afro-Caribbeans. Though similar evidence in relation to police racism is not available in Australia, the National Inquiry into Racist Violence reported that problems of racism and racist violence are 'far less significant [among Southern European communities] than that currently experienced by the Asian, Jewish and Arabic communities' (HREOC 1991, p. 140). Thus, although the following discussion focuses on some common experiences of police racism, it should not be assumed that all minority communities experience these problems to the same degree.

Assumptions by police about communities and crime

Overseas studies have documented clear evidence of prejudicial attitudes and the regular use of racist language among police officers (Bayley & Mendelsohn 1969; Gordon 1983; Holdaway 1983; Skolnick 1966; Smith 1983). Similar complaints are found in Australia. For example, police have often been accused of forming stereotypical opinions about the criminality of certain ethnic groups (ALRC 1992, p. 201; New South Wales Ethnic Affairs Commission [NSWEAC] 1992, Section 2B4). Cunneen and Robb (1987) found that Aboriginal people have been blamed by sections of the New South Wales population for various forms of social disorder. It is therefore not surprising that police officers form similar associations between Aborigines and criminality.

Since police work is largely dictated by officers' perceptions of what constitutes suspicious activities and who is considered to be respectable, stereotyping and prejudice on the part of police officers can easily lead to harassment and community resentment. Prejudicial attitudes are also obvious obstacles to gaining trust and cooperation from members of ethnic minority communities. British and US studies have found that blacks, in particular young blacks in inner cities, were more critical of police and more hostile towards police than other groups (Reiner 1985). Less systematic evidence in Australia suggests that some minorities are afraid of police and do not trust them.

Failure to use or inappropriate use of interpreters

A major problem encountered by recent immigrants and refugees to Australia is their lack of ability or confidence to communicate in English. A survey of fifty-five community organisations in New South Wales (NSWEAC 1992) found widespread concern that police did not always use interpreters when needed and that unqualified or inappropriate persons were often used as interpreters. These allegations were supported by results of a survey by Chan (1992) of New South Wales police officers. A general reluctance among the police to use professional interpreters was also reported in Victoria (Wilson & Storey 1991, p. 18), in the Northern Territory (O'Neill & Bathgate 1993, p. 142), and in other jurisdictions (ALRC 1992, p. 57).

While administrative costs—both financial and in terms of delay—have often been cited as reasons for police not to use professional interpreters, a crucial issue concerns the extent to which police discretion is appropriately exercised in these situations. In dealings with ethnic youth, for example, there were complaints that police had a tendency not to accept that interpreters were needed: 'it was commonly presumed that the youth concerned went to school [and] hence would understand English' (NSWEAC 1992, Section 2B). The assumption that someone with a reasonable grasp of conversational English would be competent to give legal evidence or answer questions in a police interrogation has already been challenged by linguistic specialists and lawyers (see Commonwealth Attorney-General's Department 1990, p. 42; Roberts-Smith 1989, p. 76). The right to an interpreter has not been uniformly established in legislation throughout Australia; some states still rely on police and judicial discretion in establishing the need for an interpreter. The Australian Law Reform Commission's consultations show, however, that statutory provisions requiring the use of interpreters may not be sufficient to remedy the problem.

Language barriers do not exist only in relation to immigrants and refugees from non-English-speaking countries. Some Aborigines also encounter difficulties in English communication. In some cases interpreters are not readily available for Aboriginal languages known by very few people (Commonwealth Attorney-General's Department 1990, p. 113). The majority of Aboriginal people also speak dialects of English which may 'differ systematically from standard English in terms of sound system, grammar, vocabulary, meaning and appropriate use of language' (Commonwealth Attorney-General's Department 1990, pp. 113–14). Foley (1984, pp. 168–9) points out that non-standard grammatical usage of tense, gender, and number in Aboriginal English could lead to confusion and misunderstandings about time, number and gender in police interrogations. In *R v. Anunga*, the Northern Territory Supreme Court set out nine guidelines which apply to the interrogation of Aborigines as suspects. These include the use of an interpreter where necessary, the presence of a 'friend' of the prisoner, the use of simple language in asking questions, the calling of legal assistance if sought, and other measures to lower the level of stress for the suspects. These guidelines are, however, not rules of law, and non-compliance did not necessarily mean exclusion of the evidence.

Over-policing: unfair targeting and harassment of minorities

One form of discriminatory policing practice is the unfair targeting and harassment of certain minority groups. The concept of over-policing encompasses both the degree and nature of police intervention (HREOC 1991, pp. 90–1). At the policy level, this may be a resource allocation decision, so that more officers than normal are directed at the policing of certain areas with a high concentration of certain minority groups. At the level of routine police work, this may reflect a strategy to single out certain minority group members regularly for questioning, or selectively enforce laws so that certain minorities are more vulnerable to arrest and prosecution than the general population.

Police harassment is a common complaint among young Aborigines and young people of non-English-speaking background (NSWEAC 1992; O'Neill & Bathgate 1993, p. 141; Wilson & Storey 1991, pp. 27–8; Youth Justice Coalition 1990, p. 232). The use of tactical response police against Aboriginal communities in Western Australia, Northern Territory and New South Wales was another category of complaints received by the Inquiry into Racist Violence (HREOC 1991). The use of 135 officers including members of the Tactical Response Group in a pre-dawn raid on Redfern in 1990 was a high-profile example of such operations in New South Wales (Landa 1991).

It has been argued that over-policing is partly responsible for the gross overrepresentation of Aborigines in the criminal justice system. The study by Cunneen and Robb (1987, p. 70) of five north-western New South Wales towns found that Aborigines were more than three times as likely to be arrested as non-Aborigines. A survey conducted in August 1988 found that Aborigines were placed in police cells at a rate of 27 times that of non-Aboriginal people. Aboriginal women were also disproportionately detained in police cells. In general, Aborigines were held in the cells for a longer period of time than non-Aborigines

(McDonald & Biles 1991). Not surprisingly, the 1986 national prison census indicated that the rate of imprisonment of Aborigines was nearly ten times higher than that of the population as a whole (Walker & Biles 1987).

Police abuse of power and excessive use of force

The National Inquiry into Racist Violence reported numerous incidents of police using intrusive and intimidatory practices and conducting searches without a warrant in their dealings with Aboriginal communities (HREOC 1991, pp. 82–3). A survey of Aboriginal households in Adelaide found that 62 per cent of respondents had been visited by police during the previous two years, even though police were not called. Of these households, 24 per cent reported that police had entered without invitation, without a warrant and with no arrest resulting, while 19 per cent alleged that a member of the household had been physically abused by police (p. 83). Discriminatory and intimidatory policing practices in relation to Aborigines in public places as well as private functions were also reported to the enquiry (pp. 85–8).

Most disturbing, however, was the 'overwhelming' evidence presented to the enquiry by Aboriginal and Islander people in relation to police violence. Consultation in six states, written submissions, and evidence received at public hearings in major cities raised serious concerns about the treatment of Aboriginal and Islander people by police (HREOC 1991, p. 80). The evidence revealed the shocking treatment of Aboriginal and Islander women and girls by police officers: there were allegations of rape while in custody, sexual threats and abuse, in addition to verbal (sexist and racist) abuse and physical violence (pp. 88–9). Similar treatment of juveniles was reported in a number of states. A survey by Cunneen (1990) of 171 Aboriginal and Islander juveniles in state detention centres in Queensland, New South Wales and Western Australia found an alarming level of alleged police violence: 85 per cent reported that they had been hit, punched, kicked or slapped, and 63 per cent hit with objects, including police batons, telephone books, torches and other objects. These assaults took place on the street, during arrest and at police stations. However, it was not only the frequency of violence, but also its nature, that was disturbing (HREOC 1991, pp. 96–7). With adult Aborigines in custody, practices such as brutal assault, hosing down detainees, denial of medical treatment, forcing detainees to drink water from toilet bowls, and other forms of abuse were reported (HREOC 1991, p. 105). Perhaps the most reprehensible of all was the finding that 'police officers had made suggestions of suicide or threatened to hang Aboriginal or Islander people when they were taken into custody' (HREOC 1991, p. 98).

The National Inquiry into Racist Violence did not receive many complaints about police abuse or violence against other ethnic minorities. However, community organisations in New South Wales did reveal concerns about 'occasional physical abuse by police, victimisation by police through the selective use of police powers, police brutality whilst youth are being detained or questioned by police' (NSWEAC 1992). Community workers consulted in the course of a New South Wales research project (Chan 1992) raised similar concerns about verbal or physical abuse during police interrogation or in police custody, and active or passive condoning of racial conflicts by the police. Workers cited incidents of harassment and brutality against young people. In Victoria, similar allegations of police misconduct—beatings in custody, property searches without warrants, harassment and abuse of individuals—were reported by the majority of community workers and some of the solicitors interviewed by Wilson and Storey (1991).

When presented with allegations of abuse and violence, police rarely took the allegations seriously. Apart from a few police officers who gave evidence at the National Inquiry into Racist Violence to confirm the existence of police abuse and police violence against Aborigines, the reactions of police forces to these complaints have tended to be defensive. The fact that very few of these allegations were taken to formal complaint bodies or criminal courts does not imply that the victims were lying or exaggerating. It is more a reflection of the inaccessibility of the complaints process and the perceived futility of complaining against a powerful body such as the police. In fact, the difficulty of getting justice in cases alleging police misconduct adds another layer of injustice to the experience of minorities. The danger is that such behaviours may be accepted as part of the routine and what the victims 'deserve', as some young people in Australia have come to expect from the police (see Cunneen 1990, p. 53).

Reform initiatives

What is disturbing about the experiences of police racism[2] described in the previous section is that all this is happening amidst a national move to professionalise the policing occupation in Australia (Etter 1992). Australian police forces have undertaken a wide range of reforms in recent years aimed at meeting the needs of ethnic minorities.

Changes include the adoption of a policy of access and equity in the delivery of police service, the recruitment of police officers from ethnic communities, the provision of cultural awareness training for police officers, and various community-based policing strategies (ABMF 1990). These strategies are not meant to be an augmentation of traditional policing, but part of a totally new approach which emphasises innovation, problem-solving, openness and accountability. Early indications are that these reform initiatives still have some way to go before they can achieve their objectives.

Policy of access and equity

Virtually all police forces in Australia are committed to the provision of accessible and equitable service to ethnic minorities. In some forces this principle is implicit in their general policy, while in others the policy is explicitly written into a formal statement. For example, in New South Wales, all government departments and statutory authorities were requested by the Premier to prepare an Ethnic Affairs Policy Statement and submit an annual report to the Ethnic Affairs Commission regarding their progress in achieving previously set objectives (see New South Wales Police Service 1988). However, these broad statements of policy do not provide adequate guidance in terms of everyday police work and, unless gross levels of discrimination against ethnic minorities can be proved, such statements will have minimal effect on police practices. A study of the New South Wales Police Service found that first attempts at implementing the Ethnic Affairs Policy Statement were disappointing; it was resisted by the organisation and treated as a bureaucratic exercise irrelevant to operational concerns (Chan 1992).

Training and recruitment

In recent years, many police forces have made substantial revisions to their training curriculum in a move away from a focus on operations towards a wider educational base, emphasising 'effective skills training in the areas of communication, negotiation, conflict resolution, cross-cultural awareness and the proper use of police discretion' (Etter 1992, 1993; NSW Police Recruit Education Programme 1991). While the intentions of these training initiatives are laudable, there is evidence to suggest that the effect of police recruit training is greatly transformed by the reality of police work and the 'commonsense' of the police occupational culture (Brogden et al. 1988, pp. 32–3; Centre for Applied

Research in Education 1990; Fielding 1988). Cross-cultural awareness training, in particular, must be conducted with great care, or it could confirm existing prejudices rather than lead to greater tolerance of minority cultures (Southgate 1984).

The recruitment of police officers from minority ethnic groups is another positive initiative, but police forces need to pay special attention to the conditions under which minority members work within the police organisation. Overseas research has suggested that minority ethnic officers are subjected to name-calling and racist prejudice within police ranks, while also being resented by white members of the public (Wilson et al. 1984; see also Holdaway 1991). In Australia, there is a marked reluctance among certain ethnic communities to join the police (Bird 1992), and those who join sometimes find themselves in a difficult position with respect to their own communities (Chan 1992).

Community policing strategies

By far the most significant ideological shift in recent years in Australian policing is the adoption of community-based and problem-solving policing strategies (see Alderson 1983; Bayley 1989; Goldstein 1979; Weatheritt 1987). This approach, modelled after overseas police forces, emphasises the importance of involving the community in a partnership relationship in policing, and de-emphasises the traditional police preoccupation with random patrol, fast car response, and retrospective criminal investigation. A partnership with the community is manifested in various community liaison activities, the appointment of liaison officers, the establishment of crime prevention measures such as Neighbourhood Watch and safety houses, the increased use of foot patrols, and the encouragement of grassroots feedback through community consultative committees. The benefit of a community-based policing strategy for multicultural communities is that police work is geared to a local level of accountability: providing quality service to ethnic minorities is no longer a marginal issue for police commanders whose jurisdictions consist of a sizeable proportion of people from minority ethnic backgrounds. In some cases, information pamphlets and phrase books are printed in community languages, multilingual liaison officers are employed, and language-specific community consultative groups are set up. Most of the efforts are directed at reducing the distance between ethnic minorities and the police, instilling confidence and building support among ethnic minorities.

In spite of its attractive rhetoric, community policing is more often talked about than practised (see Chan 1994). The evaluation by Bayley (1989) of community policing in Australia suggests a widespread confusion of community policing with public relations; a common perception of the former as a soft option; a failure by its proponents to make a convincing case for its adoption; and a tendency to view community policing as a marginal or add-on specialty rather than an integral part of all policing activities. As experienced in other countries, the concept of community-based policing is often interpreted in a tokenistic and superficial way, so that there is no real equality in partnership between the police and the minorities. Consultation of the community tends to involve respectable and established members of the community rather than those seen to be marginal or troublesome by the police, and police rarely see operational issues as an appropriate matter for consultation with the community (Youth Justice Coalition 1990, pp. 220–3; see also Morgan 1987). The establishment of specialised ethnic or Aboriginal liaison units carries the danger that police–minority relations are understood to be the responsibility of designated officers, rather than considered as mainstream police issues (Bird 1992; Chan 1992).

Conclusion: Perspectives on police reforms

The apparent ineffectiveness of police reforms in dealing with police racism should not come as a surprise. The difficulty of achieving positive changes in attitudes and practices is consistent with a range of theoretical perspectives on the nature and function of police work. Police racism, within these perspectives, is not a matter of personal prejudices, but an integral part of policing.

At the 'conservative' end of the theoretical spectrum, police forces are seen as a natural, organised response to crime and disorder in society. They 'represent the successful achievement by the modern state as a means of social control in the absence of the norms and social bonds of traditional community life' (Finnane 1994, p. 10).[3] In targeting certain minority groups, police are merely responding to illegal and disorderly conduct as the community demands. Thus police practices are 'racist' only insofar as different 'racial' groups are breaking the law. This is not to deny that social disadvantage and economic deprivation may have led to a disproportionately high rate of offending among Aborigines and other minority groups (Cunneen & Robb 1987; Devery 1991). If police racism exists, it is merely a reflection of racism in the wider society. There is no reason to expect that policy statements, cross-cultural training, recruiting police officers from minority groups, or the introduction of community policing strategies would make any difference, apart from improving the 'public relations' image of police organisations.

'Radical' interpretations of police work, on the other hand, see the police role as essentially that of carrying out a 'coercive, class-based "civilizing" function' (Jefferson 1991, p. 168; see also Brogden et al. 1988). They are 'inevitably, and usually wilfully, the agents of an oppressive state' (Finnane 1994, p. 10). Commenting on the situation in Britain, Jefferson (1993, p. 10) claims that police racism is '*not* primarily about discriminating against young black males, but rather about the production of a criminal Other in which, currently, young black males figure prominently'. Because policing is bound up with the imputation of suspicion and criminality, the demarcation between the respectable and the disreputable, the exercise of coercive force and the maintenance of the dominant social order, discriminatory practices are often 'justified' by 'utilizing a discourse of criminality routed in notions of differential crime proneness' (Jefferson 1993, p. 3). Racist policing constructs a 'reality' that certain groups are more disorderly, more deviant than others, and hence more deserving of police attention and police action, when, in fact, officers are afforded considerable discretion in relation to stop, search, arrest, and charge decisions: 'what all this amounts to is that being the wrong age, sex and class, in the wrong place at the wrong time, displaying the wrong demeanour and attitude, spells "trouble" to police, whatever the colour of your skin' (Jefferson 1993, p. 19).

Within this perspective, police racism is firmly embedded in the nature and function of police work. The prospects of changing police practices through policy directives or recruitment and training strategies seem remote indeed. Between the two polarities, a range of theoretical perspectives exists. Some recognise that what society defines as 'crime' is often biased against the poor and the powerless, hence discriminatory practices are built into our legal structures (Brogden et al. 1988). Others emphasise that police instructions and legal rules leave a great deal of room for individual officers' discretion in decisions to stop, search or arrest suspects (Cain 1973; Manning 1977). Such discretion is often informed by stereotypes of what constitutes 'normality' (e.g., middle-class nuclear family) or 'suspiciousness' (e.g., an Aboriginal person driving a red Laser). Still another view highlights the occupational culture of lower-ranking officers, those most in contact with the public. Police culture has been characterised by varying degrees of secrecy, solidarity, racial prejudice, cutting corners and distrust of the public

(Brockie 1993; Etter 1994; Reiner 1992; Sparrow et al. 1990). Given these entrenched world views, work practices and shared norms, it is therefore not surprising that policy directives and operational strategies imposed from above may have little impact on actual practice on the street.

In many ways, it is the recognition of the reality of operational police work that provides the most promise for reforms. For too long reformers have pursued the 'bureaucratic' model (Colebatch & Larmour 1993, p. 112) of organisations where police practices are expected to change simply because of the adoption of a policy or an operational strategy by the police command. The reality is that policies and directives from headquarters are often not understood: they are resisted or ignored by local police and thus have a limited impact on local police–community relations. Well documented in overseas studies of police organisations are the discrepancies between policy and practice, between the 'management cop' and the 'street cop' culture, and between the appearance of militaristic command and the reality of a mock bureaucracy (Reuss-Ianni & Ianni 1983; Van Maanen 1983). Similarly, any effect that cross-cultural awareness training may have on officers often becomes irrelevant once they are confronted with 'real' police work. Fundamental to this perspective is that top-down reforms are likely to be resisted by those working at the operational end of policing since they have developed what they feel are efficient ways of 'doing the job'.

It may be that change will come about only through a combination of incentives (the 'market' model) and officers' participation in policy-making (the 'community' model), as well as external pressure (Colebatch & Larmour 1993, pp. 112–13). To be taken seriously, policy statements must be developed with the participation of operational police, backed up by relevant programs, adequate resources, appropriate administrative support, rigorous monitoring and an effective account-ability structure. Both external and internal monitoring should be under-taken, with suitable indicators and auditing mechanisms built in. For example, to ensure that people of non-English-speaking background are not disadvantaged by the legal system, police forces need to establish detailed instructions and guidelines so that individual officers are aware of their responsibility for obtaining professional interpreters under appropriate circumstances. An adequate budget for interpreting must be allocated, and there should be close monitoring of the extent and nature of interpreter usage. Similarly, police training and education must be seen to be relevant to police operations and pitched at a practical rather than an abstract level. Training must also be reinforced and supported by peer groups and senior officers if it is to have any long-term influence on behaviour. Finally, community policing ought to be given meaningful application in practice *both* by the police and by the minority communities. Community consultative committees as presently constituted lack the expertise, the power and the resources to monitor local police practices effectively. Anti-racism strategies should take into account the fact that experiences of police racism are not uniform across minority groups. Appropriate solutions can only be successfully developed for specific communities with their active participation. Instead of discouraging criticisms and discrediting critics, police organisations should encourage feedback and take complaints as a valuable source of information about areas of community discontent, unprofessional practices, administrative deficiencies, training inadequacies, or communication failures. Community feedback may provide exactly the type of 'leverage' (Jarratt 1991) that police administrations need to bring about change.

10

Racism, reorientation and the cultural politics of Asia–Australia relations

Fazal Rizvi

> When East becomes North and West is under your feet, your compass spins frighteningly. To calm it you must find yourself a new axis (Judith Wright in Bennett 1991, p. ii).

Australia's relationship with Asia is deeply contradictory. While much has been said and written about the importance of Australia negotiating a new role for itself in the Asia-Pacific region, most Australians remain suspicious of this rhetoric, unable to determine the ways in which they must change to accommodate 'the new realities' of which the governments speak. They have been told that Australia's economic future is now inextricably tied to Asia and that they should see themselves as part of Asia. Yet they remain unclear of the extent to which this involves a rejection of the dominant European values and traditions. Australians have been asked to make a decisive ideological shift in their thinking, away from the colonialist frame that has traditionally informed their perceptions of Asia to a post-colonial outlook which challenges the racist assumptions of cultural dominance and superiority. Yet most of their attempts to revise their thinking have at best been clumsy, with the new practices of representation failing to make a decisive break from the residual racist expressions that had rendered Asians as a homogenised mass, socially inept and culturally inferior.

In this chapter, I want to examine the current contradictions of Australia–Asia relations. I argue that the links between the history of Australian racism, especially in relation to the people of Asian backgrounds, and Australia's current desire to become accepted in Asia are multi-faceted and complex; and that an examination of this complexity requires attention to the ideological frames within which our efforts to become 'Asia-literate' are located. I contend that, given new patterns and practices of migration, it is no longer possible to separate the issues of regional politics involved in our attempts to forge new relationships within the region—in trade, in education, and in the arts and cultural exchange—from the issues concerning the way Asian-Australians are treated within Australia; that is, from the issues of the racisms that reside *within* the country. I contend that an ambivalence lies at the centre of Australian attitudes towards Asia and the people of Asian backgrounds.

The notion of ambivalence I use in this chapter is derived from Homi Bhabha (1994c). Bhabha uses the idea of ambivalence to resolve a range of analytical problems associated with the work of Edward Said. Said (1978), it should be recalled, maintains in his highly influential book, *Orientalism*, that in order to understand how the West has constructed its knowledge of other cultures we must first attend to the questions of representation; of how the Orient has been constituted through a set of discursive practices. Using the insights of Foucault (1972) into the complicity of forms of knowledge with institutions of power, Said argues that the body of knowledge and beliefs with which the West has sought to understand the world constitutes a discourse that unmistakably betrays a will to cultural hegemony and repression. He calls this discourse 'Orientalist'. The grammar of Orientalism, he argues, corresponds to a system of ideas that structures power in such a fashion as to dominate and appropriate the Orient as 'the Other'.

Orientalism, suggests Said, is a colonialist project which totalises its object. It involves the West in viewing the Orient as its passive adjunct, subject to its universalising grand narrative. Said maintains that it is the historicism implicit in this narrative that originally served the West to justify in its 'accumulation of territories and population, the control of economies, the incorporation and homogenisation of histories' (1978, p. 13). He rejects the contention, however, that Orientalism was largely a historical phenomenon, no longer relevant to the way the West represents non-Western cultures. Rather, he insists that contemporary Western discourses about other cultures continue to be based on Orientalist assumptions; it is just that the 'dominant' phase of colonialism has now shifted to a 'hegemonic' phase through which attempts are still made by the West to perceive and control its Others.

In so far as it has been the dominant European ideas that have informed Australia's discursive traditions, Said's arguments apply equally to Australia's representations of Asia. There is much about these representations that can aptly be called Orientalist, particularly those that were current before World War II. Before the war, most Australians saw the world in terms of a colonial discourse inherited from Britain at the height of its power. Australia was aptly described by Humphrey McQueen (1970) as a 'New Britannia'. And as Alison Broinowski (1992, p. 15) has pointed out:

> Because European history remained a much more important component of their national identity than their Asian geography had ever been, many Australians accepted not only that China was a remote place, but that all of Asia was more distant and exotic than Europe.

Few Australians travelled to Asia, and most of those who did were either traders or missionaries, seeking to expand the Western sphere of influence in the region. Popular images of Asia homogenised the entire continent and evaluated it negatively. Australian perceptions of Asia thus emerged out of a complex dialectic between an *experienced* Other and an *imagined* Other. Myths about the allegedly inevitable differences among the races contributed to this dialectic. Race became a key explanatory factor not only in academic anthropology, but more importantly in the popular imagination of Australians.

Both religion and science contributed to the making of myths that implied a causal link between physical appearance and moral character. Christianity was a prism through which much knowledge about Asia was refracted, and as a result literal biblical explanations provided the bases for making particular judgements about Asians. Science, on the other hand, legitimated the idea of a biological hierarchy of races in which all 'Asiatics' were lumped into the same inferior category. Social Darwinism lent support to racist representations through the use of such concepts as 'natural selection' and 'competition for the survival of the fittest'. Religion and science also served effectively to silence the voices not only of the colonised indigenous people but also of the dissenters. Orientalism operated through a set of assumptions that served to define the 'normal' in the characteristics of people—their beliefs, practices and institutions. It also served to sustain the belief that non-European people needed to be tamed or civilised, made 'normal'. Most non-European customs which could not be accommodated within the scope of the 'normal' were dismissed as either primitive or exotic.

Broinowski (1992) has traced the history of Australian ideas about Asia as they have been expressed in the popular arts. Before World War II, she suggests, Asians were seldom presented as individuals. In popular films, for example, any Asian 'native' could be substituted for any other. Their clothing, habits, morals and speech were often interchangeable, suggestive of an imaginary place that was recognisable only as being *not* Australia. Asian social geography was presented either with a sense of rural tranquillity or with urban chaos—bustling, dirty and confusing. In images not dissimilar to those found in Kipling, 'natives' were presented as easy-going and half-witted, in need of control and care (see Broinowski 1992, pp. 13–15). In a sense, also, Australians viewed Asia as the Other against which their own identity was defined. For, given Australia's geographical presence in the region and its inevitable contacts with Asian countries through trade and warfare, it was necessary for Australians to develop a range of imagery, beliefs and evaluations about the Asian Other in order to understand themselves and in order to formulate their strategies of interaction.

It was not only the *imagined* Other, beyond its shores, that served to define Australia's representations of Asia, but also its *experiences* of Asian immigrants. Despite the direct contact between the Europeans and the Chinese on the goldfields of Victoria and New South Wales in the nineteenth century, most Australians retained a very narrow colonial racist perception of Asians that had been a part of their myths about the Other. When the Chinese were first encountered, the initial reaction of most Australians was that of curiosity and amusement at their 'uncouth and grotesque appearance—their peculiar features, and cunning and dexterity' (Yarwood & Knowling 1982, p. 169). Few white people doubted their superiority as a 'race' to the Chinese and other non-white people. But the extreme competition for gold ignited the latent feelings of hostility towards the Chinese. So much so that governments in all states instituted and administered a range of anti-Chinese laws with severity.

Not only did these laws prove to be the foundations upon which the White Australia policy was later to be based, but they also served to define the founding principles of the Commonwealth of Australia in 1901. The White Australia policy institutionalised racism in the practice of immigration control, and created a sense of an Australia as 'an imagined community' (Anderson 1983) that was informed by myths of biological and cultural superiority of the European race. In this sense, the ideology of racism was central to the development of Australian nationalism, which was based on the assumption that only white people could be acceptable members of the Australian 'nation' because it was only they who had the inclination and capacity for self-government by constitutional means. As Miles (1989, p. 93) has argued, 'the demand to keep out "coloured inferior races" was dialectically linked with an emerging sense of an imagined community of Australians, a collectivity that signified "whiteness" as a sign of superiority and of inclusion'.

Thus, the White Australia policy depended on the presumed 'validity and morality of the principle of nationalism' (p. 91). Racial unity was considered essential to national unity. Indeed, it was not until 1961 that 'Australia for the White Man' was finally removed as the masthead of the popular magazine, the *Bulletin*. Both militarily and culturally, it was thought necessary to protect Australia's white character, particularly from the Asians who were regarded as 'dangerous competitors'.

This perception of threat has been a consistent theme in Australian representations of Asia. Before World War II, it was the Chinese. But, during and after the war, it was the Japanese who were inserted into a specific position to construct the more generalised perception of Asianness. The Japanese were constructed as 'devilish', removed from humanity, lacking in standards of decent civilised conduct. The *Bulletin* regularly used terms like 'bloody coolies', 'apes', 'stinking yellow bastards' and 'slant-eyed golliwogs' to refer to the Japanese, who were capable only of 'gabbled conversation' and who could only be distinguished by their 'ugly shortness'. And while this abuse was certainly a part of the war propaganda, it also tapped into the deep-seated xenophobia that had existed in Australia for more than a century. For most Australians, the threat of a Japanese invasion of Darwin simply confirmed their long-held nightmare of the Asian hordes, 'the yellow peril', against which Australia had to defend itself. But the war also shattered the myth of the inevitable European military superiority. Begrudgingly, the Japanese were acknowledged as 'determined and able' fighters. But more significantly, the war also revealed to most Australians how close Australia was to Asia, and that it could no longer rely on British support.

Since World War II, the Australian representations of Asia have become ever more complex, ambiguous and contradictory, as more Australians travel to Asian countries, trade with them, and learn Asian languages. The economic context has also changed, with Japan emerging as an economic giant and with the Australian economy becoming inextricably tied to the region. The Vietnam War has also further dented the confidence Australians once had in the Western invincibility. Those constructed as the 'inferior' have shown themselves to be surprisingly enterprising. So, does this mean that Orientalism can no longer accurately describe Australian representations of Asia?

To address this issue adequately, we need to look more carefully at the theoretical structure of Said's argument, and the problems associated with the thesis of Orientalism. Perhaps the most significant of these problems is the untenable dualism Said's work assumes between the 'West' and the 'East'. Said's point that the Orientalist discourse assumes an homogenised Orient can be directed equally against his own construction of the 'West'. What has been referred to as the 'West' has never been a homogenised entity, except in a dialectical sense as that which is not the 'East'. European perceptions of the Orient have, furthermore, never been as uniform as Said's thesis might suggest. Within Australia, as Walker and Ingleson (1989) point out, there have always been conflicting views about how it should relate to its neighbours. As early as 1888, for example, a Cardinal Moran argued that Asian languages should be taught in Australian schools in order to secure the trade opportunities that existed in the region. And while he was widely dismissed and demonised as 'Chow's friend', his views did enjoy some popular support (Walker & Ingleson 1989, p. 289).

Homi Bhabha (1994c) has argued that a problem of ambivalence between universalism and particularism lies at the heart of the Orientalist project. He has suggested that at the centre of Orientalism there is not a single homogenising project but a polarity of positions—of the exercise of imperial power as well as of fantasy and fear of the Other. According to Bhabha, Orientalism cannot be regarded as a static monolithic hegemonic project, but a discourse that is constituted *ambivalently*. It does not have a single originating intention; rather, it is marked by a profound ambivalence towards 'that "Otherness", which is at once an object of desire and derision' (Bhabha 1983, p. 19). And as Young (1990, p. 142) argues, this equivocation suggests that colonial discourse is founded on anxiety, and that power is always subject to the effects of new cultural economies. Orientalist discourses are thus constantly changing as people encounter a new dialectic between power and powerlessness—new patterns of resistances and social formations.

This broader, and a more dynamic, conception of Orientalism may be used to describe how Australians have in recent years struggled to understand the new regional formations within which they are now located. An ambivalence lies at the heart of this struggle. Australians are now keenly aware of their location in the Asia-Pacific region, but find it difficult to discard the earlier racist images of Asia. They recognise Asia as inextricably linked to their critical and political objectives, but are unable to secure sufficient distance from the racial stereotyping that involved viewing Asians as a homogenised mass who posed a constant threat to Australia's national identity and to its economic well-being. Orientalism is remarkably resilient, and, in its more subtle forms, it can still be found, even in those initiatives of reorientation that are designed to forge a new relationship with Asia, in response to the changing global economic circumstances that Australia now faces.

Over the past two decades there have been major changes in the way global economic markets operate. No longer is Australia able to build walls to protect itself from the challenges of the outside world. As Castles (1992, p. 47) points out, there have been major shifts in capital accumulation strategies both at the international and local levels. These include:

> the decline in manufacturing employment in 'old' industrial areas, the rise of the newly industrialised countries, the reorganisation of production and distribution within transnational corporations, more emphasis on control and communication using new technologies, the increased role of globally mobile finance capital, and the enhanced role of 'global' cities as centres of corporate control, finance, marketing and design.

Within Australia, these changes have led to an 'internationalisation' of the Australian economy, and to a restructuring of its labour market and other domestic institutions, such as education and training.

At the same time, the structural problems associated with US and European economies have led to a decline in investment in Australia from those countries, and the gaps created have resulted in Australia becoming increasingly dependent on Japan and newly industrialising Asian countries. The end to the White Australia policy is thus explicable not only in terms of ideological changes but also of shifts in Australia's economic interests. Such shifts have been comprehensively mapped out in the Garnaut Report (1989). Interestingly, however, the language in which Garnaut couched Australia's relationship with North-East Asia is that of opportunities rather than economic interests and survival. He argued that this 'is a time when Australians have a chance to grasp the prosperity, self-confidence and independence in an interdependent world' (p. 1). The use of this language suggests that Garnaut is mindful of the ideological suspicions of Asia which continue to persist in Australia, and which need to be reoriented. Indeed, it is this recognition that leads him to stress the importance of 'knowing Asia' and of changing 'each other's minds'.

Garnaut argues that the whole world has had to come to terms with the facts of sustained and rapid, internationally oriented economic growth in North-East Asia. Australia, he suggests, is well located to take advantage of the economic dynamism in the region, not only because of its immediate neighbourhood but also because 'the North-east economies are more closely complementary to Australia in their resource endowments and in the commodity composition of their trade than any other economies on earth' (1989, p. 2). He contends further that this 'complementarity extends beyond trade in goods and services to the people and capital required for Australian development'. In this way, Garnaut acknowledges the close link that exists between Australia's economic interests in the region and its ability to secure harmonious ethnic relations within Australia. He argues that outbursts of racism—such as anti-Asian graffiti, physical violence, name-calling, as well as the media hysteria about so-called Asian crime gangs (as reported in HREOC 1991)—not only cause considerable pain to Asian immigrants: they also do considerable damage to the perceptions Asian countries have of Australia (p. 134).

Garnaut insists that Asian migration 'has a pivotal role to play in helping Australia to make maximum use of economic opportunities in Northest Asia' (1989, p. 31). His forecast is that through the 1990s Hong Kong, the People's Republic of China and Taiwan are likely to become major potential sources of young well-educated migrants whose skills in their own languages and cultures should be used deliberately and extensively in the promotion of trade opportunities, as well as in 'teacher training and retraining and education more broadly' (p. 33). Garnaut also recognises an increasing trend towards the 'internationalisation' of labour, resulting in greater movement and intermingling of people across national boundaries which are gradually losing their significance. Migrants to Australia are now more likely to retain their ties with their countries of origin and continue to conduct business across borders. This is especially true of the skilled professional migrants from Malaysia, Singapore and Hong Kong. These migrants are normally more confident in being able to negotiate two cultures at once. They are unwilling to remain in the margins and they therefore assert a new politics of representation which has more to do with an awareness of their experience as a *diasporic* experience. Stuart Hall (1992, p. 258) has noted that migrant experience is characterised by 'a process of unsettling, recombination, hybridization and the "cut-and-mix"' which takes its cue not only from local politics but also from the global movement of post-colonial ideas and aspirations.

It is within this wider context that the issues of regional and global politics and trade intersect with debates about Asian immigration and multiculturalism within Australia. Census figures indicate that in 1991 the number of Asian-born Australians was 687 850 or 4.3 per cent of the total population. Since the mid-1970s, the number of Asian immigrants has increased markedly, from 15 per cent of the total number of arrivals in 1976–77 to 34 per cent of the total intake by 1986–87, remaining around the same level today. Most of this increase has resulted from refugee settlement programs, but there has also been an increase in the migrant intake of well-educated professionals and business people. These changes in migration patterns have made the policy of multiculturalism a little more fragile than it already was. And while racially based concerns about Australia's immigration policies, such as those expressed by Blainey in 1984, have failed to capture the public imagination, it is still not inaccurate to say that the Australian community remains divided in its commitment to both a non-racial immigration policy and multiculturalism (Ip et al. 1992).

Indeed, Australians of Asian backgrounds continue to be the object of a considerable amount of overt and covert racism. The *Report of the National Inquiry into Racist Violence in Australia* (HREOC 1991, p. 140) noted that attacks on Asian-Australians were not uncommon, and that second- and third-generation Australians of Asian background were just as likely to face racism, because of the difference in their physical appearance. Furthermore, many Asians were reluctant to make official complaints or to publicise incidences of racism for the fear of greater levels of resentment. The current labour force statistics also show a pattern of discrimination against Asian-Australians. For example, the Moss Report (1993, p. 164) used research by the Bureau of Immigration and Population Research to suggest that the employment rate among the Asian-Australians was well below the national average, with the unemployment rate of the Vietnamese-born at 31.1 per cent— well above the national rate of 10.7 per cent. Furthermore, the Moss Report (p. 166) found that the key concerns for many employed Asian-Australians have been workplace racial harassment, the lack of promotion opportunities, and the lack of recognition of overseas qualifications and experience in Australia. A study by Niland and Champion (1990) has shown that even the institution of equal employment opportunity policies in New South Wales has not greatly benefited Asian-Australians. This suggests that racism may in fact be more widespread and entrenched in Australian society than is often thought.

The statistical measures, of course, cannot fully describe the scope of racism faced by Asian-Australians. Nor can they reveal its complexity and explain its origins. For racism does not express itself only in the overt practices of exclusion, marginalisation and discrimination, but also in the covert taken-for-granted generalisations about particular minorities and in the discursive constructions of the Other. It is in the media that these constructions are most evident. The Moss Report (1993, p. 163) suggested that:

the reporting of Asian-Australian criminal activities, and the use of unnecessary ethnic identifiers in media and police reports is a continuing problem. Asian offenders are depicted by local police and newspapers in the most colourful terms, using monolithic phrases and headlines such as 'Terror as Asian Gangs Rule the Streets' (*Sun-Herald*, 30 May 1993), 'CIB target Asian rackets' (*Perth Sunday Times*, 21 February 1993), or 'Asian gang preys on Japanese' (*Courier Mail*, Brisbane, 16 November 1991). With crimes committed by Anglo-Australians, the ethnicity of the offenders is rarely specified in headlines.

Media representations of Asia thus continue to be located in an Orientalist discourse that portrays Asians as morally unsound and as a major threat to harmonious social relations.

To suggest the persistence of Orientalism is not to imply, however, that the Australian discourses about Asia and Asians have remained constant. Recent theoretical works on racism have demonstrated that it does not have an essential form: it is continually changing, being challenged, interrupted and reconstructed in the discursive practices in which people engage. As Hall (1986, p. 23) has pointed out, while there are no doubt some general features to racism, what is more 'significant are the ways in which these general features are modified, and are transformed by the historical specificity of the contexts in which they become active'. Racist meaning is thus grounded in the everyday activities in which people engage, think about their options, explain their predicaments, and formulate a sense of being in the world. Their views about the Other are often disjointed, episodic, fragmentary and contradictory, and always subject to revision in light of new historical conditions.

Australians thus confront a range of contradictory messages about Asia and Asians which they have to assimilate and reconcile within the framework of the generalised set of ideas they already possess. They are constantly subjected to a rhetoric of 'new realities', but the old myths and generalisations have not entirely disappeared. The traditional Orientalist practices of representation are being challenged but in ways that are disjointed and equivocal, and often confused. The current government rhetoric suggests that major attitudinal changes are needed for Australia to become integrated into Asia. Increasing trade, immigration and the provision of Australian education for Asian students have led to calls for a reorientation of Australian educational and cultural directions, placing more stress on Asia, with an emphasis on Asian studies and languages. The notion of 'Asia literacy' has emerged as a major signifier for this reorientation. Cultural and educational organisations have been asked to provide leadership in promoting the change necessary for Australia's economic survival. In what follows, however, I argue that the initiatives designed to make Australians more 'Asia-literate' have not entirely been able to escape some of the Orientalist assumptions they seek to challenge. Indeed, there have emerged new forms of racism expressed through discourses that are predicated on an ambivalence towards Asia as an object that poses a constant threat to Australia.

Such an ambivalence is clearly evident in recent representations of Malaysia in the Australian media. Surendrini Perera (1993) has used the term 'representation wars' to refer to the issues of textuality and the crisis of meaning, and of national and popular subjectivities, surrounding the dispute over a television series, 'Embassy', presented by the Australian Broadcasting Corporation (ABC). 'Embassy' was created as a result of repeated criticisms that the ABC did not do enough to 'educate' Australians about Asian countries. It was argued throughout the 1980s that the ABC had failed to recognise important transformations in Australian society, both in terms of the ethnically diverse composition of the Australian population and in terms of Australia's economic shift towards Asia. In 1990, the ABC attempted to rectify this situation by producing 'Embassy', which sought to explore Australia's role in the Asia-Pacific region and the diplomatic impediments to its enmeshment. The series was set in a fictious South-East Asian country and adopted the conventions of the 'espionage thriller' genre. Given this genre, it was not surprising that the series evoked conflicting responses. As Bennett (1991, p. 184) has suggested, 'the sensationalism of treatment, built around a revolutionary situation, derived in part from the requirements of the genre, but also partly from the "crisis coverage" methods of presenting news about Asia and elsewhere'.

To the Malaysians, it was clear that the fictitious country in the series referred to them. They were understandably angry about the portrayal of Asians which served only to reproduce many of the residual Orientalist themes of mysterious, fanatical and untrustworthy Asiatics. Perera (1993, p. 22) has argued that:

> In a curious way, *Embassy* participates in this verbal avoidance of difference although its intertexts also evidently include the older, more imperially assured narratives of Kipling, Conrad and Maugham. In its anxiety at once to invite and evade the spectre of referentiality, the series conjures an Orient simultaneously anonymous and exhaustive, contemporary and yet effectively unchanged in its implied relations of domination, where questions of racism,

imperialism and power are both always present and almost always unasked.

'Embassy' is thus illustrative of a cultural economy which points to the anxiety many Australians have about forging a new relationship with Asia. The series pointedly depicts Malaysia as a nation that is dictatorial and corrupt, on the one hand, and yet, on the other hand, it is a country that Australia cannot afford to offend. Perera (1993, p. 16) asks: 'what is involved in the representation of another culture, when the interactions between the cultures concerned has been structured at every level by colonial and imperialist histories?'

In order to understand the complexities of contemporary Australia–Asia relations, we need to historicise Australia's unequal and uneasy relationship with its neighbours. In the past, this was a relationship predicated at once on an assumption of racial superiority and an anxiety about Australia's location in the Asia-Pacific region. Asia was represented as posing a major threat to Australia's economic security. As Perera (1993) argues, the more contemporary cultural economies are no less inscribed by this ambivalence. The heritage of anxiety continues to play an important role in the way Australians see Asia. The economic panic that swept the Australian financial media late in 1993 over Prime Minister Keating's reference to his Malaysian counterpart as 'recalcitrant' suggests that Australia lacks confidence in its regional relationships. Over the issue, while the popular media rejoiced a possible end to what it had perceived as Australia's 'kowtowing' and 'grovelling' to Asia, the financial press feared the 'downgrading' of its relationship with Malaysia and the loss of lucrative contracts. It was argued that with more than 50 per cent of Australian exports now destined to Asian countries, Australia had no option but to negotiate a new understanding of the region, even if it meant a degree of appeasement. With 'the Malaysian problem' resolved for the time being, the challenge remains, however, to develop an understanding of Asia without a reliance on the traditional racist categories.

The difficulties of such a challenge were evident in the way Australians responded to a proposal in 1990 to establish a technology research park, a Multi-function Polis, as a joint venture between Japan and Australia. Whatever the technical merits of such a proposal, what is worth noting here is the nature of the public debate surrounding the proposal, which for months continued to be surrounded by confusion, bickering, ignorance and fear. There were some legitimate environmental and economic concerns about the proposal, but it turned out to be the residual fears of a Japanese take-over of Australia that formed the basis of most of the public understanding of the proposal. Many of the arguments against the proposal were couched in highly racialised terms, with the opponents fearing the creation of a racial 'enclave' (see McCormack 1991). There was a suspicion that the original conception of the Multi-function Polis was designed to secure greater Japanese control of Australian real estate and resources. Recalled were the signs and symbols of the Japanese militarism in the region during World War II.

Such signs and symbols were most evident in the Australian media during the federal election held in March 1990. Political advertisements prepared by some of those opposed to the concept of the Multi-function Polis (see Melbourne *Herald*, 10 March 1990) utilised the imagery of the war-time Japanese flag to suggest that the danger that Japan now posed to Australia's security was similar to that which existed during World War II. Such advertisements served to illustrate how racialised images were used to express an anti-Japanese sentiment. For almost six months in 1990, the Multi-function Polis debate enabled many Australians to express their sense of frustration over the cultural changes they felt they had to endure. The comments made on talkback radio and tabloid newspapers revealed a continuity between old discredited Social Darwinist views and their more recent variants. Media reports on Asian investment, and on the Multi-function Polis, showed a clear tendency to present the Japanese in a stereotypical way, often in images that stemmed from the wartime propaganda. As McCormack (1991, p. 58) has observed, 'the buck-toothed, grinning, slightly idiotic but malevolent looking Japanese' are now in business suits, but are nevertheless 'omnipotent creatures with limitless wealth, who look on Australians with expressions of benign contempt'.

New forms of racism and images of Asians trade on their supposed 'reasonableness'. As Billig (1988) has pointed out, while the proponents of new racism are broadly committed to the Enlightenment project of an 'unprejudiced' society, they are nevertheless able to accommodate within their world view ideological beliefs that are based on racist assumptions. He has suggested that it is necessary to understand modern racist discourse in its rhetorical context, in which opposition to racism is often stated in a preliminary clause that is then followed by an expression of an overtly racist view. This rhetorical device is most evident in such phrases as 'I am not prejudiced but . . .', 'I have nothing against the Japanese but . . .' and 'some of my best friends are Asians but . . .'. A recent survey of Australian attitudes to Asians (Ip et al. 1992) has revealed precisely this tendency, with many Australians acknowledging the importance of regional realities but continuing to express their fear and derision of Asians in a fairly predictable fashion.

Nor are the attempts to construct new knowledge about Asia and Asians entirely free of this ambivalence. These attempts are predicated on the view that a fundamental shift in Australian perceptions of Asia is a matter of economic imperatives; and that insensitivities, arrogance and ignorance are a handicap in securing new contracts. The key to unlocking the door to Asian markets is assumed to be education. But what kind of education? Frost (1992) has argued that it is a particular kind of knowledge about Asia that has often been advocated in recent policy declarations in Australia. While such declarations no longer view Asia as a homogeneous mass, they nevertheless construct Asian cultures within an essentialist framework based on Australian economic interests. These constructions often assume simplistic notions of the workings of Asian societies, focusing more on newly industrialising countries rather than the economically poorer countries. As Frost (1992, p. 2) suggests, 'Asia literacy therefore includes proposals for educating our schoolchildren about the new realities of Asia where supposedly outdated notions of peasants, poverty and manual labourers are replaced by a new essentialist type: the new rich.'

According to Frost (1992), a crude form of culturalism appears to have emerged in Australian policy discourses about Asia which is economically driven, and which continues to regard Asian cultures as somehow mysterious. It is assumed that the way Asians engage in commerce is somehow culturally different, and that Australians need to develop a better understanding of Asian cultures in order to trade with them successfully. Educational programs are thus assumed to have an important role to play. However, this mode of thinking implies that the cultural differences between Australian and Asian cultures are somehow fixed. There is thus an attempt to once again reify 'Asian' values, as if they represented an uncontested terrain—no longer alien and dangerous but nonetheless mysterious and strange, needing to be comprehended for successful economic engagement.

A lack of cultural understanding of Asian cultures, it is often suggested, has jeopardised Australia's economic potential. But this assertion presupposes that the purposes of 'Asia literacy' are largely instrumental. It implies a cultural relativism that understates the massive cultural changes taking place both in Asia and in Australia, often as a result of unprecedented levels of cultural contact. It also suggests that, while Australia needs to develop a cultural sensibility, it cannot, or should not, engage in critical discourses about human rights abuses and the like. The reluctance of the Australian government to criticise the Indonesian human rights record in East Timor has recently been criticised by the Secretary-General of Amnesty International (*Austra-*

lian, 10 October 1994). It has been pointed out that Australia has failed to support the numerous oppositional voices that exist in Indonesia, and that Australia has placed its economic interests ahead of its more fundamental moral responsibilities. It seems that the discourse of 'Asia literacy' invites only a sanitised and safe understanding of Asia, which assumes a uniformity of political views within Asian societies, in a way that is not so very different from the traditional Orientalist texts. Such an understanding of Asia ignores the issues of power and politics within those societies, as well as in Australia where, with the increasing levels of Asian migration, they have become issues of major importance to the construction of Australian identity.

McQueen (1993) has raised these issues in relation to the curatorial practices surrounding the highly successful Asia-Pacific Triennial of Contemporary Art held at the Queensland Art Gallery in 1993. The significance of the Triennial lay in the fact that it was promoted as a major response to the calls for cultural organisations to play their part in promoting intercultural understanding, and in redefining Australia–Asia relations. And in so far as the Triennial and other similar artistic initiatives have promoted cultural exchange and have sought to present images of contemporary Asia, they are clearly welcome. But the questions that McQueen asks are: Which Asia is being represented in these arts exhibitions, and how do they contribute in a fundamental re-evaluation of the complex politics of Australia–Asia relations? How do they serve to disturb the axis of which Judith Wright speaks in the quotation heading this chapter?

In my view, while the show-and-tell approach to the promotion of Asian arts might help to create new markets for elite arts in both Asia and Australia, it does little to promote a critical understanding of the Orientalist assumptions that still persist in the popular Australian representations of Asia. For it is the same connoisseurs, trained in the universalising language of Western aesthetics, who still make the decisions about which of the arts from Asia are worth showing, often using criteria that are external to the aesthetic traditions in which Asian arts are embedded. As McQueen (1993) observes, the works selected for the Queensland Triennial were the safe arts which did little to disturb the cultural gaps that exist between Australia and Asia. He asks rhetorically: 'surely Indonesian women have something to say which Australians will need to learn if our relations are to prosper?' (p. 2). As it was, it was only a particular slice of Indonesian life that was presented in the exhibition, which sought to portray itself as 'conflict free', masking the authoritarianism of the Suharto regime, for example. Similarly, the debates concerning the history of Australian racism were also pushed into the background, hidden from the gaze of Asian critics. The works by Asian-Australian artists, who could have been expected to examine the contradictions of their lives in Australia, were marked by their total absence.

The Asia-Pacific Triennial is of course illustrative of the way in which arts and education have become cultural commodities that are bought and sold in commercial exchange, and are no longer viewed as practices capable of examining the contradictions of cultural difference. These practices of economic exchange of cultural goods do not disturb the Orientalist axis. It is therefore possible to suggest that Orientalism represents an axis that is protected jealously by the entrenched structures of Anglo-Australian power. Those who hold this power seem reluctant to recognise the multicultural nature of Australia, except in a very symbolic manner. Their culturalist ideologies (see Rizvi & Crowley 1993) lead them to deny multiculturalism of its transformative possibilities, for while they recognise cultural difference and change they fail to problematise them.

Initiatives designed to promote cultural understanding about Asia are, I fear, unlikely to succeed in challenging residual expressions of racism in Australia unless 'Asia literacy' and multiculturalism are much more than learning about other cultures. In my view, these projects should be about problematising the cultural politics of Asia–Australia relations or, as Viviani (1990, p. 2) has suggested, about asking 'awkward questions about ourselves and others'. We need to acknowledge that the Orientalist history of Asia–Australia relations is not something that is remote but something that continues to inform our current attempts to negotiate new cultural relations. This observation is consistent with Homi Bhabha's view that ambivalence lies at the centre of the Orientalist project. It also helps us to explain how programs of anti-racism, in the form of multicultural education and workshops in intercultural communication (see Rizvi 1993), have not always resulted in the changes they promised, but have instead often been counter-productive because they have contained residual assumptions of racism that they have not questioned. A program of anti-racism that is serious about forging a more equal and productive relation with Asia must therefore take into account the ambivalence and contradictions that seem inherent in our representations of Asia. It must also theorise the anxieties and fears that many Australians have about the changes they witness daily to the racial order which they once took for granted. Australians have to recognise that their attempts to negotiate a new relationship with Asia are tied inextricably to the way they see themselves as a multicultural society.

Endnotes

1 Introduction: Multicultural or multi-racist Australia

1 Racialisation implies the use of social power by a dominant group to ascribe undesirable characteristics to other groups defined on the basis of physical or cultural criteria. The remarks on racism and racisms in this section echo contemporary international debates, which are summarised in detail in Chapter 2. Detailed discussion of theories and definitions of racism will therefore not be presented here.

2 The racisms of globalisation

1 For a discussion of definitions of ethnicity and the ethnic group, see Castles and Miller 1993, pp. 26–9.

2 It is important to remember that any attempt at classification is arbitrary, for the boundaries between categories could be drawn in various ways, while many racist practices fit into a number of the categories used. For more detail and sources see Castles (1993). The annual Country Reports on Human Rights Practices published by the US Department of State (US DoS 1992) are a valuable source of information on racist practices in every country except the USA!

3 Dialectics of domination: Racism and multiculturalism

1 I would like to thank Stephen Castles for detailed comments on drafts of the chapter; and Lars Goran Karlsson, Department of Sociology, University of Umea, Sweden, for his helpful comments.

2 This is a comprehensive analysis of the Swedish case of multiculturalism and its paradoxes, and raises some of the issues analysed in this chapter.

5 Mis/taken identity

1   Special thanks to Janie Conway and Vicki Crowley who provided ongoing support and encouragement during the writing of this chapter.

2   Where my mother's aboriginal family are from in south-western queensland, aboriginal people often refer to themselves as *murris*. Aboriginal people name themselves differently depending on what part of mainland australia they are from, for example, many people from new south wales often refer to themselves as *kooris*, in south australia they're *nungas*, *nyoongas* are from western australia, etc. The use of the word *aboriginal* is somewhat problematic in that it is a colonial and social construct that negates many peoples', particularly east coast peoples', experiences. In contrast, naming myself a murri enables me to acknowledge my indigenous australian heritage as much as my african, english and irish australian heritages.

   For the purposes of this chapter, I move between the use of the words *murri* and *aboriginal people*, in reference to myself as well as in reference to other aboriginal people when appropriate. In order to play down the importance placed on naming nationhood, national institutions and places, it is my preference to move away from capitalisation.

3   *Mabo and Others v. State of Queensland* provides the first determination by the australian high court of the rights of indigenous people to land at common law. The decision that was handed down on 3 June 1992 rejected the doctrine that this country was *terra nullius* (empty land) at the time of british settlement. Any murri group who can prove their continued relationship to land are entitled to reclaim it. To date, no compensation package has been offered to any murri group who were forcibly removed and dispossessed of their land. (See Richard H. Bartlett 1993.)

4   See Verity Burgman 1993; Jan Pettman 1992; Henry Reynolds 1989.

5   The fear of being swamped with asian immigrants created unease in australia, causing the government to resolve to keep australia white and european. The white australia policy existed for over seventy years and was officially scrapped in 1972.

6 Aboriginal Rural Education Program: A case study in anti-racist strategies

1   The word *Aboriginal* is used in this text because it reflects an ongoing relationship with the state and is included in the nomenclature of the program under discussion.

2   The nomenclature used in this chapter shifts between *Aboriginal* and *indigenous*. The term *Aboriginal* will be used in relation to the AREP program and *indigenous* used at other times. The term *indigenous* is seen to be more inclusive of the indigenous diaspora within and around the Australian geographic boundaries. *Non-indigenous* is also more inclusive and situates the non-indigenous Other as heterogeneous, in contrast to terms such as *black* and *white*.

3   Miles argues that scientific racism uses scientific legitimation of a biolog-

ical hierarchy. Scientific racism has been largely discredited but still appears in the understandings and 'commonsense' notions of difference.

4 Mayer (1992) outlined seven employment-related key competencies: collecting, analysing and organising information; communicating ideas and information; planning and organising activities; working with others and in teams; using mathematical ideas and techniques; solving problems; using technology.

5 The Centre for Australian Indigenous Cultural Studies was set up in 1994 as a UWS initiative, suggesting a renewed commitment to indigenous education. This marks a new phase where indigenous involvement in course development and research is institutionalised.

7 Liberal multiculturalism's 'NESB Women'

1 I wish to acknowledge Ian Bedford and Barbara Holloway for reading and commenting on this chapter.

2 See, for instance, the many volumes on the castes and tribes of India by colonial ethnologists such as Thurston (1909) and Crooke (1896).

3 The more fluid and processual approach argued by several of the contemporary social sciences and literary approaches is well exemplified in several collections: de Lepervanche and Bottomley (1988), Donald and Rattansi (1992); Bottomley (1992); Gates (1986); La Capra (1991).

4 But see the discussion of post-colonialism and the multicultural arts in Gertsakis 1994.

5 The scholarship on this aspect of British rule alone is voluminous. But see the collection of essays in Sanghari and Vaid 1989, especially the papers by Mani and Chakravarty.

6 See also the recent collection of essays entitled *After Colonialism* (Prakash 1995), which attempt to pursue questions of identity transformations.

7 In an earlier paper, I explore some of these dissatisfactions which arise from an uncritical mapping of poststructuralist theses on to the situation of post-colonial and immigrant women: see Ram 1993.

8 Signs of the time: Race, sex and media representations

1 This chapter is not concerned with Aboriginal populations, who are the subject of other chapters in this book, and anyway should not be subsumed to an NESB category. (See Goodall, H. et al. 1990.) Many of the examples used in this chapter were collected for the project 'Racism and the Media' at the University of Technology, Sydney. See Jakubowicz et al. 1994.

2 Astonishingly, the Australian mass media continued to beat the drum on anti-Asian migration well after it became apparent that it was neither a public issue nor an election issue. Two further well-documented incidents were: the diplomatic incident attendant on the screening of the ABC series 'Embassy' 1991–92 (Perera, S. 1993), and the use of file tape from the Salman Rushdie riots in the UK to background media coverage of demonstrations by Islamic Australians to build a mosque in Lakemba (Jakubowicz et al. 1994).

3   Or the general category 'black' in contrast to the general category 'white' as the case may be. It should be noted that in the *realpolitik* of migrant politics, categories such as 'Anglo' and 'NESB' are often appropriated rhetorical terms whose content is empty, or whose content is historically and situationally specific: that is, the terms refer to positions, not fixed categories of identity, and do not imply a general theory of domination in a society.
    It seems foolish to have to point this out, but Anglo is relevant only to the Australian situation. For all I know, non-Anglos, where dominant, may well proceed in much the same way. *Anglo* is used to mean Anglo-Australian in an Australian context.

4   See for example Liebes & Katz 1988 on different audience readings of 'Dallas'.

5   Although not the subject of this chapter, the preference for Afro blacks over Aboriginal characters should be noted. Although there had been an obvious shift preceding 1994, the period was marked by the inclusion of Afro blacks in ads and in dramatic shows, in response to a demand for a black presence. Until 1992, Afro black men in particular clearly had greater sexual and moral currency than Aboriginal populations (Goodall et al. 1990; Jakubowicz et al. 1994).

6   Aboriginal women *qua* Aboriginal women are barely represented at all (although Aboriginal men may be). Aboriginal women are therefore foreignised in their own country (as a tourist site); or merge into a natural 'empty' landscape.

7   Endogamy does not prevail in actual social practices, as class affiliations override.

8   Class is not the subject of this paper. However, it should be noted that working-class Anglo men are often feminised in relation to middle-class Anglo men in much the same way. They are not, however, sexualised in the same way as some groups (Afro-American, Southern European) of foreign men.

9   Police racism: Experiences and reforms

1   Acknowledgment: This chapter draws on the findings of a research project 'Policing in a Multicultural Society', which is partly funded by the Sir Maurice Byers Fellowship of the NSW Police Service.

2   This section is based partly on a conference paper (Chan 1993).

3   See also Reiner (1992), and the review by Brogden et al. (1988) of the histories of policing in Britain.

Bibliography

ABMF (Australian Bicentennial Multicultural Foundation) 1990, *The Proceedings of the National Conference on Police Services in a Multicultural Australia, 28–31 August 1990*, Melbourne

Aboriginal Rural Education Program Review Document 1994, (unpublished). Prepared by the Macarthur Aboriginal Liaison Unit, University of Western Sydney Macarthur, Sydney

Ackland, R. and Williams, L. 1992, *Immigrants and the Australian Labour Market: The Experience of Three Recessions*, Bureau of Immigration Research, AGPS, Canberra

ACPEA (Australian Council on Population and Ethnic Affairs) 1982, *Multiculturalism for All Australians: Our Developing Nationhood*, AGPS, Canberra

ACTU (Australian Council of Trade Unions) 1995, *Combating Racism: Discrimination and Racism During 1994—How far in fact have we come*, ACTU, Melbourne

ADL (Anti-Defamation League) 1988, *Hate Groups in America*, B'nai B'rith, New York

AEAC (Australian Ethnic Affairs Council) 1977, *Australia as a Multicultural Society*, AGPS, Canberra

Alcorso, C. 1991, *Newly Arrived Non-English Speaking Background Women in the Workforce*, Centre for Multicultural Studies, University of Wollongong, for the Office of Multicultural Affairs, Wollongong

—— 1993, 'Economic Stocktake: Trends and Issues for Non-English Speaking Background Women Since 1982', *Australian Feminist Studies*, no. 18, Summer, pp. 49–66

Alderson, J. 1983, 'Community Policing', *The Future of Policing*, ed. T. Bennett, Institute of Criminology, University of Cambridge, Cambridge

ALRC (Australian Law Reform Commission) 1992, *Multiculturalism and the Law*, Report no. 57, Commonwealth of Australia

Alund, A. and Schierup, C.-U. 1991, *Paradoxes of Multiculturalism*, Avebury, Aldershot

Anderson, B. 1983, *Imagined Communities*, Verso, London

Andric, I. 1994, *The Bridge Over the Drina*, Havill, London

Anthias, F. and Yuval-Davis, N. 1983, 'Contextualising Feminism: Gender, Ethnic and Class Divisions', *Feminist Review*, no. 15, pp. 62–75

Arrow, K. 1972, 'Models of Job Discrimination', *Racial Discrimination in Economic Life*, ed. A. H. Pascal, Heath-Lexington Books, Lexington, Mass.

Attwood, B. and Arnold, J. eds 1992, *Power, Knowledge and Aborigines, special edition of Journal of Australian Studies*, La Trobe University Press, Bundoora, Vic.

Australia. Parliamentary Joint Standing Committee on Migration 1994, *Australians All: Enhancing Australian Citizenship*, AGPS, Canberra

Australia. Royal Commission into Aboriginal Deaths in Custody 1991, *National Report*, by Commissioner Elliott Johnston, AGPS, Canberra

Australian Bureau of Statistics 1991 Census of Population and Housing 1993, Commonwealth of Australia, Canberra

Awasthi, S. P. and Chandra, A. 1993, 'Migration from India to Australia', paper to the Conference on Asia-Pacific Migration Affecting Australia, Darwin, 14–17 September

Baker, M. and Wooden, M. 1992, *Immigrant Workers in the Communication Industry*, Bureau of Immigration Research, AGPS, Canberra

Balibar, E. 1991a, 'Is There a "Neo-racism?"', *Race, Nation, Class: Ambiguous Identities*, eds E. Balibar & I. Wallerstein, Verso, London

—— 1991b, 'Racism and Nationalism', *Race, Nation, Class: Ambiguous Identities*, eds E. Balibar & I. Wallerstein, Verso, London

—— 1991c, 'Class Racism', *Race, Nation, Class: Ambiguous Identities*, eds E. Balibar & I. Wallerstein, Verso, London

Ball, W. and Solomos, J. eds 1990, *Race and Local Politics,* Macmillan, London

Barker, M. 1981, *The New Racism*, Junction Books, London

Barrett, M. 1980, *Women's Oppression Today*, Verso, London

Bartlett, R. H. 1993, *The Mabo Decision*, Butterworths, Sydney

Bayley, D. H. 1989, 'Community Policing in Australia: An Appraisal', *Australian Policing: Contemporary Issues*, eds D. Chappell & P. Wilson, Butterworths, Sydney

Bayley, D. H. and Mendelsohn, H. 1969, *Minorities and the Police: Confrontation in America*, The Free Press, New York

Becker, G. 1957, *The Economics of Discrimination*, University of Chicago Press, Chicago

Bedford, I. 1985, 'Stalin on Linguistics', *Canberra Anthropology*, Special Volume on Minorities and the State, vol. 8, no. 1–2, pp. 58–86

Bell, D. 1992a, *Faces at the Bottom of the Well: The Permanence of Racism*, Basic Books, New York

Bell, P. 1992b, *Multicultural Australia in the Media*, Report to the Office of Multicultural Affairs, Canberra

Bennett, B. 1991, *An Australian Compass: Essays on Place and Directions in Australian Literature*, Fremantle Arts Centre Press, Perth

Bennett, S. 1989, *Aborigines and Political Power*, Allen & Unwin, Sydney

Bennie, A. 1994, 'Poetry's Redneck Rebel', *Sydney Morning Herald: Spectrum* 10 September 1994

Berry, G.L. and Mitchell-Kernan, C. 1982, *Television and the Socialisation of the Minority Group Child*, Academic Press, San Diego

Bhabha, H. K. 1983, 'The Other Question', *Screen*, vol. 24, no. 6, pp. 18–35

—— 1994a, 'The Commitment to Theory', *The Location of Culture*, Routledge, London and New York

—— 1994b, 'Signs Taken for Wonders', *The Location of Culture*, Routledge, London and New York

—— 1994c, *The Location of Culture*, Routledge, London and New York

Billig, M. 1988, 'Prejudice and Tolerance', *Ideological Dilemmas: A Social Psychology of Everyday Thinking*, eds M. Billig, S. Condor, D. Edwards, M. Gane, D. Middleton & A. Radley, Sage, London

Bird, G. 1992, 'The Times They are a "Changing": Policing Multicultural Australia', *Policing Australia: Old Issues, New Perspectives*, eds P. Moir & H. Eijkman, Macmillan, South Melbourne

Blainey, G. 1984, *All For Australia*, Methuen Haynes, Sydney

Bolaria, B. S. and Li, P. eds 1988, *Racial Oppression in Canada*, 2nd edn, Garamond Press, Toronto

Borowski, A. 1992, 'Business Migration to Australia', paper to Conference on Immigration and Refugee Policy: The Australian and Canadian Experiences, York University, Toronto, Canada, 2–5 May, pp. 1–11

Bottomley, G. 1984, 'Women on the Move: Migration and Feminism', *Ethnicity, Class and Gender in Australia*, eds G. Bottomley & M. de Lepervanche, George Allen & Unwin, Sydney

—— 1992, *From Another Place*, Cambridge University Press, Cambridge

Bottomley, G. and de Lepervanche, M. eds 1984, *Ethnicity, Class and Gender in Australia*, George Allen & Unwin, Sydney

Bottomley, G., de Lepervanche, M. and Martin, J. eds 1991, *Intersexions: Gender/Class/Culture/Ethnicity*, Allen & Unwin, Sydney

Bourdieu, P. 1984, *Distinctions: A Social Critique of the Judgement of Taste*, Routledge & Kegan Paul, London

—— 1991, *Language and Symbolic Power*, Harvard University Press, Cambridge, Mass.

Brah, A. 1991, 'Difference, Diversity, Differentiation', *'Race', Culture and Difference*, eds J. Donald & A. Rattansi, Sage, London, Newbury Park and New Delhi

Bridges, L. 1994, 'Tory Education: Exclusion and the Black Child', *Race and Class*, vol. 36, no. 1, pp. 33–48

Brockie, J. 1993, 'Police and Minority Groups', paper to the Royal Institute of Public Administration National Conference 'Keeping the Peace: Police Accountability and Oversight', 20–21 May, Sydney

Brogden, M., Jefferson, T. and Walklate, S. 1988, *Introducing Policework*, Unwin Hyman, London

Broinowski, A. 1992, *The Yellow Lady: Australian Impressions of Asia*, Oxford University Press, Melbourne

Brubaker, W.R. 1990, 'Citizenship and Nationhood in France and Germany', PhD thesis, Columbia University, New York

—— 1992, 'Citizenship Struggles in Soviet Successor States', *International*

Migration Review, Special Issue on the New Europe and International Migration, vol. 26, no. 2, pp. 269–91

Bureau of Immigration Research 1993, *Immigration Update, June Quarter*, AGPS, Canberra

Burgman, V. 1993, *Power and Protest: Movements for Change in Australian Society*, Allen & Unwin, Sydney

Burton, C. 1988, *Gender Bias in Job Evaluation*, AGPS, Canberra

Cain, M. 1973, *Society and the Policeman's Role*, Routledge & Kegan Paul, London

Carmichael, L. 1992, *Australian Vocational Certificate Training System, Employment and Skills Formation Council*, National Board of Employment and Training, AGPS, Canberra

Castles, S. 1992, 'The "New" Migration and Australian Immigration Policy', *Asians in Australia: The Dynamics of Migration and Settlement*, eds C. Inglis, S. Gunasekran, G. Sullivan & Chung-Tong Wu, Institute of Southeast Asian Studies, Singapore

—— 1993, *Racism: A Global Analysis*, Centre for Multicultural Studies, University of Wollongong, Occasional Paper no. 28

—— 1994, 'Democracy and Multicultural Citizenship: Australian Debates and their Relevance for Western Europe', *From Aliens to Citizens*, ed. R. Baubock, Avebury, Aldershot

Castles, S. and Kalantzis, M. eds 1994, *Access to Excellence: A Review of Issues Affecting Artists from Non-English Speaking Backgrounds*, Office of Multicultural Affairs, Canberra

Castles, S. and Miller, M.J. 1993, *The Age of Migration: International Population Movements in the Modern World*, Macmillan, London, and Guilford Books, New York

Castles, S., Alcorso, C., Rando, G. and Vasta, E. eds 1992a, *Australia's Italians: Culture and Community in a Changing Society*, Allen & Unwin, Sydney

Castles, S., Collins, J., Gibson, K., Tait, D. and Alcorso, C. 1991, *The Global Milkbar and the Local Sweatshop: Ethnic Small Business and the Economic Restructuring of Sydney*, Office of Multicultural Affairs and Centre for Multicultural Studies, University of Wollongong

Castles, S., Kalantzis, M., Cope, B., Morrissey, M. 1992b, *Mistaken Identity: Multiculturalism and the Demise of Nationalism in Australia*, 3rd edn, Pluto Press, Sydney

Castles, S., Mitchell, C., Morrissey, M. and Alcorso, C. 1989, *The Recognition of Overseas Trade Qualifications*, AGPS, Canberra

Centre for Applied Research in Education 1990, *The New South Wales Police Recruitment Education Programme: An Independent Evaluation*, University of East Anglia, Norwich

Centre for Urban Research and Action 1978, *Outwork: An Alternative Mode of Employment*, Centre for Urban Research and Action, Melbourne

Centre for Working Women's Co-operative Limited 1986, *Women Outworkers: A Report Documenting Sweated Labour in the 1980s*, Centre for Working Women's Co-operative Limited, Melbourne

Chan, J. 1992, *Policing in a Multicultural Society: A Study of the New South Wales Police*, Final Report to the New South Wales Police Service, New South Wales Police Board, Sydney

—— 1993, 'Police Accountability in a Multicultural Society', paper to the Australian Institute of Criminology Conference 'The Criminal Justice System in a Multicultural Society', 4–6 May, Melbourne

—— 1994, 'Policing Youth in "Ethnic" Communities: Is Community Policing the Answer?', *The Police and Young People in Australia*, eds R. White & C. Alder, Cambridge University Press, Oakleigh, Vic.

Chapman, B.J. and Iredale, R.R. 1990, *Immigrant Qualifications: Recognition and Relative Wage Outcomes*, Centre for Economic Policy Research, Australian National University, Discussion Paper no. 240

Chapman, B.J. and Miller, P.W. 1983, 'Determination of Earnings in Australia: An Analysis of the 1976 Census', *Japanese and Australian Labour Markets: A Comparative Study*, eds K. Hancock, Y. Sano, B. Chapman & P. Fayle, Australia–Japan Research Centre, Canberra

Chatterjee, P. 1986, *Nationalist Thought and the Colonial World: A Derivative Discourse*, Zed Press, London

Cohen, P. and Bains, H.S. eds 1988, *Multi-Racist Britain*, Macmillan Education, Basingstoke and London

Cohen, R. 1987, *The New Helots: Migrants in the International Division of Labour*, Avebury, Aldershot

Colebatch, H. and Larmour, P. 1993, *Market, Bureaucracy and Community*, Pluto Press, London

Collins, J. 1989, 'Immigrants in New South Wales: A Profile of Recent Settlement and Labour Market Patterns', Kuring-gai CAE Centre for Labour Studies, Working Paper no. 4, September

—— 1990, 'Labour Market Deregulation in New South Wales: A Critique', UTS Centre for Labour Studies, Working Paper no. 6, August

—— 1991, *Migrant Hands in a Distant Land: Australia's Post-War Immigration*, 2nd edn, Pluto Press, Sydney

—— 1993, 'Cohesion with Diversity? Immigration and Multiculturalism in Canada and Australia', UTS School of Finance and Economics, Working Paper no. 28, March

—— 1994, 'Asians in Australia', *The Cambridge Survey of World Migration*, ed. Robin Cohen, Cambridge University Press, Cambridge

Collins, J. and Castles, S. 1992, 'Restructuring, Migrant Labour Markets and Small Business in Australia', *Migration: A European Journal of International Migration and Ethnic Relations*, no. 10, pp. 7–34

Committee of Arab Australians & Committee on Discrimination Against Arab Australians 1990, *Documentation of Incidents of Harassment and Racism towards Australians of Arab Descent and Australian Muslims*, Committee of Arab Australians & Committee on Discrimination Against Arab Australians, NSW

Commonwealth Attorney-General's Department 1990, *Access to Interpreters in the Australian Legal System. Draft Report*, AGPS, Canberra

Connell, R.W. 1987, *Gender, Culture and Power*, Allen & Unwin, Sydney

—— 1993, *Schools and Social Justice*, Pluto Press, Sydney

Cope, W. and Kalantzis, M. eds 1993, *The Powers of Literacy: A Genre Approach to Teaching Writing*, Falmer Press, London

Coward, R. 1987, 'Sexual Violence and Sexuality', *Sexuality: a Reader*, ed. Feminist Review, Virago, London

Cowlishaw, G. 1988, *Black, White or Brindle*, Cambridge University Press, Cambridge

—— 1993, 'Introduction: Representing Racial Issues', *Oceania*, vol. 63, no. 3, March, pp. 183–94

Cox, E. and Laura, S. 1992, *What Do I Wear for a Hurricane: Women in Australian Film, Relevision, Video and Radio*, Australian Film Commission and National Working Party on the Portrayal of Women in the Media, Canberra

Cox, O.C. 1959, *Caste, Class and Race*, Monthly Review Press, New York

Crooke, W. 1896, *The Tribes and Castes of the North-Western Provinces and Oudh*, 4 vols, Office of the Superintendent of Government Printing, Calcutta

Cross, M. and Keith, M. eds 1993, *Racism, the City and the State*, Routledge, London and New York

Cunneen, C. 1990, *A Study of Aboriginal Juveniles and Police Violence*, Report commissioned by the National Inquiry into Racist Violence, Human Rights and Equal Opportunity Commission, Sydney

Cunneen, C. and Robb, T. 1987, *Criminal Justice in North-West New South Wales*, NSW Bureau of Crime Statistics and Research, Sydney

Daly, A.E. 1991, 'Aboriginal Women in the Labour Market', *Aboriginal Employment Equity by the Year 2000*, ed. J.C. Altman, Centre for Aboriginal Economic Policy Research, Australian National University, Research Monograph no. 2

Daniels, D. 1986, 'The Coming Crisis in the Indigenous Rights Movement: From Colonialism to Neo-colonialism to Renaissance', *Native Studies Review*, vol. 2, no. 2, pp. 97–115

Das, V. 1994, 'Modernity and Biography: Women's Lives in Contemporary India', *Thesis Eleven*, no. 39, pp. 52–62

Davis, M. 1990, *City of Quarz: Excavating the Future in Los Angeles*, Vintage, London

de Certeau, M. 1988, *The Practice of Everyday Life*, University of California Press, Berkeley, California

de Lepervanche, M. 1975, 'Australian Immigrants, 1788–1940: Desired and Unwanted', *Essays in the Political Economy of Australian Capitalism*, vol. 1, eds E.L. Wheelright & K. Buckley, Australia & New Zealand Book Company, Sydney

—— 1980, 'From Race to Ethnicity', *Australia and New Zealand Journal of Sociology*, vol. 1, no. 16, pp. 4–37

—— 1989, 'Women, Nation and the State in Australia', *Woman, Nation, State*, eds N. Yuval-Davis & F. Anthias, Macmillan, London

—— 1990, 'Holding it all Together: Multiculturalism, Nationalism and the State in Australia', paper presented at XII World Congress of Sociology, Madrid

de Lepervanche, M. and Bottomley, G. eds 1988, *The Cultural Construction of Race*, Sydney Association for Studies in Society and Culture, University of Sydney, Australia

Department of Foreign Affairs and Trade 1992, *Australia's Business Challenge: South-East Asia in the 1990s*, AGPS, Canberra

Devery, C. 1991, *Disadvantage and Crime in New South Wales*, NSW Bureau of Crime Statistics and Research, Sydney

DIEA (Department of Immigration and Ethnic Affairs) 1986, *Report of the Review of Migrant and Multicultural Programs and Services Don't Settle For Less*, AGPS, Canberra

Donald, J. and Rattansi, A. 1992, 'Introduction', *'Race', Culture and Difference*, eds J. Donald & A. Rattansi, Sage Publications, London

Dubet, F. and Lapeyronnie, D. 1992, *Les Quartiers d'Exil*, Seuil, Paris

Durand, J. 1983, 'Rhetoric and the Advertising Image', *Australian Journal of Cultural Studies*, vol. 1, no. 2, pp. 29–53

Eades, D. 1981, 'That's Our Way of Talking: Aborigines in South-East Queensland', *Social Alternatives*, vol. 2, no. 2, Diamond Press, Brisbane, p. 11

—— 1993, 'The Case for Condren: Aboriginal English, Pragmatics and the Law', *Journal of Pragmatics*, vol. 20, no. 2, pp. 141–62

—— 1994, 'A Case of Communicative Clash: Aboriginal English and the Legal System', *Language and the Law*, ed. J. Gibbons, Longman, London

—— 1995, 'The Langwij Gets Understood', *Sydney Morning Herald*, 11 March

Esman, M.J. 1992, 'The Political Fallout of International Migration', *Diaspora*, vol. 2, no. 1, pp. 3–41

Essed, P. 1991, *Understanding Everyday Racism*, Sage Publications, Newbury Park, London and New Delhi

Etter, B. 1992, 'The Future Direction of Policing in Australia', paper to the Australian and New Zealand Society of Criminology Conference, 20 September – 2 October, Melbourne

—— 1993, 'The Culture Clash: Police and Multicultural Australia', paper to the 9th Annual Conference of the Australian and New Zealand Society of Criminology, 28 September – 1 October 1993, Sydney

—— 1994, 'Cross Cultural and Race Relations Training for Operational Police Officers', MBA thesis, Northern Territory University, Darwin

Evans, M., Jones, F. and Kelley, J. 1988, 'Job Discrimination Against Immigrants?', *Australian Attitudes: Social and Political Analyses from the National Social Science Survey*, eds J. Kelley & C. Bean, Allen & Unwin, Sydney

Featherston, E. ed. 1994, *Skin Deep: Women Writing on Color, Culture and Identity*, The Crossing Press, California

Featherstone, M. ed. 1990, *Global Culture: Nationalism, Globalization and Modernity*, Sage Publications, Newbury Park, London and New Delhi

Federation of Ethnic Communities' Council of Australia (FECCA) 1991, 'Background Paper on Ethnic Youth' prepared for FECCA's Multicultural Youth Conference, FECCA, Sydney

Fielding, N. 1988, *Joining Forces: Police Training, Socialization, and Occupational Competence*, Routledge, London and New York

Finn, B. 1991, *Young People's Participation in Post-compulsory Education and Training*, Australian Education Council Review Committee, Canberra

Finnane, M. 1994, *Police and Government: Histories of Policing in Australia*, Oxford University Press, Melbourne

Fletcher, J.J. 1989, *Clean, Clad and Courteous: A History of Aboriginal Education in New South Wales*, Fletcher, Carlton, Vic.

Foley, M. 1984, 'Aborigines and the Police', *Aborigines and the Law*, eds P. Hanks & B. Keon-Cohen, Allen & Unwin, Sydney

Forbes, G. H. 1979, 'Women and Modernity: The Issue of Child Marriage in India', *Women's Studies International Quarterly*, vol. 2, pp. 407–19

Foster, L. and Seitz, A. 1993, 'Intended and Unintended Consequences of Measures Against Racial Vilification', paper to the Conference on Confronting Racism in Australia, New Zealand and Canada, University of Technology, Sydney, 9–11 December

Foster, L. and Stockley, D. 1988, *Australian Multiculturalism: A Documentary History and Critique*, Multilingual Matters, Clevedon and Philadelphia

Foster, L., Marshall, A. and Williams, L. 1991, *Discrimination Against Immigrant Workers in Australia*, AGPS, Canberra

Foucault, M. 1972, *The Archaeology of Knowledge*, Tavistock, London

Freeman, G.P. and Jupp, J. eds 1992, *Nations of Immigrants: Australia, the United States and International Migration*, Oxford University Press, Melbourne

Freire, P. 1972, *Pedagogy of the Oppressed*, Penguin, London

Frost, S. 1992, 'Economic Rationalism, Cultural Relativism and the Policy Discourse of "Asia Literacy"', paper to the Asia Research Centre, Murdoch University, Perth, 15 October

Furtie, F. and Donohoue-Clyne, I. 1994, 'Whose Body? The Cultural Agenda of How Migrant Women are Perceived', paper to the Conference on Linking our Histories: Asian and Pacific Women as Migrants, University of Melbourne, 9 September–2 October

Galtung, J. 1988, 'On Violence in General and Terrorism in Particular', *Transarmament and the Cold War: Essays in Peace Research*, ed. J. Galtung, vol. 6, Christian Ejlers, Copenhagen

Garnaut, R. 1989, *Australia and the Northeast Asian Ascendancy*, AGPS, Canberra

Gaspard, F. and Khosrow-Khavar, F. 1995, *Le Foulard et la République*, La Découverte, Paris

Gates, H. L. Jr ed. 1986, *'Race', Writing and Difference*, University of Chicago Press, Chicago

Gellner, E. 1983, *Nations and Nationalism*, Blackwell, Oxford

Gertsakis, E. 1994, 'An Inconstant Politics: Thinking about the Traditional and the Contemporary', *Culture, Difference, and the Arts*, eds S. Gunew & F. Rizvi, Allen & Unwin, Sydney

Gilroy, P. 1987, *There Ain't no Black in the Union Jack*, Hutchinson, London

—— 1992, 'The End of Antiracism', *Race, Culture and Difference*, eds J. Donald & A. Rattansi, Sage Publications, Newbury Park, London and New Delhi

—— 1993, *The Black Atlantis: Modernity and Double Consciousness*, Maynard University Press, Cambridge, Mass.

Giroux, H. 1992, 'Beyond the Politics of Pluralism', *Border Crossings: Cultural Workers and the Politics of Education*, Routledge, London

—— 1994, 'The Cultural Studies Classroom', *Disturbing Pleasures: Learning Popular Culture*, Routledge, London

Goldberg, D. 1993, *Racist Culture: Philosophy and the Politics of Meaning*, Blackwell, Oxford

Goldstein, H. 1979, 'Improving Policing: A Problem-oriented Approach', *Crime and Delinquency*, April, no. 25, pp. 236–58

Goodall, H., Jakubowicz, A., Martin, J., Mitchell, T., Randall, L. and Seneviratne, K. 1990, *Racism, Cultural Pluralism and the Media: Report to the Office of Multicultural Affairs*, University of Technology, Sydney

Goot, M. and Rowse, T. 1994, *Make a Better Offer: The Politics of Mabo*, Pluto Press, Sydney

Gordon, P. 1983, *White Law: Racism in the Police, Courts and Prisons,* Pluto Press, London

Gunew, S. and Rizvi, F. 1994, *Culture, Difference and the Arts*, Allen & Unwin, Sydney

Gutmann, A. ed. 1994, *Multiculturalism: Examining the Politics of Recognition*, Princeton University Press, Princeton

Habermas, J. 1994, 'Struggles for Recognition in the Democratic Constitutional State', *Multiculturalism: Examining the Politics of Recognition*, ed A. Gutmann, Princeton University Press, Princeton

Hacker, A. 1992, *Two Nations: Black and White, Separate, Hostile, Unequal*, Charles Scribner's Sons, New York

Hall, S. 1986, 'Gramsci's Relevance to the Analysis of Racism and Ethnicity', *Journal of Communication Studies*, vol. 10, no. 2, pp. 5–27

—— 1992a, 'The Question of Cultural Identity', *Modernity and its Futures*, eds S. Hall, D. Held & T. McGrew, Polity Press, Cambridge

—— 1992b, 'New Ethnicities', *Race, Culture and Difference,* eds J. Donald & A. Rattansi, Sage Publications, London

Hamilton, A. 1990, 'Fear and Desire: Aborigines, Asians and the National Imaginary', *Australian Cultural History*, no. 9, Special Edition, pp. 14–35

Hartmann, H. 1979, 'The Unhappy Marriage of Marxism and Feminism: Towards a More Progressive Union', *Capital and Class*, no. 8, pp. 1–33

Hegel, G. W. F. 1967, *The Phenomenology of Mind*, Harper & Row, New York (trans. J. B. Baille)

Holdaway, S. 1983, *Inside British Police: A Force at Work*, Blackwell, Oxford

—— 1991, *Recruiting a Multi-racial Police Force: A Research Study*, Home Office, HMSO, London

Hollingworth, P. 1994, 'Moral Vacuum Threatens Liberal State', *Australian,* 8 September

Hollinsworth, D. 1992, 'Discourses on Aboriginality and the Politics of Identity in Urban Australia', *Oceania*, vol. 63, no. 2, December, pp. 137–55

Holt, L. 1993, 'One Aboriginal Woman's Identity: Walking in Both Worlds', *Australian Feminist Studies*, no. 18, Research Centre for Women's Studies, Adelaide University, South Australia, pp. 175–9

HREOC (Human Rights and Equal Opportunity Commission) 1991, *Racist Violence: Report of the National Inquiry into Racist Violence in Australia*, AGPS, Canberra

Husband, C. 1982, 'Introduction: "Race", The Continuity of a Concept', *Race in Britain—Continuity and Change*, ed. C. Husband, Hutchinson, London

Inglis, C. 1992, 'An Overview of Australian Migration Policy and Flows', paper to the Conference on Immigration and Refugee Policy: The Australian and Canadian Experiences, York University, Toronto, Canada, 2–5 May

Ip, D., Berthier, R. and Kawakami, I. 1992, *Asians in Multicultural Australia*, a report submitted to the Toyota Foundation, Sydney

Iredale, R. 1992, 'Where Are We Now in Overseas Qualifications Recognition? A Decade of Review and Changes', Centre for Multicultural Studies, University of Wollongong, Occasional Paper no. 26

Jakubowicz, A. 1981, 'State and Ethnicity: Multiculturalism as Ideology', *Australian–New Zealand Journal of Sociology*, vol. 17, no. 3, pp. 4–13

—— 1989a, 'The State and the Welfare of Immigrants in Australia', *Ethnic and Racial Studies*, vol. 12, no. 1, pp. 1–35

—— 1989b, 'Speaking in Tongues: Multicultural Media and the Construction of a Socially Homogenous Australian', *Communication and the Public Sphere*, ed. H. Wilson, Allen & Unwin, Sydney

Jakubowicz, A. et al. 1994, *Race, Ethnicity and the Media*, Allen & Unwin, Sydney

Jakubowicz, A., Morrissey, M. and Palser, J. 1984, *Ethnicity, Class and Social Policy in Australia*, Social Welfare Research Centre, UNSW, Report no. 46

Jarratt, J. 1991, 'Pitfalls of the Introduction of Community Policing', *The Police and the Community in the 1990s*, Proceedings of Conference, 23–25 October 1990, eds S. McKillop & J. Vernon, Australian Institute of Criminology, Canberra

Jefferson, T. 1991, 'Discrimination, Disadvantage and Police-work', *Out of Order? Policing Black People*, eds E. Cashmore & E. McLaughlin, Routledge, London

—— 1993, 'The Racism of Criminalization: Policing and the Reproduction of the Criminal Other', *Ethnic Minorities and the Criminal Justice System*, ed. L. Gelsthorpe, 21st Cropwood Round Table Conference, Institute of Criminology, Cambridge

Jefferson, T. and Walker, M.A. 1992, 'Ethnic Minorities in the Criminal Justice System', *Criminal Law Review*, pp. 83–95

Johnson, P. 1994, *Feminism as Radical Humanism*, Allen & Unwin, Sydney

Johnston, E. 1991, *Review of the Training for Aboriginals Program*, AGPS, Canberra

Johnston, K. 1990, 'Dealing with Difference', *Education Links*, no. 38, pp. 26–9

Jones, F. 1991, 'Economic Status of Aboriginal and Other Australians: A Comparison', *Aboriginal Employment Equity by the Year 2000*, ed. J.C. Altman, Centre for Aboriginal Economic Policy Research, Australian National University, Research Monograph no. 2

Jones, R. and McAllister, I. 1991, *Migrant Unemployment and Labour Market Programs*, AGPS, Canberra

Junankar, P. N. and Pope, D. 1990, *Immigration, Wages and Price Stability*, AGPS, Canberra

Jupp, J. 1984, 'Power in Ethnic Australia', *Ethnic Politics in Australia*, ed. J. Jupp, George Allen & Unwin, Sydney

Jupp, J. and Kabala, M. 1993, *The Politics of Australian Immigration*, Bureau of Immigration Research, AGPS, Canberra

Kalantzis, M., Cope, B., Noble, G. and Poynting, S. 1990, *Cultures of Schooling: Pedagogies for Cultural Difference and Social Access*, Falmer Press, U.K.

Kalantzis, M. 1992, 'Competencies, Credentials and Cultures', paper to joint NSW Ethnic Affairs Commission and Office of Multicultural Affairs Seminar on the Mayer Committee's Proposals, July 18, pp. 1–10

—— 1994, *Cultural Understandings as the Eighth Key Competency, Final Report to the Queensland Department of Education and the Queensland Vocational Education, Training and Employment Commission*, James Cook University, Townsville

Khoo, S-E., Pookong, K., Dang, T. and Shu Jing 1993, 'Asian Immigrant Settlement and Adjustment in Australia', paper to the Conference on Asia-Pacific Migration Affecting Australia, Darwin, 14–17 September

Kidd, M.P. 1991, 'Immigrant Wage Differentials and the Role of Self-employment in Australia', Department of Economics, University of Tasmania, Discussion Paper

King, A.D. ed. 1991, *Culture, Globalization and the World-System*, Macmillan, London

La Capra, D. ed. *The Bounds of Race*, Cornell University Press, Ithaca & London

Landa, P. 1991, *Operation Sue*, Report Under Section 26 of the Ombudsman Act, NSW Ombudsman's Office, Sydney

Langton, M. 1993, '*Well, I heard it on the radio and I saw it on the television . . .*', Australian Film Commission, North Sydney

Lapeyronnie, D., Frybes, M., Couper, K. and Joly, D. 1990, *L'Intégration des Minorités Immigrées: Etude Comparative: France—Grande Bretagne*, Agence pour le Développement des Relations Interculturelles, Paris

Lattas, A. 1993, 'Essentialism, Memory and Resistance: Aboriginality and the Politics of Authenticity', *Oceania*, vol. 63, no. 3, March, pp. 240–67

Law Reform Commission, see ALRC (Australian Law Reform Commission)

Layton-Henry, Z. 1992, *The Politics of Immigration*, Blackwell, Oxford

Legge, K. 1994, 'Living Two Lives', *The Australian Magazine*, 3–4 September, pp. 20–7.

Lever-Tracy, C. and Quinlan, M. 1988, *A Divided Working Class*, Routledge, London

Levine, M., McLellan, P. and Pearce, J. 1992, *Immigrant Workers in the Automotive Industry*, Bureau of Immigration Research, AGPS, Canberra

Liebes, T. and Katz, E. 1988, 'Dallas and Genesis: Primordiality and Seriality in Popular Culture', *Media Myths and Narratives*, ed. J. Cary, Sage Publications, Newbury Park

Lippmann, L. 1973, *Words or Blow. Racial Attitudes in Australia*, Penguin, Ringwood, Vic.

Lloyd, P. 1993, 'The Political Economy of Immigration', *The Politics of Australian Immigration*, eds J. Jupp & M. Kabala, AGPS, Canberra

Lutz, H. 1993, 'Migrant Women, Racism and the Dutch Labour Market', *Racism and Migration in Western Europe*, eds John Wrench & John Solomos, Berg, Oxford

Lynch, H. M. 1990, 'Aboriginal Education Centres in Institutions of Higher Education: A Case Study', thesis submitted to the Faculty of Education, University of New England, Armidale

Manning, P. 1977, *Police Work*, MIT Press, Cambridge, Mass.

Manyarrows, V. 1994, 'Colorism in the Indian Community', *Skin Deep: Women Writing on Color, Culture and Identity*, ed. Elena Featherston, The Crossing Press, California

Marable, M. and Mullings, L. 1994, 'The Divided Mind of Black America: Ideology and Politics in the Post-Civil Rights Era', *Race and Class*, vol. 36, no. 1, pp. 61–72

Marginson, S. 1993, *Education and Public Policy in Australia*, University of Cambridge Press, Oakleigh, Vic.

Markus, A. 1988, 'How Australians See Each Other', *Commitment to Australia:*

Consultants' Report, Committee to Assess Australia's Immigration Policies, AGPS, Canberra

—— 1994, *Australian Race Relations*, Allen & Unwin, Sydney

Martin, J. 1978, *The Migrant Presence*, George Allen & Unwin, Sydney

—— 1984, 'Non English-speaking Women: Production and Social Reproduction', *Ethnicity, Class and Gender in Australia*, eds G. Bottomley & M. de Lepervanche, George Allen & Unwin, Sydney

—— 1986, 'Non-English-speaking Migrant Women in Australia', *Australian Women: New Feminist Perspectives*, eds N. Grieve & A. Burns, Oxford University Press, Melbourne

—— 1990, 'David Jones and the Tropics', *Bulletin of the Olive Pink Society*, vol. 2, no. 1, pp. 18–27

—— 1991a, 'Multiculturalism and Feminism', *Intersexions*, eds G. Bottomley, M. de Lepervanche & J. Martin, Allen & Unwin, Sydney

—— 1991b, 'Aussie-Mums and Television Ads', *Refractory Girl*, no. 38, pp. 12–18

—— 1991c, 'The Politics of Stereotypes', paper to the Annual Conference of the Australian Sociological Association, Brisbane

—— 1993, 'The Culture of the Exotic', in *Proceedings of the 2nd Documentary Film Conference*, Australian Film Institute, Sydney and Canberra

Mayer, K. 1992, *Key Competencies*, Report of the Committee to Advise the Australian Education Commission and Ministry of Vocational Education, Employment and Training on Employment-related Competencies for Post-compulsory Education and Training, Australian Education Council, Victoria

McConaghy, C. 1994, 'Fashion and Prescription in Representations of Indigenous Education', *Discourse*, vol. 15, no. 2, University of Queensland, pp. 81–4

McConnochie, K. 1990, *Report on Staff Development Workshop Aboriginal Education Unit*, University of Western Sydney Macarthur, 19–23 February

McCormack, G. 1991, 'Coping with Japan: The MFP Proposal and the Australian Response', *Bonsai Australia Bonzai*, ed. G. McCormack, Pluto Press, Sydney

McDonald, D. and Biles, D. 1991, 'Who Got Locked Up? The Australian Police Custody Survey', *ANZ Journal of Criminology*, vol. 24, no. 3, pp. 190–203

McLaren, P. 1995, 'Multiculturalism and the Postmodern Critique: Towards a Pedagogy of Resistance and Transformation', *Critical Pedagogy and Predatory Culture*, ed. Peter McLaren, Routledge, London, pp. 201–8

McQueen, H. 1970, *A New Britannia*, Penguin, Melbourne

—— 1993, 'Asia's Cultures Lie Waiting to be Discovered', *Weekend Australian*, 16 October, p. 22

Miles, R. 1989, *Racism*, Routledge, London

—— 1993, *Racism after Race Relations*, Routledge, London

Miles, R. 1982, *Racism and Migrant Labour*, Routledge & Kegan Paul, Boston

Miller, M. (Chair) 1985, *Report of the Committee of Review of Aboriginal Employment and Training Programs*, AGPS, Canberra

Miller, P.W. 1991, 'Aboriginal and Non-Aboriginal Youth Unemployment', *Aboriginal Employment Equity by the Year 2000*, ed. J.C. Altman, Centre for Aboriginal Economic Policy Research, Australian National University, Research Monograph no. 2

Montagu, A. 1974, *Man's Most Dangerous Myth: The Fallacy of Race*, Oxford University Press, New York

Morgan, R. 1987, 'The Local Determinants of Policing Policy', *Policing and the Community*, ed. P. Wilmott, Policy Studies Institute, London

Morrissey, M., Dibden, M. and Mitchell, C. 1992, *Immigration and Industry Restructuring in the Illawarra*, Bureau of Immigration Research, Melbourne

Moss, I. 1993, *State of the Nation: A Report on the People of Non-English Speaking Background*, AGPS, Canberra

Mudrooroo, Atwood, B., Lattas, A. and Beckett, J. 1992, 'Comments on Hollinsworth', *Oceania*, vol. 63, no. 2, pp. 156–71

Murphy, R. 1972, *The Dialectics of Social Life*, George Allen & Unwin, London

Nairn, T. 1980, *The Break-up of Britain*, New Left Books, London

New South Wales Ethnic Affairs Commission (NSWEAC) 1992, 'Policing and Ethnicity in NSW', unpublished report

New South Wales Ombudsman 1992, *Annual Report*, Office of the Ombudsman, Sydney

New South Wales Police Board 1992, *Annual Report 1991–92*, NSW Police Board, Sydney

New South Wales Police Recruit Education Programme 1991, *Course Documentation*, NSW Police Service, Sydney

New South Wales Police Service 1988, *Ethnic Affairs Policy Statement*, NSW Police Service, Sydney

Niland, C. and Champion, R. 1990, *EEO Programs for Immigrants*, AGPS, Canberra

Nord, S. 1984, *Migrant Women Workers—These Are Your Rights*, South Coast Labour Council, Wollongong

Norris, K. 1993, *The Economics of Australian Labour Markets*, Longman Cheshire, Melbourne

NPC (National Population Council) 1991, *Refugee Review*, National Population Council, Canberra

O'Neill, S. and Bathgate, J. 1993, *Policing Strategies in Aboriginal and Non-English Speaking Background Communities: A Community Relations Project*, Final Report, Northern Territory Police, Winnellie, NT

OMA (Office of Multicultural Affairs) 1989, *National Agenda for a Multicultural Australia*, AGPS, Canberra

OSW (Office of the Status of Women) 1993, *Women and the Media*, National Working Party on the Portrayal of Women in the Media, OSW, Canberra

Parrella, L. 1993, 'Participation in Government Structures: Progress or Co-Option?', *Australian Feminist Studies*, no. 18, Summer, pp. 67–9

Pearson, N. 1994, 'From Remnant Title to Social Justice', *Make a Better Offer: The Politics of Mabo*, eds M. Goot & T. Rowse, Pluto Press, Sydney

Perera, S. 1993, 'Representation Wars: Malaysia, "Embassy" and Australian *Corps Diplomatique*', *Australian Cultural Studies: A Reader*, eds J. Frow & M. Morris, Allen & Unwin, Sydney

Pettman, J. 1992, *Living in the Margins: Racism: Sexism and Feminism in Australia*, Allen & Unwin, Sydney

Piore, M. 1980, *Birds of Passage*, Cambridge University Press, London

Pollard, D. 1989, *Give and Take: The Losing Partnership in Aboriginal Poverty*, Hale & Iremonger, Sydney

Pope, D. and Withers, G. 1990, 'Do Migrants Rob Jobs? Lessons from Australian History', Department of Economic History, Australian National University, Canberra, Working Paper in Economic History, no. 133

Poster, M. 1990, *The Mode of Information: Poststructuralism and Social Context*, Polity Press, Cambridge

Potts, L. 1990, *The World Labour Market: A History of Migration*, Zed Books, London

Prakash, G. 1992, 'Science "Gone Native" in Colonial India', *Representations*, no. 40, Fall, pp. 153–78

—— ed. 1995, *After Colonialism. Imperial Histories and Postcolonial Displacements*, Princeton

'Racism: The Touchy Subject that Leaves a Blot on our Schools', *Weekend Australian*, 7 November 1992, pp. 1–2

Ram, K. 1993, ' "Too Traditional Once Again": Some Poststructuralists on the Aspirations of the Immigrant/Third World Female Subject'. *Australian Feminist Studies*, no. 17, pp. 5–28

—— 1995, 'Migrating Dances', *Writings on Dance*, no. 13, Special Issue on Performance Across Cultures, pp. 35–54

Raman, P. 1993, 'Dealing with Difference. Arranged Marriages and the Law of Duress in Multicultural Australia', BA Hons. Thesis, Faculty of Law, Australian National University

Rath, J. 1993, 'The Ideological Representation of Migrant Workers in Europe: A Matter of Racialisation?', *Racism and Migration in Western Europe*, eds J. Wrench & J. Solomos, Berg, Oxford

Reiner, R. 1985, 'The Police and Race Relations', *Police: The Constitution and the Community*, eds J. Baxter & L. Koffman, Professional Books, London

—— 1992, *The Politics of the Police*, 2nd edn, Harvester Wheatsheaf, London

Reuss-Ianni, E. and Ianni, F. 1983, 'Street Cops and Management Cops: The Two Cultures of Policing', *Control in the Police Organization*, ed. M. Punch, MIT Press, Cambridge, Mass.

Rex, J. and Mason, D. eds 1986, *Theories of Race and Ethnic Relations*, Cambridge University Press, Cambridge

Reynolds, H. 1981, *The Other Side of the Frontier*, Penguin, Ringwood, Vic.

—— 1987a, *Frontier*, Allen & Unwin, Sydney

—— 1987b, *The Law of the Land*, Penguin, Ringwood, Vic.

—— 1989, *Dispossession: Black Australians and White Invaders*, Allen & Unwin, Sydney

—— 1995, *Fate of a Free People: A Radical Re-examination of the Tasmanian Wars*, Penguin, Ringwood, Vic.

Ricca, S. 1990, *Migrations internationales en Afrique*, L'Harmattan, Paris

Rivett, K. ed. 1962, *Immigration: Control or Colour Bar?*, Melbourne University Press, Carlton, Vic.

Rizvi, F. 1987, *Multiculturalism as an Educational Policy*, Deakin University, Victoria

—— 1993, 'Educative Leadership in a Multicultural Society', *Educative Leadership: A Practical Theory for New Administrators and Managers*, eds P. Duignan, & R. J. S. McPherson, The Falmer Press, London

Rizvi, F. and Crowley, V. 1993, 'Teachers and the Contradictions of Culturalism',

Inequality and Teacher Education, ed. G.K. Verma, The Falmer Press, London

Roberts-Smith, L.W. 1989, 'Communication Breakdown', *Legal Services Bulletin*, vol. 14, no. 2, pp. 75–8

Robertson, R. 1992, *Globalisation: Social Theory and Global Culture*, Sage Publications, London, Newbury Park and New Delhi

Rowe, D. 1984, 'Media Beat up Migrants: News Values on the Small Screen', *Journal of Intercultural Studies*, vol. 5, no. 11, pp. 5–21

Rowley, C. 1970, *The Destruction of Aboriginal Society*, Australian National University Press, Canberra

Rowse, T. 1993, *After Mabo: Interpreting Indigenous Traditions*, Melbourne University Press, Carlton, Vic.

Royal Commission into Aboriginal Deaths in Custody, see Australia. Royal Commission into Aboriginal Deaths in Custody

Said, E. 1978, *Orientalism*, Routledge & Kegan Paul, London

Sanghari, K. and Vaid, S. eds 1989, *Recasting Women: Essays in Colonial History*, Kali for Women, New Delhi

Sassen, S. 1988, *The Mobility of Labor and Capital*, Cambridge University Press, Cambridge

Schierup, C.-U. 1993, 'Prelude to the Inferno—Economic Disintegration and the Political Fragmentation of Yugoslavia', *Migration*, vol. 19, no. 93, pp. 5–40

Schnapper, D. 1991, 'A Host Country of Immigrants that Does Not Know Itself', *Diaspora*, vol. 1, no. 3, pp. 353–63

Sekine, M. 1990, *Guest Workers in Japan*, Centre for Multicultural Studies, University of Wollongong, Occasional Paper no. 21

Sherwood, J. ed. 1982, *Aboriginal Education: Issues and Innovations*, Creative Research, Perth

Silverstone, R. 1988, 'Television Myth and Culture', *Media Myths and Narratives*, ed. J. Cary, Sage, Newbury Park

Skolnick, J. 1966, *Justice Without Trial*, John Wiley & Sons, New York

Smith, D.J. 1983, *Police and People in London I: A Survey of Londoners*, Policy Studies Institute, London

Social Justice for Indigenous Australians 1993–1994, 1993, circulated by the Honourable Robert Tickner, MP, Minister for Aboriginal and Torres Strait Islander Affairs, AGPS, Canberra

Solomos, J. 1993, *Race and Racism in Contemporary Britain*, 2nd edn, Macmillan, London

Solomos, J. & Back, L. 1994, 'Conceptualising Racisms: Social Theory, Politics & Research', *Sociology*, vol. 28, no. 1, pp. 143–61

Sontag, S. ed. 1988, *A Barthes Reader*, McGraw-Hill, USA/Toronto

Southgate, P. 1984, *Racism Awareness Training for the Police: Report of a Pilot Study by the Home Office*, Research and Planning Unit Paper no. 29, Home Office, London

Sparrow, M. K., Moore, M. H. and Kennedy, D. M. 1990, *Beyond 911: A New Era for Policing*, Basic Books, New York

Spindler, K. 1987, 'Australian Immigration: Some Factor Market Consequences and the Implications for Community Attitudes to Immigration Policy', Research report for Master of Commerce degree, University of Melbourne

Stahl, C., Ball, R., Inglis, C. and Gutman, P. 1993, *Global Population Movements and their Implications for Australia*, Bureau of Immigration and Population Research, AGPS, Canberra

Stevens, F. S. ed. 1970, *Racism. The Australian Experience*, 3 vols, ANZ Book Co., Sydney

Storer, D. 1976, *But I Wouldn't Want My Wife to Work Here: A Study of Migrant Women in Melbourne Industry*, Centre for Urban Research and Action, Fitzroy, Vic.

Stratton, J. and Ang, I. 1994, 'Multicultural Imagined Communities: Cultural Difference and National Identity in Australia and the USA', *Continuum*, vol. 8, no. 2, pp. 124–58

Stricker, P. and Sheehan, P. 1981, *Hidden Unemployment: The Australian Experience*, University of Melbourne Press, Carlton, Vic.

Stromback, T. and Williams, T. 1985, 'Do Migrants Earn What They Should?', *Bulletin of Labour Market Research*, no. 15, June

Taguieff, P.-A. 1988, *La Force du Préjugé*, La Découverte, Paris

Taylor, C. 1975, *Hegel*, Cambridge University Press, Cambridge

—— 1992, *Multiculturalism and the Politics of Recognition*, Princeton University Press, Princeton

—— 1994, 'The Politics of Recognition', in ed. A. Gutmann, *Multiculturalism: Examining the Politics of Recognition*, Princeton University Press, Princeton

Taylor, J. 1992, 'Occupational Segregation: A Comparison between Employed Aborigines, Torres Strait Islanders and Other Australians', Centre for Aboriginal Economic Policy Research, Australian National University, Discussion Paper no. 33

Thompson, J. 1990, *Ideology and Modern Culture*, Polity Press, Cambridge

Thurow, L.C. 1975, *Generating Inequality*, Macmillan, Melbourne

Thurston, E. 1909, *Castes and Tribes of Southern India*, Government Press, Madras

Troyna, B. 1993, *Racism and Education*, Open University Press, Buckingham

Uberoi, P. 1995, (in press) 'When is a Marriage not a Marriage? Sex, Sacrament and Contract in Hindu Marriage', *Contributions to Indian Sociology*, Special Issue on Social Reform, Sexuality and the State, vol. 29, nos. 1–2

UNFPA (United Nations Population Fund) 1993, *The State of World Population*, United Nations, New York

US DoS (US Department of State) 1992, *Country Reports on Human Rights Practices for 1990*, US Government Printing Office, Washington

van Dijk, T. 1993, *Elite Discourse and Racism*, Sage, Newbury Park, London, New Delhi

Van Maanen, J. 1983, 'The Boss: First-line Supervision in an American Police Agency', *Control in the Police Organization*, ed. M. Punch, MIT Press, Cambridge, Mass.

Vasta, E. 1991, 'Gender, Class and Ethnic Relations: The Domestic and Work Experiences of Italian Migrant women in Australia', *Intersexions*, eds G. Bottomley, M. de Lepervanche & J. Martin, Allen & Unwin, Sydney

—— 1993a, 'Multiculturalism and Ethnic Identity: The Relationship between Racism and Resistance', *Australia–New Zealand Journal of Sociology*, vol. 29, no. 2, pp. 209–25

—— 1993b, 'Immigrant Women and the Politics of Resistance', *Australian Feminist Studies*, no. 18, Summer, pp. 5–23

Viswanathan, G. 1989, *Masks of Conquest. Literary Study and British Rule in India*, Columbia University Press, New York

—— 1992, 'The Beginnings of English Literary Study in British India', eds J. Donald & A. Rattansi *'Race', Culture and Difference*, Sage Publications, London

Viviani, N. 1990, 'Australia's Future in Asia: People, Politics and Culture', *Australian Cultural History*, no. 9, pp. 103–17

Viviani, N., Coughlan, J. and Rowland, T. 1993, *Indochinese in Australia: The Issues of Unemployment and Residential Concentration*, AGPS, Canberra

WAF Editorial Group 1994, *Women Against Fundamentalism*, vol. 1, no. 5, p. 1

Walker, D. and Ingleson, J. 1989, 'The Impact of Asia', *Under New Heavens: Cultural Transmission and the Making of Australia*, ed. J. Meaney, Heinemann Educational Australia, Port Melbourne

Walker, J. and Biles, D. 1987, *Australian Prisoners 1986*, Australian Institute of Criminology, Canberra

Wallerstein, I. 1991, 'The Ideological Tensions of Capitalism: Universalism versus Racism and Sexism', *Race, Nation, Class: Ambiguous Identities*, eds E. Balibar & I. Wallerstein, Verso, London

Weatheritt, M. 1987, 'Community Policing Now', *Policing and the Community*, ed. P. Wilmott, Policy Studies Institute, London

Weil, P. 1991, *La France et ses Étrangers*, Calmann-Lévy, Paris

Whatman, S. 1995, 'Promoting Indigenous Participation at Tertiary Institutions: Past Attempts and Future Strategies', *The Aboriginal Child At School: A National Journal for Teachers of Aborigines and Torres Strait Islanders*, vol. 23, no. 1, pp. 36–43

White, N. and White, P. 1978, *Immigrants in the Media*, Longman Cheshire, Melbourne

Wieviorka, M. 1991, *L'Espace du Racisme*, Seuil, Paris

—— 1992, *La France Raciste*, Seuil, Paris

—— 1993, 'Tendencies to Racism in Europe: Does France Represent a Unique Case, or Is It Representative of a Trend?', *Racism and Migration in Western Europe*, eds J. Wrench & J. Solomos, Berg, Oxford and Providence

—— 1994, 'Introduction', *Racisme et Xenophobie en Europe: une comparaison internationale*, eds M. Wieviorka, P. Bataille, K. Couper, D. Martucelli & A. Peralva, La Découverte, Paris

Willard, M. 1923, *History of the White Australia Policy*, Melbourne University Press, Carlton, Vic.

Williamson, J. 1978, *Decoding Advertisements: Ideology and Meaning in Advertising*, Marion Boyas, London

Wilson, D., Holdaway, S. and Spencer, C. 1984, 'Black Police in the UK', *Policing*, vol. 1, no. 1, pp. 20–30

Wilson, P.L. and Storey, L. 1991, *Migrants and the Law—The Vietnamese: A Case Study*, Footscray Community Centre, Vic.

Wooden, M. 1993, *Underemployment, Hidden Unemployment and Immigration*, AGPS, Canberra

—— 1994, 'The Economic Impact of Immigration', *Australian Immigration: A*

Survey of the Issues, 2nd edn, eds M. Wooden, R. Holton, G. Hugo & J. Sloan, Bureau of Immigration Research, AGPS, Canberra

Wrench, J. and Solomos, J. eds 1993, *Racism and Migration in Europe*, Berg, Oxford and New York

Yarwood, A. and Knowling, M. 1982, *Race Relations in Australia*, Methuen, Sydney

Yarwood, A.T. 1964, *Asian Migration to Australia. The Background to Exclusion*, Melbourne University Press, Carlton, Vic.

Yeatman, A. 1992, *NESB Migrant Women and Award Restructuring: A Case Study of the Clothing Industry*, Report to the Office of Multicultural Affairs, AGPS, Canberra

Young, I.M. 1990a, *Justice and the Politics of Difference*, Princeton University Press, Princeton

—— 1990b, *White Mythologies: Writing History and the West*, Routledge, London

Youth Justice Coalition (NSW) 1990, *Kids in Justice: A Blueprint for the 90s*, Youth Justice Coalition, Sydney

Yuval-Davis, N. and Anthias, F. eds 1989, *Woman–Nation–State*, Macmillan, London

Zegers de Beijl, R. 1990, 'Discrimination of Migrant Workers in Western Europe', World Employment Working Paper, International Labour Office, Geneva, December

Zolberg, A., Suhrke, A. and Aguayo, S. 1989, *Escape from Violence*, Oxford University Press, New York

Zubrzycki, J. 1977, 'Towards a Multicultural Society in Australia', *Australia 2000: The Ethnic Impact*, ed. M. Bowen, University of New England, Armidale, NSW

INDEX

Aboriginal and Torres Strait Islander Commission, 50
Aboriginal English, 124
Aboriginal Reconciliation Council, 51–2
Aboriginal Rural Education Program (AREP), 114–19, 120, 123, 125–8
Aboriginal Studies, 9–10, 121
Aborigines: 'Aboriginal protection', 51; education for, 81, 112–29; employment of Aboriginal teachers, 121–3; English language difficulties, 163–4; essentialist notions of aboriginality, 97–8, 105–6, 108–11, 125; exploration of identity in education, 126; fixed notions of culture, 125; granted citizenship (1967), 104; in the labour market, 73–4, 82–3, 85–6, 112; interrogation of, 164; living standards, 94; *Mabo* case, 2; 'myths of blackness', 123–6; 'myths of whiteness', 127–8; over-policing of, 164–5; personal experience of racism, 2, 50–1, 100–4, 106–10, 120–3; police treatment of, 161–2, 164–6; portrayal of in textbooks, 101; priority employment, 120–1; rate of imprisonment, 165; reconciliation process, 73; relation to multiculturalism, 50–2; removal of children from families, 51; representation of in the media, 192n; self-determination, 16; stereotypes of, 106–7, 108, 121, 123–6, 127–8; studies of Aboriginal resistance, 9–10; unemployment, 79–81, 82; use of term 'aboriginal', 104–5, 190n
absenteeism, 93
Access and Equity, 58–9
Accord, 73
Ackland, R., 78
advertising: in television, 148, 149–55; preference for Afro blacks in, 153, 192n; sexuality in, 154–5, 156
affirmative action programs, 18, 44, 120–1
Afro-Americans, in advertising, 153, 192n
Air Pacific, 152, 155
Albania, 34
Ang, I., 70
Anglo-Australians: defined, 192n; dominance in the media, 158; identity, 48; loss of culture, 54–7; representation of on television, 150–2, 156, 157
annulment of marriage, 132
anthropology, 6, 9–10
anti-discrimination legislation, 15, 75
anti-racism, 43–4, 59
anti-Semitism, 3, 21, 26, 27
anti-vilification legislation, 15